Performing Neurology

Jonathan W. Marshall

Performing Neurology

The Dramaturgy of Dr Jean-Martin Charcot

Jonathan W. Marshall
Edith Cowan University
West Australian Academy of Performing Arts
Perth, West Australia, Australia

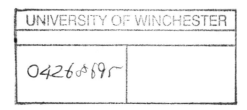
ISBN 978-1-137-51761-6   ISBN 978-1-137-51762-3   (eBook)
DOI 10.1057/978-1-137-51762-3

Library of Congress Control Number: 2016943538

Cover illustration: © World History Archive / Alamy Stock Photo (from *La Nature*, 7.1, 1879: 104)

Printed on acid-free paper

This Palgrave Macmillan imprint is published by Springer Nature
The registered company is Nature Americ Inc. New York

Preface and Acknowledgments

As an undergraduate, I attended a lecture on Michel Foucault's concept of the "hystericization" of the female body. In order to provide a context, Professor Charles Chips Sowerwine detailed to us Charcot's lessons at the Salpêtrière during the 1880s. Here, doctors prodded partially-dressed hysterical women in order to stage the patients' seizures and delusions for the apparent edification and teaching of the audience. It sounded like theatre to me. My later discovery of a massive photographic archive detailing these poses sealed my interest. Chips was to supervise my masters thesis on a related subject, and acted as the secondary supervisor on the beginnings of this project also. I am grateful for his support in these and other endeavours. It was, however, Professor Joy Damousi who supervised my doctoral studies on this subject, and it is to her I owe the greatest thanks. I remain in her debt today. Invaluable notes on my doctorate were provided by Robert Nye and David Garrioch, who I again thank here.

The material published here has therefore been under development for some time. Amongst the many individuals who supported and assisted me through iterations of this research, I wish to acknowledge the former archivist and librarian at the Bibliothèque Charcot, Véronique Leroux-Hugon, whose own publications provide excellent background material for any study of Charcot. I often had occasions to draw on the skills of Jack Eckert, senior librarian at the Rare Books collection of the Francis F. Countway Medical Library, Boston. Philippe Comar and Catherine Mathon at ENSBA, Paris, and Elizabeth Ihrig at the Bakken Museum and Library of the History of Electricity in Life, Minneapolis, were equally helpful and generous with their time. My family, whose expertise crosses the fields of medicine, aphasiology, and art history, have provided critical assistance, especially Helen Patricia Marshall, Vernon Marshall, Christopher Marshall, and Louise Marshall. Professional translator and sometime actor Alice Garner vetted many of my translations. I have benefited greatly from the editorial advice provided when I published some of the earlier versions of this work, notably Christopher E. Forth, Peter Cryle, Amy Wygant, Catriona MacLeod, Ian Maxwell, and Christopher Green, as well as the advice of my colleagues and associates Suzanne Little, Cat Hope, Maggie Phillips, Hilary Radner, Erika Wolf, and Sharon Matthews. To them all, I give my sincerest thanks.

An earlier version of Chap. 5 of this book was published as "The Theatre of the Athletic Nude: The Teaching and Study of Anatomy at the École des Beaux-Arts, Paris, 1873–1940," *Being There: ADSA (Australasian Association for theatre and Drama Studies) Conference Proceedings* (June 2008), <http:ses.library.usyd.edu.aubitstream212325111 ADSA2006 _ Marshall.pdf>, and an earlier version of Chap. 4 was published as "Dynamic Medicine and Theatrical Form at the *fin de siècle*: A Formal Analysis of Dr Jean-Martin Charcot's Pedagogy, 1862–1893," *Modernism/Modernity,* 15.1 (January 2008): 131–153. The material on Munthe in Chap. 8 was first published as "Hypnotic Performance and the Falsity of Appearances: The Aesthetics of Medical Spectatorship and Axel Munthe's Critique of Jean-Martin Charcot," in Catriona MacLeod et al., eds, *Elective Affinities* (Amsterdam: Rodopi, 2009), 221–242. Material in Chaps. 6 and 7 has appeared in "Beyond the Theatre of Desire: Hysterical Performativity and Perverse Choreography in the Writings of the Salpêtrière School, 1862–1893," in Peter Cryle and Christopher E. Forth, eds, *Fin de siècle Sexuality: The Making of a Central Problem* (Newark: Delaware University Press, 2008), 42–60, and "The Priestesses of Apollo and the Heirs of Aesculapius: Medical Art-Historical Approaches to Ancient Choreography After Charcot," *Forum for Modern Language Studies,* 43.4 (October 2007): 410–426. These materials have been reworked for reproduction here by kind permission of the original publishers, the Australasian Drama Studies Association, Johns Hopkins University Press, Rodopi and Brill publishing, Delaware University Press, and Oxford University Press, correspondingly.

CONTENTS

LIST OF FIGURES

List of Tables

CHAPTER 1

Introduction

1   THE WEB OF MEANING

On 18 April 1883, the headline of the French newspaper *Le Figaro* read, in bold capitals, "HAMMING IT UP" ("CABOTINAGE"). Below followed a damning attack on the famous neuropathologist, Professor Jean-Martin Charcot (1825–1893). Here and in other articles, columnist Félix Platel likened Charcot to the fashionable German opera composer, Richard Wagner, claiming that Charcot:

> monopolized hysteria. He astonished men. He frightened women. He practiced in sum scientific *cabotinage*.

> His success has been enormous. Oh the great allure of hamming it up! It has profited Charcot, but science also. He advanced science in the manner of Wagner, the great musical *cabotin*.

> Charcot and Wagner seem to me to be of the same race.[1]

Wagner was famous for championing the *Gesamtkunstwerk*, or total art work, in which all of the senses were simultaneously assaulted by different elements of performance: sound, music, voice, acting, lighting, spectacle, and design.[2] Charcot and his acolytes warned against the potential ill effects of such intense neuro-affective stimulation, claiming that it could bring on hysteria or other diseases. France had, moreover, been defeated by Germany, 1870–1871, making the popularity of Wagner's work highly

© The Editor(s) (if applicable) and The Author(s) 2016
J.W. Marshall, *Performing Neurology*,
DOI 10.1057/978-1-137-51762-3_1

problematic for nationalists like Charcot and Platel. To call Charcot a Wagnerian was, therefore, to call him "a wog" and a histrionic ham, an actor rather than a doctor—or more precisely, to classify him as a director and dramaturg, rather than an objective scientist.

Platel's insulting but revealing account serves as a frame for my discussion of Charcot. The reading offered above also offers, in condensed form, an example of my approach to the topic. Anthropologist Clifford Geertz christened this "thick description," whereby concepts drawn from a social milieu may be read against each other to reveal the complex meanings which lie embedded within commonplace terms. Geertz's first examples of thick description were indeed theatrical scenarios. According to Geertz, the aim of thick description was to determine the difference between a reflexive act such as spasmodic contracture of the eyelid, versus the communicative act of winking which resembles this otherwise meaningless pathological action, each of which have different nuances and significance.[3] Robert Darnton employed Geertz's concept in his now classic examination of how the staged execution of cats by eighteenth century apprentices was a remarkably complex symbolic act, having social consequences whilst remaining within the realm of fiction and the symbolic. It is in the space between fiction and action, between gesture and its contextual force, that I deploy thick description to bring out such contradictions and paradoxes within Charcot's rhetoric.

Although Charcot rarely wrote about the theatrical practices of his day, his work is redolent with theatrical concepts. This was part of Charcot's genius: to deploy a fundamentally choreographic analysis of the body to diagnose neurological illnesses, and derivations of this remain at the heart of neurology today. This was also Charcot's Achilles heel, drawing him into uncertain territory. Charcot conceived his approach in the final years prior to the invention of cinema. His close collaborators Paul Richer and Albert Londe indeed produced proto-cinematic stop-motion analyses of the moving body.[4] Nor did Charcot himself have access to X-rays, though X-ray technology was also pioneered at the Salpêtrière immediately after Charcot's death. In the context of this paucity of bio-imaging technologies, Charcot's recourse to models of theatrical spectatorship and visual caricature (the exaggeration of bodily form to highlight diagnostic detail) was inspired. Charcot was, however, then faced with the problem of differentiating between illness and the mere performance of illness; between outward theatrical display and essence, which in turn implicitly raised the question of whether illness was *itself* a kind of performance. If this was the case, how does the neurologist remain aloof from fictional performance, or is the neurologist a flawed ballet master, a Svengali, or Wagnerian dramaturg, who fosters the very diseases he seeks to diagnose? These questions are implicit in the criticism which Platel offers. My aim in what follows is to show how such uncertainties came into play within the writings of Charcot and his followers, and to sketch some of the consequences.

This relationship between theatre and medicine was paradoxical—one might say dialectical—not only because theatre and medicine are usually seen as discrete practices. The chief feature of Charcot's career was to make distinctions between things, not simply between the actor and the diseased individual, but between diseases. Charcot experimented with many treatments, but there were few effective therapies for major neurological illness during the late nineteenth century. What Charcot excelled at was the differential identification of disease and the isolation of the tissues or processes which lay at the root cause of illnesses. Charcot's exceptional work on the description of illness types laid the foundations of neurology as we know it, but was at the time a novel discipline. Only by naming can one begin to search for causes and solutions. Even so, Charcot himself was, at the level of aesthetics, thoroughly imbricated in the practices and phenomena from which he sought to distance himself.

Ironically, these uncertainties at the heart of Charcot's discourse contributed to his renown. Critics, artists, and theatre-makers exploited the confusions which this implicitly Wagnerian aesthetic offered. The writings of Léon Daudet and Axel Munthe, together with plays produced under the aegis of the horror theatre of the Grand Guignol, are particularly notable as they were authored in part by Charcot's former students. At the Guignol and in the work of Munthe and Daudet, a Charcot-figure is depicted as a diseased performer or histrionic actor within the staging or mise en scène which that character had forged for his own medical practice. Platel's critique is developed in more detail in these and other accounts. By contrast, Charcot's former students and art historians Richer and Henry Meige sought to locate a realm within which healthy performance could be readily identified. They concluded that the aesthetic ideals embodied within Ancient Greek athletics provided the most reliable model for spectatorship of the healthy moving body, and championed such sportive events in opposition to those of the aesthetic avant-garde, the Grand Guignol, and of illness itself. This antimony within Charcot's own circle between the dramatization of highly innervating, sensorially shocking events by Daudet, Munthe, and the Guignol's Alfred Binet and André de Lorde, versus the measured Greek athletics of Richer and Meige, illustrates the fraught nature of the rapprochement between theatre and medicine which Charcot strove to maintain during his lifetime.

In his lectures and writings, Charcot developed a way of presenting his patients in the lecture theatre and in his publications that not only suited, but paradoxically echoed, the symptoms of his subjects. He nevertheless attempted to maintain a distinction between the performance of medical knowledge in the lectures, as opposed to the pathological performativity of his patients themselves. The instability of this opposition is the subject of this text as a whole. The focus of the first two sections of this book (Chaps. 2–7) is fin de siècle neurology itself: a discourse which describes and pathologizes physical acts. The first section describes the frames, contexts, and evocative sites—including the Salpêtrière and its texts, all of which acted as stages for these events—wherein neurology was performed (Chaps. 2–5). In the second section I move to pathological performance itself, drawing especially on Richer's *Études cliniques sur la grande hystérie* (1881; 1885) and the *Iconographie photographique de la Salpêtrière* (1875–1880), the latter of which is considered here less as a collection of static images than as a flip-book representation of performance itself (Chaps. 6 and 7). The closing section reveals how the theatricality of Charcot's practice was critiqued in three main sources authored by former students of Charcot, namely Daudet and Munthe (Chap. 8), and Binet's collaboration with de Lorde as part of the Théâtre du Grand Guignol (Chap. 9). Here the inversions hinted at within Charcot's practice erupt in horrifying narratives of the doctor as patient.

As a work of thick description, my sources consist primarily of the works of the Charcot school from the 1870s through to 1925, when a flurry of eulogies and biographies was issued to mark the centenary of Charcot's birth. Unpublished archival works have also been sparingly used. Key biographies include that authored by Charcot's former student Paul Peugniez as well as Georges Guillain's study of 1959.[5] Although Guillain never met Charcot, he interned with Charcot's students Fulgence Raymond, Pierre Marie, and Achilles Souques, as well as encountering former patients when he came to occupy Charcot's professorial chair at the Salpêtrière, 1925–1948. Guillain's work is treated here as a primary source, as far as discourse and imagery is concerned.

Charcot's own output was prolific and varied. It was anthologized several times, whilst scholar Christopher Goetz has added to this material by republishing some of Charcot's Tuesday lectures.[6] The most extensive collection of Charcot's writings includes not only the first nine volumes of the *Oeuvres complètes* which was edited by his associate Désiré Bourneville, but also the *Hospice de la Salpêtrière* series (*Oeuvres complètes*, volumes ten and eleven) which was collated by Charcot's secretary Georges Guinon. These texts are sometimes put together with Charcot's *Leçons du mardi*, edited by his students Emery Blin and Henri Colin, and Charcot's son Jean-Baptiste (*Oeuvres complètes*, volumes twelve and thirteen). Collectively, they make up a thirteen volume set, although the binding of such serialized publications was not always consistent in the late nineteenth century.[7]

As demonstrated within the *Oeuvres complètes*, Charcot's work was a collaborative effort, in which his concepts were transcribed and edited by students, assistants, and secretaries, before further revision at the hands of the master. Of Charcot's famous lectures, his leading pupil Georges Gilles de la Tourette recalled that, "He never gave a lesson without first preparing it in long hand, documenting it to excess. Upon leaving the amphitheatre … he said to one of his students: 'Here are my notes, write them out,'" whilst in other cases Charcot stated that he "wrote it entirely myself"—hardly necessary if Tourette's description of Charcot's notes was an accurate one.[8] Whilst the precise give and take between Charcot's lecture scripts and subsequent notation varied somewhat, the work of Charcot's associates and supporters can be identified as that of a broadly unified school.

Charcot's work, then, was inseparable from that of his acolytes. I draw here particularly upon the work of Paul Richer, Henry Meige, Alfred Binet, and Max Nordau. Richer and Meige both served as professors of artistic anatomy at the national academy of fine arts (École Nationale Supérieure des Beaux-Arts), 1903–1922 and 1922–1940, respectively, whilst Binet wrote for the Grand Guignol, 1905–1911. Nordau produced a tract on nervous degeneration and art in 1892, drawing heavily on his studies with Charcot of 1885. These materials provide invaluable data on the aesthetic values of Charcot's school. Such sources are here used as a framework through which to re-read Charcot's own pronouncements, rendering in more visible terms themes initially derived from Charcot's discourse.

Although I employ concepts drawn from feminist psychoanalysis, linguistics, and performance studies, my approach is chiefly hermeneutic. My focus is on concepts, words, and theatrical acts; on their mutations and implications across texts, images, and between authors. As a discursive analysis of the Charcotian perspective in context, I do not focus upon the evolution of Charcot's concepts over time. This is a horizontal study, not a vertical analysis. It is an "archaeology" in Michel Foucault's terms.[9] As a study in the history of ideas and representation, my attention is less directed towards determining any underlying facts which may or may not be possible to recognize today—such as what Charcot's patients may have suffered from—than with what was at stake within the discursive concepts and turns of phrase that Charcot and his peers deployed. To quote Geertz, I employ "essentially a semiotic" model because:

> man is an animal suspended in webs of significance he himself has spun, I take culture to be those webs, and the analysis of it to be ... an interpretive one in search of meaning.[10]

Charcot's fame has ensured that his work was highly influential in the arts. Janet Beizer and Jann Matlock have examined how various hysterical bodies seemed to resist full description within literary and theatrical texts of Charcot's time, whilst Rae Beth Gordon has shown that actors, comedians, dancers, and singers within the cabarets and films of the 1890s and 1900s drew extensively upon Charcot's ideas to enact neuropathology as radical entertainment.[11] Felicia McCarren has noted a similar influence upon the choreography of dancer-projectionist Loïe Fuller. The stages of the relatively novel, bohemian venues of Paris' *café-concérts* or Fuller's specially designed dance-and-light shows were teeming with performers whose extraordinary movements, staggered gait, grimaces, or song lyrics, reflected or commented upon the disorder of the neuropathological body. These figures from early French cabaret rapidly crossed over to cinema, a form which burst onto the scene in 1894, one year after Charcot's death. Jaqueline Carroy has also examined the careers of a number of former medical patients or "trance dancers" who appeared on the stages of Europe in the late nineteenth and early twentieth century.[12] Fascinating though these various developments are, they left Charcot and his circle relatively untouched. The neurologists took a dim view of such performances, with the exception of the Grand Guignol, which was supported by several of Charcot's acolytes. In Nordau's terms, the *café-concért* described by Gordon was nothing but a site for the debased display of that which should have remained strictly under the protective and therapeutic ministrations of medicine.

In the years that followed Charcot's death in 1893, there were to be many significant literary and aesthetic works touching upon his career, including the Surrealist essay by Louis Aragon and André Breton, "The Fiftieth Anniversary of Hysteria" (1928), Per Olov Enquist's fictional account of Charcot's patients *Blanche and Marie* (2007), Alice Winocour's film *Augustine* (2012), the plays of Anna Furse and Dianne

Hunter (*Big Hysteria*, 1991, and *Dr Charcot's Hysteria Shows*, 1988), as well as the work of photomedia artists such as Mary Kelly, Anne Ferran, and Pat Brassington, who draw upon the vast photographic output of the Salpêtrière.[13] Christina Wald argues that the dramatization of these historic hysterical subjects might now be considered a genre within feminist theatre.[14]

These creative interpretations, as well as much of the scholarship on Charcot, tend to exhibit a moderate to high level of generality. Charcot appears within these and other studies as a representative of broader trends within fin de siècle culture, its gender relations, French medicine, visual technology, and the emergence of cinema, psychiatric history, or other key issues upon which his practice touched. Although Charcot's work is routinely noted to have been highly theatrical, critical analyses of what this might mean, and what this observation might imply, are thin on the ground outside of Gordon's study of cabaret and film. Wald is concerned with later plays about the neurologist, whilst Hunter's exegetical comments are primarily addressed to theatre-makers. Beyond this, the theatricality of Charcot's practice is treated as a secondary outgrowth of late nineteenth century approaches to hysteria. Indeed, attention to hysteria tends to obfuscate the diversity of Charcot's practice as a general neurologist—although it is true that Charcot's popular reputation was in large part built on his diagnosis of hysteria. My aim is to return to the scholarship a close attention on the particularities and words of Charcot and of those who worked so closely with him, moving beyond hysteria and its psychology to describe the performative aesthetics of neuropathology itself. The intricacies of hysterical seizure and the different nuances of the paralytic contracture receive detailed analysis here. My aim is to return the full richness of these corporeal and performative phenomena to the historiography.

2   HYSTERIA AND PSYCHOANALYSIS

Much of scholarship on Charcot issuing from the humanities has focused on his role as a precursor for psychoanalysis. Sigmund Freud studied with Charcot, 1885–1886, and he paid homage to his former teacher by placing an illustration of Charcot above his famous couch.[15] Whilst Freud took much from Charcot, he broke with the neurologist to argue that the chief concern of physicians should be on the patients' psychological development. For Freud, the body is emotionally organized by our lusts and desires. Over time, individuals associate particular parts of the body with sexual and affective responses, linking certain desires, memories, or conflicts with various locations and sensations. For Charcot, however, psychological factors were only significant inasmuch as they were derived from identifiable underlying neuro-physical conditions. In deference to Charcot, I direct my attention first and foremost towards muscles and nerves, gestures and tics, stimuli and reaction, over and above psyche, sexuality, or psychology.

The 1980s saw an explosion of scholarship dealing with hysteria, inspired by feminist psychoanalysis such as Julia Kristeva's *Powers of Horror* (1980), as well as the collaboration of playwright Hélène Cixous with critic Catherine Clément, *La jeune née* (1975)—a text whose punning reference in the title to gay playwright Jean Genet ("La Genet") reveals how close issues of theatricality have remained in such discussions.[16] Echoing Carroll Smith Rosenberg's groundbreaking study of middle class female hysterics in late nineteenth century America, these authors have identified hysteria as a form of resistance to social pressures and barriers, notably those on women's participation in the public sphere. Kristeva, Clement, and Cixous argue that this resistance was expressed primarily through the relation of these patients to language. As a form of revolt, hysteria is inchoate, having no proper language or logical set of pronouncements or speech acts. Hysteria is expressed via the illogical or grotesque body and its acts. Rather than speaking, the hysteric erupts in fits and seizures. Whilst the corporeal illogic of the hysterical body was a chief concern of Charcot, too, Mark Micale and others have pointed out that this model cannot be applied wholesale to inmates of the Salpêtrière.[17] Most of Charcot's patients were not denied the ability to work, for example. The vast majority toiled as servants, as maids, or in other low paid professions. They were not the frustrated bourgeois women one sees in Smith-Rosenberg, within Freud's practice, or even Gustave Flaubert's novel *Madame Bovary* (1856)—notwithstanding that Flaubert and Freud were well read in the medical literature of their day.

Nevertheless, the psychoanalytic association of chaotic bodily gestures with an anti-language of the body is insightful. It accurately characterizes not just Charcot's hysterioepileptic patients, but neuropathology more broadly as a group of disorderly behaviours and gestures. My contention is that hysteria should not be seen as a distinct or clearly gendered concept within Charcot's practice. As Micale has pointed out, Charcot had a particular interest in working class labourers and soldiers afflicted with hysteria despite their manliness. Nor can Charcot be retrospectively dismissed as a misogynist, although Charcot was criticized for his treatment of women during his own lifetime. As Goetz has demonstrated, Charcot mentored several of the first women to study at the Paris medical school.[18] I draw on the scholarship of hysteria throughout this study—notably the work of Elizabeth Bronfen, Elizabeth Showalter, Étienne Trillat, and Sander Gilman—and I discuss gender issues as they arise, but my focus is elsewhere.[19] My concern is the body's resistance to neurological classification and the underlying aesthetics this implies. I am interested in the dynamic fungibility and choreographic patterning of the body, rather than issues of psychology and desire. My contention is that within Charcot's practice, hysteria acted as the ultimate expression of neuropathology in terms of its near unmanageable variability and performative excess.

In addition to Goetz's translations, my study owes much to the critical biography of Charcot, which was written by Goetz in collaboration with fellow neurologists and historians Michel Bonduelle and Toby Gelfand. Titled *Charcot: Constructing Neurology* (1995), it sketches the trajectory and medical data behind Charcot's practice. In terms of argument and methodology though, I owe a greater debt to art historian Georges Didi-Huberman and his masterful *Invention of Hysteria* (2003).[20]

Describing how Charcot's associates compiled a vast collection of photographs and images of their patients, Didi-Huberman concludes that:

> Charcot rediscovered hysteria. I attempt to retrace how he did so, amidst all the various clinical and experimental procedures, through hypnosis and the spectacular presentations of patients having hysterical attacks in the amphitheater where he held his famous Tuesday Lectures. With Charcot we discover the capacity of the hysterical body, which is, in fact, prodigious. It is prodigious; it surpasses the imagination, surpasses "all hopes," as they say.[21]

For Didi-Huberman, the collection of photographs published within the *Iconographie photographique de la Salpêtrière* "contains everything: poses, attacks, cries, 'passionate attitudes,' 'crucifixions,' 'ecstasy,' and all the postures of delirium" or what might be called "theatricalized bodies."

Didi-Huberman surveys the extensive iconographic archive produced by Charcot and his associates, concluding that the act of medical visualization through photographic capture and other means generated a mutual seduction at the level of the image between doctor and subject. The production of images elicited responses, generating an ever expanding spiral of relations, until the body itself came to function as an image. This is one of Didi-Huberman's most significant observations: hysterics became art objects. One of the main characteristics of hysterioepilepsy was its capacity to replicate the symptoms of other diseases. The hysterical body was a sort of photograph or sculpture, which manifested other illnesses of neuromotor control. This in turn echoed the way in which the physicians themselves produced drawings and photographs of the patients in these states. In a particularly telling note, Didi-Huberman explains that it was through such means that "hysteria in the clinic became the spectacle, the *invention of hysteria*. Indeed, hysteria was covertly identified with something like an art, close to theater or painting."[22] Didi-Huberman sees this as a "paradoxical situation" because it threatens the normal separation of an image from that which it represents: the hysterical body is both an image, and that which the image depicts. My point is that the diseased neurological body is therefore a kind of *fiction*, very close to theatre, as Didi-Huberman registers.

Extending Didi-Huberman's insight that the hysterical body served as a kind of camera or painting of those motions which constituted illness, I argue that Charcot and his peers saw in the patient not just an *image* of the disorderly body. Rather, Charcot's patients rendered in the wards and upon the stage of the demonstration theatre a series of acts and expressions which might be linked to each illness type—a Wagnerian *Gesamtkunstwerk* if you will. Whilst neuropathology might have constituted something *like* a theatre for Charcot, it was equally important for the neurologist to be able to establish that to be afflicted with a disease was not just "acting." In the face of such manifold terminological challenges, Charcot and his associates developed a complex aesthetic understanding of their practice and of disease. As I outline below, disease was defined by performance without causality, performance in denial of the usual rules of classical Aristotelian theatre, or performance whose gestures were asymmetrical or highly exaggerated—prodigiously exceeding all hopes, in Didi-Huberman's phrasing. This is examined in Chaps. 6 and 7.

The living body was, moreover, conceptualized as the absolute ground from which authority was derived and from which diagnosis flowed. But such bodies were effectively displaced from the scene of lecturing. The body was a stage property which, once it had been introduced, could be substituted with an array of more idealized, instructive representations. Patients appeared onstage, but as in any theatrical spectacle, their role and function was closely directed, functioning within a complex set of other dramaturgical devices (speech, text, projection, image, staging). Charcot's lectures are discussed in Chap. 4.

By laying out the writings and practice of Charcot's school in this way, I aim to show how Charcot's analysis of sensorial flows and passages, of neural linkages and disruptions, implicitly evoked the spatial and temporal mise en scène within which each body might act. Certain stages elicited certain responses within the patient, particularly for the hysteric. The neurological body was nothing if not responsive; it was a feedback loop. The action of nerves and muscles generated sensory information as the body moved, felt, touched, heard, and even smelled, and each of these sensory nodes generated a change in the original action. Neuromotor behaviour is, at least in part, conditional, and to describe the body and its responses was always at some level to describe a theatre within which it performs. Whilst this construction is not unique to Charcot, his oeuvre offers a particularly striking case study of how this discovery by nineteenth century physicians led to a series of rhetorical problems which had the potential to subvert medicine as a discipline.

3   FRENCH MEDICINE AND THE CLASSICAL TRADITION

Charcot and his associates were associated with the Republican government of France, founded in 1870 amidst the ruins of military defeat at the hands of the Prussians. Charcot remained in Paris whilst it was under siege, and several of his colleagues such as Richer and Charles Richet manned the ambulance facilities in Paris and its surrounds. Most of Charcot's peers professed strong nationalist positions and styled themselves as defenders of the French tradition. This was typically associated with the conviction that France was the centre of Latinate learning throughout the medieval and early modern period, and so was the true heir to the classical traditions of the Ancients.[23] Central to French Neoclassicism was adherence to the laws of Greek drama as laid down by Aristotle in his *Poetics* (c. 335 BC). Aristotle argued that theatre depended on the mirroring, or mimesis, of plausible events and their outward features. Theatre could deal with suffering and other pathetic events, but this was to be measured and restrained. Violence was alluded to, rather than enacted onstage. Theatre also had to exhibit a high level of structural and dramaturgical unity.[24]

Aristotle's most rigid precept was the model of the three unities. Drama should accord with a unity of time, a unity of space, and a unity of character. Unity of time meant that all events within a single scene, or better yet the whole play should be continuous, and that one minute of stage time should be equivalent to one minute of time in the audience's reception. Most high classical works were, therefore, set over the course of a single night or afternoon, although elisions between acts were acceptable. Unity of space likewise meant that any given scene should only be set in one location. Symbolist, Modernist, and Expressionist playwrights objected to these rules, preferring to echo the temporal and spatial agility of human thought. Finally, unity of character implied that great characters changed little in their psychological make-up over the course of the narrative. They might be presented with various challenges, but characters would respond in a predictable fashion determined by their essential features. Whilst these ideas had been under assault for centuries, it was the art movements of Romanticism, Symbolism, and Modernism that provided the greatest challenges to them during Charcot's own time. Needless to say, Charcot himself preferred the work of Neoclassical playwrights like Jean Baptiste Molière over that of more avant-garde theatre-makers such as Wagner or Aurélien Lugné-Poe. Significantly, though, Charcot often went to cabarets such as the Folies Bergère with students and friends, where he was particularly taken by the acrobatic feats performed by clowns.[25] The significance of these models for diagnosis is discussed in Chaps. 6 and 7. To deny the rules of classicism within one's own performance was, according to Charcot, to be diseased.

The ordered beauty of Neoclassical aesthetics was also threatened by popular lay forms such as the carnival. Theorists such as Mikhail Bakhtin and Victor Turner have argued that theatrical scenarios such as carnivals offer a space wherein normal separations can break down.[26] Drawing on the European tradition of the King for a Day or Lord of Misrule, these authors contend that carnivals and carnival-like venues (clowns at the cabaret, urban and rural fairs, waxwork displays, and so on) take social conventions and tropes and stage them in a grotesque, burlesque, or otherwise distorted and inverted form.[27] Indeed, the association between the bodily excesses of carnival with medical practice dates back to the Renaissance, where early Italian anatomical demonstrations tended to occur during carnival and were frequented by rowdy students and revellers in masks.[28] As we shall see, a number of Salpêtrière patients worked in fairs or freak shows, and the neurologists were keen to re-establish the proper boundaries and hierarchies which such practices flaunted. The "remarkable abilities" of the freaks were shown to be egregious symptoms of illness, and attempts were made to close down these performances and shift the subjects from the carnival to the hospital. Charcot's attacks on these aesthetic forums were, therefore, defensive acts aimed at minimizing any confusion between Charcot's aesthetic practices and values, and those of such carnivalesque practices. This was especially true of his attempts to ban lay hypnotic displays at carnivals, fairs, and in theatres. One may take from this that something like a carnival, or the inversion of the distinction between performer and doctor, between patient and physician, was always in the offing within Charcot's practice. The carnivalesque is, therefore, here discussed as a potentiality which threatens to erupt from within scenarios of control and order such as psychiatry, neurology, and psychoanalysis, as well as from within the hysterical body.[29] Bodily forms and aesthetic tropes associated with such carnivalesque excess emerge at several times within the study below.

4   BUTLER AND PERFORMATIVITY

The valency of the terms "performance" and "to perform" are crucial to my analysis. Central here is the concept of performativity, as it was developed by Judith Butler from the work of James Austin and Jacques Derrida.[30] Butler is acknowledged by historians as one of several authors who draws attention to how the linking of one's gender identity with one's genital sex is neither unequivocal nor universal. Her theory of performativity itself, however, has received little attention in the historical literature. Butler's concept of iteration, or the repetition of a prior speech act to make it better established, has only been seriously considered by scholars of early modern gender such as Belinda Johnson—though Nina Auerbach comes close in her analysis of the distrust Victorian writers had for anything which might smack of potentially deceitful practices of acting or theatricality.[31]

Butler's model derives in the first instance from linguistic theory. A "performative" is a statement or other speech act which renders actual that which it describes. The typical example is when an official says, "I pronounce you man and wife," or when a judge reads out a sentence. By saying "I pronounce you man and wife," those addressed actually become a married couple. Equally important is that this classifies them as individuals. A performative not only does something, it names and defines the subject who is addressed. Even if the man addressed was not previously known as a man, from this point onwards he will be seen, in social terms at least, as a heterosexual husband. As Austin noted, all language has some performative character. Seen in this light, Charcot's discourse is also performative, being designed to identify and name the subjects whom the neurologist addresses as either "Tourette's sufferer" or "hysteric." Reversing the direction of this relationship, one can also discern how for Charcot, certain gestures or types of seizure are performatives. To have a seizure of a particular kind identifies for the doctor that the subject is a patient of a particular type; it defines and reveals their bodily nature.

Butler complicates this model by noting that performativity can at times have a certain thinness. The heterosexual fiancé may in fact be homosexual, and could perform other acts in other contexts which might define him differently. Derrida explains this by reference to language itself. For any word to make sense, it must have been said before, and the association of this word with a particular object or concept have been recognized. Every time this word is subsequently said, it becomes more clearly associated with the object it names—the more one is called "man," the more this designation becomes, in Butler's phrasing, "sedimented" and "concretized" in social, physical, and subjective terms. One "becomes" a man through such performances. This raises, however, the possibility that the subject was not a man at some time or other, and hence that it was always possible that another designation could have been applied. The iteration of an original act of naming is, in a sense, a shared fiction or convention which is sustained and reinforced by each reiteration or performance. Performatives must, therefore, be constantly invoked and consolidated to dispel such notions. Each performance serves both to reinforce the truth of the identity being performed, whilst allowing the possibility that this performed identity might fall apart.

This model resonates strongly with Charcot's practice. Repetitive evidence and re-performance rendered Charcot's ideas forceful, and conditioned those bodies on display and in the wards to be read more clearly in these terms. However, on other occasions, this very reiteration seemed to suggest that the pathologies which were staged within the lecture theatre and in the hospital were not so much effective *performatives*, but empty *performances*. This danger within performative diagnosis was most pronounced within hypnotic behaviour—a set of actions and gestures which Charcot and his peers saw as symptomatic of hysteria and neuropathology. This topic is discussed in Chap. 7.

In a posthumous homage to Charcot, the medical journalist Jules Bois claimed that:

> The Salpêtrière seems … to have been above all a wonderful field of experimentation, a sort of theatre where the ancient convulsive dramas of the middle ages were played out.

But is there not a profound difference between living, breathing reality and the scenic pretense?

Bois conceded that Charcot offered the "spectacle of Satanism" and other spasmodic dramas, but perhaps that was all. Caught between "reality" and "scenic pretense," therapy and diagnosis, Charcot's novel fusion of aesthetics and diagnosis did not survive him—though this outcome was far from assured when he began giving his lectures in 1872.[32]

NOTES

1. Félix Platel (Ignotus), "Le cabotinage," *Figaro* (18 April 1883): 1; also Platel, "M. Charcot," *Les hommes de mon temps* (Paris: Bureau du Figaro, from 1878; dating incomplete), 377–388.
2. Richard Wagner, *Wagner on Music and Drama* (London: Victor Gollancz, 1970); Thomas Grey, ed., *Richard Wagner and his World* (Princeton: Princeton University Press, 2009).
3. Clifford Geertz, *The Interpretation of Cultures* (NY: Basic, 1973), 6–12, 412–454; Robert Darnton, *The Great Cat Massacre* (London: Penguin, 1991).
4. Albert Londe, *La photographie médical*, préface Jean-Martin Charcot (Paris: Gauthier-Villars, 1893).
5. Paul Peugniez, *J.-M. Charcot (1825–1893)* (Amiens: Picarde, 1893); Georges Guillain, *J.-M. Charcot 1825–1893: His Life—His Work*, trans. Pearce Bailey (NY: Paul Hoeber, 1959).
6. Jean-Martin Charcot, *Charcot the Clinician: The Tuesday Lessons: Excerpts From Nine Case Presentations on General Neurology Delivered at the Salpêtrière Hospital in 1887–1888*, trans., ed. and commentary Christopher Goetz (NY: Raven, 1987). Also excellent on the general neurological context is Anne Harrington, *Medicine, Mind, and the Double Brain* (Princeton: Princeton University Press, 1987).
7. I follow the Francis F. Countway Harvard Medical Library, and list all as part of the total *Oeuvres complètes* (Paris: Progrès médical, 1888–1894), 13 vols.
8. Georges Gilles de la Tourette, "Jean-Martin Charcot," *Nouvelle iconographie photographique de la Salpêtrière* [hereafter *NIPS*], 6 (1893): 248; Toby Gelfand, "Mon cher docteur Freud," *Bulletin of the History of Medicine*, 62.4 (Winter 1988): 578–9.
9. Michel Foucault, *Archaeology of Knowledge*, trans. A.M. Sheridan Smith (NY: Pantheon, 1972).
10. Geertz, 5.

11. Janet Beizer, *Ventriloquized Bodies* (Ithaca: Cornell University Press, 1994); Jann Matlock, *Scenes of Seduction* (NY: Columbia University Press, 1994); Rae Beth Gordon, *Why the French Love Jerry Lewis* (Stanford: Stanford University Press, 2002); Felicia McCarren, "The 'Symptomatic Act' circa 1900: Hysteria, Hypnosis, Electricity and Dance," *Critical Inquiry* (Summer 1995): 748–774; Jonathan W. Marshall, "'The World of the Neurological Pavilion': Hauntology and European Modernism *'mal tourné*,'" *TDR: The Drama Review*, 57.4 (Winter 2013): 60–85. The definitive history of the influence of neuropsychology on acting theory remains Joseph Roach, *The Player's Passion* (Delaware: Delaware University Press, 1985).

12. Jaqueline Carroy[-Thirard], *Hypnose, suggestion et psychologie* (Paris: Presses universitaires de France, 1991), "Hystérie, théâtre, littérature au dix-neuvième siècle," *Psychanalyse à l'université*, 7.26 (March 1982): 299–317; Jonathan W. Marshall, "Kleist's *Übermarionetten* and Schrenck-Notzing's *Traumtänzerin*: Nervous Mechanics and Hypnotic Performance Under Modernism," in Bernd Fischer and Tim Mehigan, eds, *Heinrich von Kleist and Modernity* (Rochester: Camden House, 2011), 261–281.

13. Louis Aragon and André Breton, "Le cinquantenaire de l'hystérie," *Révolution surréaliste*, 4 (15 March 1928): 20–22; Per Olov Enquist, *The Book About Blanche and Marie* (NY: Overlook, 2007); Dianne Hunter, *The Makings of "Dr. Charcot's Hysteria Shows"* (NY: Mellen, 1998); Anna Furse, *Augustine (Big Hysteria)* (Oxford: Routledge, 2013); Felicity Johnson et al., *Anne Ferran* (Perth: Lawrence Wilson Art Gallery, 2014); Mary Kelly et al., *Interim* (NY: New Museum of Contemporary Art, 1997); Anne Marsh, *Pat Brassington* (Hobart: Quintus, 2006); Alice Winocour, dir., *Augustine*, film (France: 2012).

14. Christina Wald, *Hysteria, Trauma and Melancholia* (Houndmills: Palgrave Macmillan, 2007).

15. The definitive work remains Henri Ellenberger, *The Discovery of the Unconscious* (London: Penguin, 1970). Jan Goldstein's *Console and Classify* (Cambridge: Cambridge University Press, 1987) also positions Charcot within psychiatry, whilst the best accounts of Freud's debt to Charcot are Julian Miller et al., "Some Aspects of Charcot's Influence on Freud," *Journal of the American Psychoanalytic Association* 17.2 (1969): 608–23, and Daphne de Marneffe, "Looking and Listening: The Construction of Clinical Knowledge in Charcot and Freud," *Signs*, 17.1 (Autumn 1991): 71–111.

16. Julia Kristeva, *Powers of Horror*, trans. Leon Roudiez (NY: Columbia University Press, 1980); Barbara Creed, *The Monstrous Feminine* (NY: Routledge, 1993); Hélène Cixous and Catherine Clément, *The Newly Born Woman*, trans. Betsy Wing (Minneapolis: Minnesota University Press,

1975); Carroll Smith-Rosenberg, "The Hysterical Woman," *Social Research*, 39 (Winter, 1975): 652–678; Luce Irigaray, *That Sex Which is Not One*, trans Catherine Porter and Carolyn Burke (Ithaca: Cornell University Press, 1977).

17. See Mark Micale, *Approaching Hysteria* (Princeton: Princeton University Press, 1995), "Charcot and the Idea of Hysteria in the Male," *Medical History*, 34 (1990): 363–411, "Hysteria Male / Hysteria Female," in Marina Benjamin, ed., *Science and Sensibility* (Oxford: Blackwell, 1991), 200–242.
18. Christopher Goetz, "Charcot and the Myth of Misogyny," *Neurology*, 52 (May 1999): 1678–1685; C. Reenooz, "Charcot devoilé," *Revue scientifique des femmes*, 1.6 (December 1888): 241–7; Berthe de Courrière, "Néron: Prince de la science," *Mercure de France* (9 October 1893): 144–6.
19. Elisabeth Bronfen, *The Knotted Subject* (Princeton: Princeton University Press, 1998); Étienne Trillat, *Histoire de l'hystérie* (Paris: Seghers, 1986); Elaine Showalter, *Hystories* (NY: Columbia University Press, 1997), *The Female Malady* (London: Virago, 1988); Sander Gilman et al., *Hysteria Beyond Freud* (LA: California, 1993); Sander Gilman, *Seeing the Insane* (NY: Wiley, 1982).
20. Christopher Goetz, Michel Bonduelle, and Toby Gelfand, *Charcot: Constructing Neurology* (NY: Oxford University Press, 1995); Georges Didi-Huberman, *Invention of Hysteria*, trans. Alisa Hartz (Boston, MA: MIT, 2003). Also useful for the general narrative of the Charcot school is Nadine Simon-Dhouailly, ed., *Le leçon de Charcot: Voyage dans une toile*, catalogue d'exposition (Paris: Musée de l'Assistance publique des hôpitaux de Paris, 1986).
21. Didi-Huberman, *Invention*, xi.
22. Ibid., xi.
23. Jonathan W. Marshall, "The Priestesses of Apollo and the Heirs of Aesculapius: Medical Art-Historical Approaches to Ancient Choreography After Charcot," *Forum for Modern Language Studies*, 43.4 (October 2007): 410–426.
24. Philip Freund, *The Birth of Theatre* (London: Peter Owen, 2003), 41–61, 270–286.
25. Guillain, x.
26. Richard Schechner, *Performance Studies* (London: Routledge, 2013); Mikhail Bakhtin, Mikhailovich, *Rabelais and His World*, trans. Hélène Iswolsky (Bloomington: Indiana University Press, 1984).
27. On the freak show, see Michael Chemers, *Staging Stigma* (New York: Palgrave Macmillan, 2008).
28. Cynthia Klestinec, "Civility, Comportment, and the Anatomy Theater," *Renaissance Quarterly*, 60 (2007): 434–463.

29. Peter Stallybrass and Allon White, *The Politics and Poetics of Transgression* (London: Methuen, 1986), 171–190; Umberto Eco, *On Ugliness* (London: Harvil Seeker, 2007), 135–153.
30. Judith Butler, *Bodies That Matter* (NY: Routledge, 1993), *Excitable Speech* (NY: Routledge, 1997).
31. Belinda Johnson, "Renaissance Body Matters," *International Journal of Sexuality and Gender Studies*, 6.1 (2001): 77–94; Nina Auerbach, *Private Theatricals* (Cambridge, MA: Harvard University Press, 1990).
32. Jules Bois, *Le monde invisible* (Paris: Flammarion, 1902), 368.

CHAPTER 2

Charcot, Spectacle, and the Mise en Scène of the Salpêtrière

1 VISION AND DRAMATURGY

For Charcot, vision was paramount. The act of looking served as an entry point into comprehending the totality of neuropathological action and sensation. Even for Charcot, though, ocular information was but one of a number of tools for theatrical analysis. In performance analysis, the structural principles which dictate theatrical reception collectively make up what is called the dramaturgy of the work, and it is my contention that Charcot's oeuvre functioned through, and was in turn criticized for, its dramaturgical qualities. Dramaturgy is closely related to mise en scène, a phrase which literally means "to put in place." The mise en scène is the total stage picture, or more generally, how the ensemble of material onstage has arisen from previous scenes, conditions, events, and so on. Within this chapter I bring forward some of the characters who drove the narrative of Charcot's career, whilst emphasizing the place of the image and the role of location and scenography within Charcot's dramaturgical reception: the place which framed the mise en scène of Charcot's career and practice. Whilst the extensive use of iconographic and photographic material at the Salpêtrière is frequently commented on, this is rarely seen as functioning within a larger framework of physical, theatrical, and choreographic analysis. The image, then, is a problematic mode of interpretation and analysis for Charcot, at once essential but also partial, tied as it is to the physical embodiment and temporal qualities which exceed the image itself.

© The Editor(s) (if applicable) and The Author(s) 2016   19
J.W. Marshall, *Performing Neurology*,
DOI 10.1057/978-1-137-51762-3_2

Whilst Charcot's approach may well have seemed "theatrical" no matter where it might have been deployed, it became more so because of where these acts and interpretive gambits were staged. The important characters of the drama I lay out here include: Charcot, his technology of vision and the means with which he constructed this drama, and the scenography of the Salpêtrière itself. We follow some of the key developments that Charcot pioneered, notably the shift from the hospice as a centre for the study of psychiatry—or alienism as the French called it—to the Salpêtrière as a dramatic site for the study of neurology. I close with a discussion of the ambivalent, melancholy ambience which the Salpêtrière generated in the writings of several commentators, a location that echoed in many ways the impression which visitors to Charcot's house, such as the neurologist's former student Léon Daudet, found so alarming. Charcot and others would go on to try and counter this impression by decorating the Salpêtrière with memorials to the glorious history of Positivist science, as we shall see in Chap. 3—but many figures such as Jules Claretie found such efforts unconvincing.

2   THE STAGE MANAGER OF THE SALPÊTRIÈRE

Charcot's biography provides an overview of the major political and social events of his lifetime, and the nature of the medical world within which he practiced. Charcot was a well-known public figure with personal connections to the Republican government, a status which enabled him to develop the Salpêtrière as a world centre for the development of neurology as a new specialist practice. Charcot remained, however, a physician-polymath, active in virtually all branches of medicine. The place of hysteria, as well as hypnosis (which Charcot saw as a hysterical symptom) featured prominently within his diverse career. His 1883 application to join the Academy of Sciences was made on the basis of a paper related to this topic, causing Platel to respond with his virulent attack in *Le Figaro*. One eulogy in the *Gazette de France* after Charcot's death contained the opinion that Charcot "owed to hypnotism not his reputation, but his fame, and his alleged discoveries [in hypnosis] are precisely those which are least remarkable in his career."[1] Another English commentator responded that such a dismissal of Charcot's work on hypnosis was "astonishing," a debate which reflected the vexed position this topic occupied within Charcot's practice. It is, moreover, important to note here that one of the main reasons Charcot initially became involved with the study of hysteria arose from his efforts to manage the *space* of the hospital itself.

Born in 1825, Jean-Martin was the oldest of the four sons of Simon-Pierre Charcot, a Parisian builder of luxury carriages.[2] As the child of an artisan, Jean-Martin enjoyed a well-to-do but far from wealthy upbringing. Myth had it that Simon-Pierre gathered his sons together in a dramatic scene which reads as if from the Bible or a folk tale, and explained to them that only one could afford to be sent to university. Émile-Martin was to join the army (he died in Senegal in 1869), Eugène-Martin enlisted in the navy, whilst Pierre-Martin successfully carried on the family business. As the brightest, Jean-Martin was given the choice of enrolling either in the arts or medicine. Jean-Martin chose the latter, though he retained the draftsman's skills which had prompted his father's offer.

Charcot began his career during Louis Napoleon III's Second Empire, 1852–1870. The student's early papers set the tone for his later work, covering topics which ranged from rheumatism to hemiplegia, pathological anatomy, faith-healing, and his doctoral thesis on "Primitive Asthenic Gout" (1853).[3] His 1857 aggregation thesis was on "expectation," or how the beliefs of a patient could affect their nervous disposition, a long term interest which Charcot eventually developed into the posthumous publication *The Faith Which Heals* (1897).[4] Presaging the hostility Charcot was later to encounter on the ambiguous relationship between behaviour and physical illness, he was not passed on this first thesis. It was a subsequent, more sedate essay on chronic pneumonia which allowed him to proceed up the medical hierarchy.

Charcot enjoyed the patronage of Pierre Rayer, a general physician best remembered today for assisting in identifying the anthrax bacillus. In 1862 a professorial chair in comparative pathology was created specifically for Rayer, who later became dean of the Paris Faculty of Medicine.[5] Rayer proved adept at moving through the growing medico-bureaucratic systems which had developed since the 1789 Revolution. He was physician to Bonaparte's brother Jêrome Napoleon and was friendly with influential physicians such as the renowned experimental physiologist Claude Bernard and neurophysiologist Charles-Édouard Brown-Séquard. Charcot followed the traditional career path for medical interns of writing up the cases of their patrons for medical journals, a pattern which was later replicated by Charcot's own students. Charcot in fact surpassed Rayer in developing such patronage networks. However, commentators like Pont-Calé from *Les hommes d'aujourd'hui* and Platel did not allow the neuropathologist to completely escape his former association with Rayer and the Imperial medical fraternity. Charcot was often compared to Napoleon, whilst Platel and Pont-Calé claimed that Charcot's allegiance had simply shifted from the Bonapartists to the radical left—although they conceded that this was more due to the changes which had occurred in French politics than Charcot's own convictions. Neither assessment was entirely fair. Charcot grew into a staunch Republican like most of his peers, but he was never a radical.[6]

The journalists' comments revealed both the political tensions of Charcot's time and the rapprochement which had been established by the 1880s. The years 1789–1852 saw numerous revolts, two republics, a novel imperial regime, and two monarchies. The Second Empire, therefore, marked a period of relative political stability and—perhaps more importantly—economic and cultural growth. A rising patrician consensus grew out of the preceding July Monarchy period, favouring a statist, paternalistic regime in which physicians and scientists played a growing role in industrialization, social hygiene, mental health, sexuality, and jurisprudence. Divisions of class, ideology, and religion nevertheless continued to fester throughout Charcot's lifetime, as General George Ernest Boulanger's abortive 1889 coup based on right-wing populist ideology demonstrated.

The most dramatic political event of Charcot's lifetime came in 1870. Charcot had by now worked at the major combined hospital-asylums of Charité, Pitié, and the Salpêtrière. He and his early collaborator Alfred Vulpian had begun cataloguing the disorders found in the patients at the Salpêtrière. Vulpian succeeded Jean Cruveilhier to the teaching position of professor of pathological anatomy in 1867—a post which Charcot was to hold when Vulpian became professor of experimental pathology in 1872. Both men presented lectures at the hospice and other teaching institutions. In 1869 Vulpian accepted a position at the nearby Pitié Hospital, whilst Charcot stayed on at the Salpêtrière. Vulpian became a successful neuroanatomist and physician in his own right, though he remained one of Charcot's strongest supporters.

In 1870 the Imperial regime suffered a humiliating defeat at the hands of Prussia, with Napoleon III himself being captured by the enemy. The Empire collapsed and a new government was declared outside of Paris. In the capital, the ensuing uncertainty and divisions precipitated the radical left-wing revolt in the form of the Paris Commune.[7] The city had been first besieged by the German forces, after which the new conservative national government fled the growing political activity of the urban crowds and the

National Guardsmen for Versailles. This culminated in the revolt of the Communards, bloodily suppressed by the national government in 1871, after which the regime returned to Paris. The Third Republic came out of this conflict.

The less than propitious birth of the Republic largely explained the social anxiety which figures such as Charcot both reflected upon and perpetrated. Commentators uttered dark predictions regarding spread of hereditary illness and racial degeneration, the hysterical mimicry of anarchism, the potentially psychotic affects of social trauma, the scourge of modern poisons ranging from mercury to cocaine, the dangers of mechanized transport, and a growing mania for incendiarism. In 1881 the author Guy de Maupassant (a neighbour of Charcot who also attended the neuropathologist's lectures) went so far as to describe the Commune as "nothing other than a hysterical crisis of Paris," and Charcot's former students such as Max Nordau and Léon Daudet were to become significant commentators on these scourges and the role of neuropathology in them.[8] Charcot himself noted that his patients had "seen their malady born in the midst of the political commotions which have agitated our country."[9] The hospital served in part as a mnemonic theatre where the internees' nightmarish delusions indirectly replayed the history of French political terror. As we shall see, the hallucinations experienced by hysterics and others often recalled scenes of political violence and disorder. The institutional effects of the socio-political struggles which followed 1870 were less dramatic, however, and such events influenced but did not determine Charcot's career.

Charcot remained studiously aloof from the virtual civil war which surrounded the Salpêtrière in 1870–1871. He continued to treat the general populace throughout the bombardment, but refused to offer succour to combatants from either side. The subsequent Republican regime expanded many of the paternalistic policies of its predecessors. The major innovation of the Third Republic was an increasingly powerful anticlerical, laicizing trend—enthusiastically endorsed by Charcot and his peers such as Charcot's collaborator, the physician-politician Désiré Bourneville, whose work I discuss in Chap. 6. The Republic was also witness to a rise in materialist, scientific explanations, particularly with regard to mental pathology, rather than the more abstract psychological approaches which had dominated psychiatry and other disciplines during the eighteenth and early nineteenth centuries.

French economic and cultural life recovered quickly from the nadir of 1871, giving rise to what has been retrospectively christened "*la Belle époque.*" Charcot's star ascended with that of the new regime. Rayer had referred the banker Achille Fould to Charcot's care, and Fould later became Finance Minister under the Republic. Charcot knew many other senior Republicans personally, including the most influential of them all: Léon Gambetta. Charcot's almost unequalled position as senior physician of the Third Republic led him and his associate, professor of legal medicine Paul-Camille-Hippolyte Brouardel, to attend at Gambetta's autopsy in 1883. In 1893 the pair were appointed to determine if the main defendant in the financial scandal of the French Panama Canal Company float—Cornelius Herz—was fit to return from Britain to France to stand trial. Charcot was even said to have facilitated the Franco-Russian alliance by bringing together his patient the Grand Duke Nicholas and Gambetta at Charcot's Neuilly residence. Though many physicians were well known and widely respected under the Third Republic, few could rival him in fame or influence, except perhaps the physiologist Claude Bernard and the Catholic surgeon Jules Émile Péan. No matter what Charcot did, he was always performing for an audience.

Charcot was thus a model for social mobility under the Republic, having risen from the artisan-class to become one of the most influential and well-known physicians of his day. In 1864 he married the young widow Augustine-Victoire Durvis, daughter of the celebrated collector M. Laurent-Richard who had made his fortune as a tailor. Laurent had in fact begun the association between the two families by employing Simon-Pierre to build a lavish carriage. Jean-Martin and Augustine shared a love of the arts. They collaborated on the "common oeuvre" of the furnishings for their increasingly opulent living quarters, collectively designing and producing many decorative objects themselves and patronizing prominent artists such as Émile Gallé and Auguste Rodin.[10] As a member of the Union centrale des arts décoratifs, Augustine played a role in the encouragement of national revival through the promotion of an identifiably French domestic taste (largely neo-Rococo and neo-Gothic furnishings, although classical and Latinate motifs also featured prominently). The Charcots were, therefore, amongst those who helped set the standard for patrician taste during the Third Republic, with one of Augustine's pieces featuring in the first Exposition of Women's Arts of 1892.

After the Siege the family moved from the avenue du Coq on the Right Bank, to the Hôtel Chimay on the Seine's quai Malaquais (1875–1884, following which the Hôtel Chimay was acquired to house the National School of Fine Arts, where Paul Richer was later to teach), before eventually settling in the Hôtel Varangeville on the boulevard St Germain (a room from which is now held at New York's Metropolitan Museum of Art). The Hôtel Varangeville was close to the medical consulting rooms of Jean-Martin's peers, legal practices, the homes of writers such as the Daudets and Jean-Baptiste Dumas, as well as aristocratic and diplomatic residences (notably the Imperial Russian property of the Hôtel d'Estrées) and those of physicians like Pierre-Carl Potain. The Charcots also owned a summer home in Neuilly-sur-Seine. The social networks which the couple maintained in these sumptuous surrounds reached their summit with the marriage of Marie Durvis—Augustine's daughter by her first marriage—to Gambetta's protégé René Waldeck-Rosseau, who was to become head of government 1899–1902. For the son of a carriage builder to marry into a wealthy bourgeois family and later become part of a Republican political dynasty was no small feat. Charcot, however, apparently never felt entirely at ease in social gatherings with his more high-born peers, and this may have explained his famously cool demeanour.[11] As a performer, Charcot remained restrained.

Charcot's preeminence as a famous doctor proved short lived, however. In the last years before his demise in 1893 it became clear that Charcot's construction of hypnosis as an essentially pathological, hysterical disorder was indefensible in light of rival theories promoted by Hippolyte Bernheim. The Nancy based physician insisted—correctly as it turned out—that normal individuals were susceptible to hypnotic suggestion as well as those who suffered from neurological impairments. Significant though this distinction was, it is important to remember that both Bernheim and Charcot associated hypnosis with a special state of the nervous system, and both argued that it was associated with illness to the degree that it either existed in tandem with, or could be used to treat, illness. For many lay commentators then, this impassioned medical debate was of less significance than the scientific recognition that hypnosis was a *real* phenomenon which could affect a variety of subjects.[12]

The power vacuum in the Medical Faculty subsequent to Charcot's death by heart attack was followed by a rapid devaluing of the neurologist's status. Jean-Martin's son Jean-Baptiste (1867–1936) had obeyed his father's wishes by becoming a neurologist. After Charcot *père*'s demise however, Jean-Baptiste moved from the mapping of the body to the mapping of space and exploration. This was not an entirely decisive break though. Jean-Baptiste procured valuable financial support from his former colleagues at the Salpêtrière to whom he continued to send photographs and accounts of interesting medical cases he encountered. It is his untimely demise in 1936 whilst off the coast of Iceland on board the *Pourquoi pas?* that now most often captures the popular imagination when the name Charcot is heard.

At the height of his career Charcot gathered considerable support for the development of a specialist neuropathological practice at the Salpêtrière. From the mid 1870s he lobbied the Medical Faculty, international physicians such as Wilheim Erb and Carl Westphall, the Assistance publique, the Paris Municipal Council, as well as leading politicians like Gambetta and Jules Ferry. Charcot was rewarded for these efforts by assuming France's first chair of neuropathology in 1882.

Prior to occupying the chair of diseases of the nervous system, Charcot held the more general teaching position of professor of pathological anatomy at the Salpêtrière, formerly occupied by Cruveilhier and Vulpian. Charcot's *Oeuvres complètes* charted his transition through various medical specialties. Volumes one to four and volume ten dealt specifically with the neuropathological ideas Charcot developed largely during the 1880s, focusing on matters related to nervous tissue, the spinal cord, and general neuromotor function. The contemporaneous ninth volume, however, moved into the related field of brain function, which was becoming increasingly important for psychiatric diagnoses as well as for neuropathology proper. The fifth volume reproduced his lectures on diseases of the cardiovascular system and lungs from his 1877–1878 course in pathological anatomy, the sixth those on the liver and kidneys, the seventh chronic illness associated with ageing including rheumatism and gout as well as Charcot's lectures on medical thermometry first published during the 1860s, whilst the eighth covered infectious diseases such as pneumonia, dermatological conditions, and gastrointestinal states. Nor did the *Oeuvres complètes* represent an exhaustive survey of his interests. Charcot's senior assistants Edouard Brissaud and Pierre Marie reflected: "There is not ... a branch of medicine in which he did not excel."[13] Charcot's specialization in neuropathology represented the conclusion to an extensive and varied career covering clinical anatomy, microbiology, and even abstract concerns like the nature of aphasia. His practice sat astride several discourses which had both a lay and a professional audience.

Charcot's tenure at the Salpêtrière marked the eclipse of the alienist models which had reached their height under Jean-Étienne Dominique

Esquirol in the 1830s. Charcot was at the forefront of the more material-ist approaches to mental function of the Paris school of medicine, build-ing especially on the work of his senior colleague and early collaborator Guillaume-Benjamin Duchenne de Boulogne, with whom Charcot worked from 1862 until de Boulogne's death in 1875.[14]

After Philippe Pinel moved from the Bicêtre Men's Asylum to the Salpêtrière in 1795, he pioneered the alienist techniques later formalized by his successor Esquirol. Although Charcot served in a different depart-ment than Esquirol, both Charcot and Pinel originally occupied the same position at the Salpêtrière: that of general physician to the patients of the Salpêtrière infirmary.

Alienists considered mental disorder to be derived from the alienation of the psyche or soul from itself; madness was a form of mental self-alienation. Alienism was concerned with mental conditions which often had physical or hereditary causes. These pathologies could also have sec-ondary somatic symptomatic signs. Charcot's neuropathological approach inverted this schema. It dealt with primarily physical conditions, which could have psychic symptoms or secondary characteristics. Charcot's diag-nostic method did not, therefore, begin with a verbal interrogation to determine the mental state of the subject, as was the case in alienist psy-chiatry. On the contrary Charcot's examination characteristically took the form of a laconic visual analysis of the body of the patient. The neuropa-thologist himself reflected that often "a single glance at the patient, his movements, his speech, or his gait will suffice to give the case away."[15] Subjects were ushered into Charcot's modest consultation office and the patients were asked to strip. Charcot would regard the nude individual whilst his interns read out the case history and preliminary observations. In the words of his contemporary, the Amiens physician-neurologist Paul Peugniez, Charcot's eyes would "fix the patient with an extraordinary pen-etrative force."[16] Charcot would then confirm the details of the notes by asking his subject a number of short questions, before instructing the suf-ferer to attempt to reproduce certain movements—particularly walking.

Charcot's consulting room was laid out not only so as to resemble the studio of a photographer or painter, but also so as to resemble a the-atre. One later visitor noted that: "The entire room and its furnishings were painted black," whilst another reflected that Charcot typically, "sits before the window, from which light falls on the faces of the two or three patients ... occupying chairs in front of him."[17] Though Charcot doubtless savoured the aloof, mysterious air he enjoyed by having his patients view him shadowed or in silhouette in this dark chamber, the primary function of this placing was to enable Charcot to see his subjects in the best possible illumination. This same scenario also existed in his home office. Although Charcot regularly toured the rest of the Salpêtrière, he preferred to confine his consultations to this highly stage-managed office space.

The preface to the *Nouvelle iconographie de la Salpêtrière* gave a sense of this interplay between the iconographic approach of visual arts and performativity, stating:

> When a patient demonstrates signs of particular interest ... he is ... drawn or photographed. With the aid of this immediate record, we are able to freeze the abnormality, to decompose the various abnormal movements one by one, and thereby capture the disorder with precision. These vignettes from the Salpêtrière complement the clinical examination to form a collection of great significance.[18]

Despite the fact that both the *Nouvelle iconographie de la Salpêtrière* and the preceding *Iconographie photographique de la Salpêtrière* featured a wealth of photographs and engravings, these visual materials were deemed to have little value on their own. They were rather complementary "vignettes" taken from the disordered body; fragments captured and frozen in time. It was from the "collection" itself that the utility of these otherwise disparate images and observations was derived. These "vignettes" were used in tandem with "the clinical examination" so as to construct a performative narrative. Charcot's practice constituted an expansive archive of materials which was then sewn together through various diagnostic strategies.

It was, therefore, highly significant that some of the earliest work in French cinematic technologies was produced at the Salpêtrière by Charcot's senior associates and collaborators. Amongst the most important figures involved was the professor of medicine at the Collège de France, Étienne-Jules Marey.[19] Marey constructed an extensive array of devices for measuring bodily movement which were employed by the Salpêtrière physicians. He designed some of the first sphygmomanometers or blood pressure monitors, a project also explored by the first head of the Salpêtrière's photographic laboratory, Paul Régnard. Marey later made available to Charcot and his associates "pneumographic" machines or "tambours" with counterweighted arms which wavered in time to bodily movement. These mechanisms were then connected to a revolving barrel of graphite-coated paper, or in some cases fitted with an internal

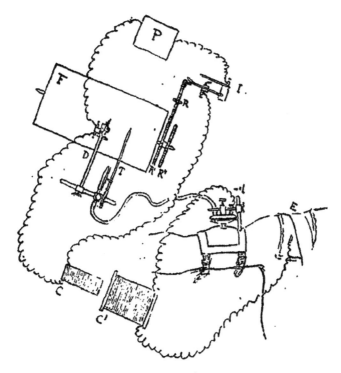

Fig. 2.1   Marey tambour; *Source*: Richer, *Études* (1885), 630. Courtesy of the Boston Medical Library in the Francis A. Countway Library of Medicine

surface for recording tremors. The smallest of these contraptions could be strapped directly to the body (Fig. 2.1). Régnard's successor, Albert Londe, also crafted an adaptation of one of Marey's inventions using a small lamp attached to the patient. The movement of the light beam was recorded upon a roll of photosensitive paper. The traces produced under the direction of Marey, Régnard, Londe, and Richer were employed by Charcot to distinguish between mercury poisoning and other tremulous conditions, including hysteria (see Chap. 6). Reproductions of these graphs appeared throughout the writings of the Salpêtrière school, especially the case histories, both published and unpublished.[20] The purpose was to produce an objective, quantifiable image of temporal movement or performance in the living patient.

In addition to these ingenious apparatuses, Marey pioneered the construction of shuttering devices which allowed cinematic stills to be created. Londe began work on his own version of the shutters developed by Marey and US photographer Eadweard Muybridge, later enlisting Marey's assistance at the Salpêtrière itself. Richer collaborated with Londe using Marey's method of "chronophotography" (stop-motion photography) to produce a precise, quantitative breakdown of each part of the body in movement. Richer published their initial findings in the *Nouvelle iconographie de la Salpêtrière* during the 1880s. This culminated in Richer's 1895 *Artistic Physiology of Man in Movement*. Although Charcot died two years before its publication, his legacy remained present in the form of his athletic son Jean-Baptiste, who served as one of the early subjects. Nor were Marey, Richer, and Londe the only scientists associated with the Salpêtrière school to work in this field. The *Nouvelle iconographie* published several other similar studies, including a "cinematographic" examination of hemiplegic stagger by Charcot's former student, the Romanian Georges Marinesco. The full cinematic capture of the moving body represented the logical culmination of Charcot's otherwise apparently iconographic process. Images were not primarily important in themselves. They were rather used as an aid for the description of action, or that which occurred in the realm of performance and movement. To quote the *Nouvelle iconographie*, illustrations "complement the clinical examination."

Charcot and his followers were not so concerned with an idealized image or architecture of shapes, forms, or static geometric relations captured within the frame of the gaze. Rather they sought to identify the temporal phenomena which existed between or across individual images. Charcot's work only partly conformed to the aesthetics of classical painting and sculpture. An image isolated in space and time was comparatively unhelpful from a diagnostic point of view. Its full significance was only evident when such images were placed side by side. Photography helped Charcot to link together the otherwise contradictory imperatives of materialist dissection (the decomposition of abnormal movement referred to in the *Nouvelle iconographie de la Salpêtrière*) with the aggregation of more immaterial phenomena such as gait. The aim was to reconcile a universally applicable set of diagnostic criteria with the idiosyncratic, contingent shapes found in living, moving bodies. Charcot's desire for an immediate record pointed to the way his practice functioned both within time (movement and living physiology) whilst also defying time (recording ephemera).

The camera was a particularly useful tool in this creative endeavour. Even the sequential arrangement of the photographs in the *Iconographie photographique de la Salpêtrière* and the *Nouvelle iconographie* resembled pre-cinematic technologies such as flip-book animation or Eadweard Muybridge's zoetropes. The logical culmination of Charcot's diagnostic method was the equivalent of a filmic archive for a society in which cinematic techniques had yet to be perfected. Charcot created a reiterative theatre in which the physical repetition of movements, captured and analysed through photography and drawing, was invoked in the lecture theatre so as to clarify, stabilize, and order that which lay at the margins of orderly conduct—namely the living, pathological body. Little wonder Charcot's work so intrigued the Surrealists in their project of championing the creative potential of such psychophysical disorders.

Richer distinguished between the dissociated, moribund forms isolated through post-mortem, and the analysis of performance which he helped to pioneer at the Salpêtrière. He proclaimed that for physiologists the "principal objective" of study was "the exterior form during the movement."[21] Richer observed that photography allowed scientists to wed dissection with theatrical observations; it enabled one to "fix in a durable image the most fugitive moment of a movement."

Charcot made the same point in his lectures for the Medical Faculty's 1877–1878 course in anatomy. Anatomical dissection only enabled one "to constitute a sort of museum more or less encumbered by specimens catalogued following an arrangement which is necessarily arbitrary."[22] The lesion which one viewed in the autopsy merely represented "the static condition" of the diseased body. The dynamic function of the observed organs could only be surmised. To truly understand illness however: "the doctor must know not only the impaired, dead organ, but also the impaired, living organ, active, exercising its normal functions"—a point to which we shall return in Chap. 4. Thus, although Charcot noted that "brilliant advances" had been "furnished, in these last few years, by histological pathological anatomy," these scopic innovations had been preceded by "another anatomy, the most ancient, that which is produced with the naked eye" gazing upon the clinical body.

Charcot proclaimed that his purpose was:

> to place before your eyes anatomical specimens with which you are able to study the imperfections revealed by the naked eye. In their absence, I will present you with plates ... from the best authors ... [in which] these lesions

will be represented as faithfully as possible. No doubt a good plate, no matter how faithful it is, can never completely replace the direct contemplation of the diseased organ; but by placing in relief, if it is cleverly devised, the important, fundamental characteristics, it [the plate] helps us to see and to see better. Moreover, since one is able to hold it always before one's eyes, it offers the advantage of quickly and efficaciously fixing one's memories which fade quickly if one does not have the opportunity of frequently reviving them.[23]

Charcot's discourse, however, put into relief the very tensions which he sought to overcome. Photography was characterized here as both superior to, and inferior to, the theatrical viewing of the living body. The neuropathologist extolled photography for enabling one to see that which was difficult to revive, whilst simultaneously conceding that images could only stand in for the living body. Photographs acted merely as mnemonic aids. The photograph was able to remain "always before our eyes"—yet ideally so too would the moving body itself. Photography, therefore, took over only "when one does not have the opportunity" to stage pathologies before one's eyes.

Images repeated, emulated, replaced, annihilated, evoked, and gestured towards (all in the one action) that which was made manifest in time and space. The physician had, in Charcot's words, to constantly draw together "the laboratory work and the autopsy of the amphitheatre."[24] Charcot thus characterized medicine as a fraught creative practice in which materials derived from different sources were united in the mind of the physician, producing a descriptive language, or nosography, of the living, breathing, moving body. Only in the theatre of the clinic could one hope to bring all of these elements together.

3   The Versailles of Misery, the Bastille of Medicine

The Salpêtrière was well known to the European public as the setting for dramatic encounters. Walter Benjamin and others have noted how late nineteenth century Paris was often seen as a spectacle through which the curious wanderer or *flâneur* might proceed, taking in its various scenes and sights.[25] The Salpêtrière itself featured prominently in newspaper articles and even tourist guidebooks. In addition to acting as a frame for Charcot's own practice, the hospice was a common setting for commentaries which drew upon the Catholic ideal of redemptive suffering, the piteous spectacle which this provided, as well as the popular interest in recent scientific discoveries and innovations. The Salpêtrière was routinely described as a "city of misery" in both popular and medical commentary. Charcot himself described the hospice as "that great refuge" or "emporium of human miseries."[26] Jules Claretie's account was perhaps the most famous in this genre of medical pathos. Claretie had set his novel, *The Loves of an Intern* (1902), in this "women's hell," whilst in his regular column for *Le temps*, Claretie noted that Charcot's practice was centred around that "doleful city populated like a town within a town" which was the Salpêtrière.[27] In a eulogy devoted to Charcot, Claretie described the hospice as "picturesque and admirable like a theatre set, fully equipped" so as to house the dramas it had contained, including those of Charcot's life and practice.[28]

The hospice was indeed remarkable for its scale and design. It had its own general store and market (where tobacco and sweets were amongst the most sought after supplies), a post-office, a brasserie and other drinking establishments, public wells, laundries (where many of the patients were employed washing linen from the other Parisian hospitals), roads named after local landmarks (rue de la Cuisine, rue de la Pharmacie), rail-carts for deliveries, as well as a cemetery.[29] In addition to the semi-permanent, destitute adult female patient population, one could also find patients' children and a small number of young internees, transitory patients both male and female from the infirmary—a hospital within a hospital—plus a large, resident working population of both sexes, drawn especially from the neighbouring poor *faubourgs*. Although these individuals doubtless shared some sense of community and happiness, Claretie and his peers found nothing but "misery, madness, broken old age, all of that which engenders not only vice and debauchery, but also—more tragically—virtue itself, impoverished virtue, poverty, work!"[30]

Despite these depressing commentaries, the major Parisian hospitals were also routinely associated with progressive developments in the history of French medicine. The Salpêtrière was an especially rich site for such evocations, its buildings replaying French medical history and the vexed, controversial transition from Catholic charity administered by the absolutist, monarchical regime of the seventeenth century, to modern Republican medicine. The hospital was initially constructed in the late sixteenth century to house a gunpowder manufactory beyond the main population centres of Paris.[31] Vincent de Paul petitioned government minister Cardinal Mazarin to assist foundlings, the poor, and the destitute, which led Louis XIV to establish the *hôpitaux généraux* in 1656. The Salpêtrière arsenal was one of several structures transformed into a hospice for those without a fixed address—"the Great Confinement" as Foucault christened it.[32] Itinerants and non-working members of the public were placed into institutions established by royal edict. Women, prostitutes, and the aged in particular were served by the Salpêtrière. An important distinguishing feature of the Salpêtrière, however, was that, unlike some other Parisian hospices such as the Hôtel Dieu near Notre Dame cathedral, the Salpêtrière was staffed by a state-employed order of lay surveillants, and not nuns.

Louis devoted considerable resources to this state institutionalization of charity. In 1657 the royal architects began work on the immense dome of the Salpêtrière chapel, following the model employed for the cupola of the state military hospice of the Hôtel des Invalides. The new chapel was dedicated to the King's patron saint, St Louis. The Salpêtrière's impressive facade was set back behind the main gate, which enclosed a large, tree-lined courtyard—the *cour d'honneur*—leading up to the two main wings which flanked the chapel. Maurice Guillemot noted in *Le Paris illustré* of 1887 how the long, framed views of Salpêtrière's verdant boulevards resembled those built under royal patronage at both Invalides and the palace of Versailles: "all that greenery gives the general atmosphere almost an air of gaiety, something of the impression of a retreat, a holiday house in the middle of the country."[33] Claretie, however, saw little "gaiety" in the Old Regime design of Salpêtrière gardens and their immediate surrounds on boulevard de l'Hôpital:

> Immediately after crossing the sad square, planted with trees which give no shade, projecting their spindly silhouettes on the bare grass which grows in this spot, trodden down by the feet of the old women who walk around outside the hospice, we passed through the door where a tricolour flag flaps, above it the lugubrious inscription: Hospice for Aged-Women, it is as though one is enveloped by the great melancholy silence of that doleful city.[34]

The skeletal forms of the trees and the venerable entrance only evoked in Claretie a sense of suffocating silence and hidden misery which united the decayed patients with their surrounds. What is significant here is the tendency to read bodies in terms of their mise en scène, and vice versa. Barely within the walls of the hospice, Claretie already began to feel the doleful effects of the space. The buildings and the sick treated within them were in "melancholy" harmony with each other, enveloping visitors with their ambience.

Claretie's dour response was indicative of how the once bucolic locale of the Salpêtrière had long since disappeared by the Third Republic. As Paris grew, the *faubourgs* near the hospice came to house a large working-class population, especially workers from the nearby Gobelins' royal tapestry manufactory. Victor Hugo set part of *Les misérables* (1862) in the streets beside what he called "the unknown country of the Salpêtrière ... where it might be said that Paris disappeared."[35] The hospice lay at the edges of the main districts of Paris, a deteriorating relic of royal extravagance, its gardens overlooking contemporary urban poverty and industry. This squalor caused the asylum's doctors to see patients of both sexes from not only the local district, but also further afield. The outpatient facility was eventually formalized by Charcot as the policlinique, with beds furnished within the infirmary. There Charcot saw working-class subjects, often free of charge, whilst his more prestigious clients paid substantial fees.

This history of accretions and changes recorded in stone was evoked by journalist Alexandre Guérin in his article for *La revue illustrée* of 1887. Noting its origins under Louis XIV, Guérin reflected that:

> Despite the modifications that it has undergone for more than two centuries, the Salpêtrière still preserves, in the ensemble of its principal buildings, the magisterial and glacial aspect which it had in the time of the great King.[36]

Perhaps because of this "as one passes through the vestibule of this immense refuge, one is struck by an impression analogous to what one would feel upon entering a dead town." The Salpêtrière was a space haunted by the ghosts of the Old Regime and the subsequent revolutions which overthrew it, the hospice's once "magisterial" royal grandeur in decline, "glacial" and reminiscent of a "dead town." Guérin's words took on greater significance in light of the fact that his 1887 article united both popular and professional discourse. Guérin, like Claretie, had trained as a doctor—though Guérin went on to practice medicine, whilst Claretie did not. The latter made this link between the modern Salpêtrière and the edifice's once regal history still more explicit, noting that:

> Behind these bare walls lives, swarming and dragging themselves along the ground, a special population: old men, poor women, resting on a bench as they await death ... The thick, grey walls of this *citta dolorosa* seem to have

conserved their dilapidated solemnity, the magisterial character of a district from Louis XIV's time, forgotten in the Paris of electric tramways. There [at the Salpêtrière] it is like the Versailles of pain.[37]

The Salpêtrière did not, however, simply represent a spatio-architectural concretization of history and Gothic suffering. It was, on the contrary, a realm where modern scientific therapy and its antithesis collided; where an acceptance of pain and suffering cohabited with novel methods deployed in order to diagnose, control, and eliminate such phenomena. Modernism and the pre-modern faced off against each other within the venue. The Salpêtrière was a space well known to doctors and the newspaper-reading public alike, defined in large part by a confluence of medical, literary, and theatrical tropes.

Medical and lay commentators routinely described the Salpêtrière by taking the reader through a virtual tour of the buildings, recreating the space upon the reader's mental stage. Claretie, for example, traced the path of the patients as they moved down from the "chalets of the mad" built during Pinel's time in the northeast of the grounds, and then south to the main garden behind the chapel, traversing:

> this immense building ... the Salpêtrière ... with six thousand souls breathing inside that pile of walls, in the shadow of the black, slate-dome which is the church; at the end of the great courtyards where, on the wooden benches, they miserably ruminate on their existence ... over there, after having followed the flowerbeds, thick with lilacs in spring, [but which are] melancholic in autumn; at the end of the successive arcades which open, one after the other, onto new courtyards, courtyard Sainte-Claire, courtyard Saint-Félix.[38]

Here the aged patients became indistinguishable from the structures they inhabited. The inmates resembled tragic "shadows" playing about the greying walls. Space and architecture came to define identity.

Visiting the Salpêtrière did not, however, necessarily produce such a melancholy tone. The first stop for many authors was the statue of Pinel which stood before the front gate—an attraction which even featured in the 1910 Hachette guide to strolls in Paris.[39] Pinel had famously unchained the insane at the Hospice de la Bicêtre and at the Salpêtrière, and, as we shall see, this event recurred throughout the iconography of both alienism and Charcot's practice. Under the Old Regime, patients were incarcerated at the Salpêtrière through a magistrate's *lettre de cachet. Lettres de cachets* were deployed for a range of public offences, varying from insurrection to insanity. Not only were these diverse crimes grouped together by judicial process, but insanity could be invoked to hasten the transfer of assets to dissatisfied heirs or to incarcerate political dissidents without trial. Consequently *lettres de cachet* became primary signifiers of royal absolutism. The link between the sequestration of the insane and criminal behavior led to the addition of the prison ward (a *"maison de force"*) to the Salpêtrière complex in 1680. Even in 1925, Georges Guillain and Pierre Mathieu had to concede that "the appearance" of this section "has remained lugubrious."[40] The inmates of Salpêtrière's *maison de force* consisted of various miscreants identified first by the royal regime, then later by the Revolution. The 1792 massacre of inmates which occurred there was one of the darker memories of Revolutionary Terror associated with the grounds of the Salpêtrière.

Pinel's actions in the years immediately following the overthrow of the King were soon incorporated into Republican hagiography, coming to represent the pinnacle of enlightened reform. Pinel's tenure at the Salpêtrière was a medical parallel to the fall of the Bastille. The presence of Pinel's statue at the entrance to this place of allegedly enlightened sequestration implied that post-Revolutionary science had overcome such misdeeds. Guérin, Claretie, Hugo, and others, however, mitigated these claims by invoking the architectural style, history, and poor condition of the buildings—Guérin noting, for example, the historical contradiction of the "the coat of arms of the kings of France" resting below the Tricolour and the inscription "Liberty, Equality, Fraternity" upon the main gateway.[41]

The contradictory meanings inherent in what Charcot's former student and New York physician Moses Allen Starr aptly described as "the theatre of his wonderful activity" were of more than passing interest to hospital physicians.[42] Charcot's student Louis Boucher, for example, devoted his 1883 thesis to the hospice's pre-Revolutionary past. Boucher observed that: "Just as the ancient Gothic cathedrals were the work of several centuries, so the Salpêtrière has been enlarged successively at different periods."[43] Fulgence Raymond—Charcot's immediate successor as professor of neuropathology—made the same observation in his 1894 opening lecture: "this place, with its immense buildings, from different ages, all like the old Gothic cathedrals, already has the import of a small city."[44] The hospital design itself, therefore, served to dramatize the conflict between

objective social hygiene and the piecemeal additions made to an institution originally based upon royal charity. Despite modern advances, the
Salpêtrière remained a decaying, under-resourced town within a town,
home to 4383 residents in 1873.[45] Before Charcot and his colleagues
even came onstage, the manipulation of space was of primary importance
in determining the meaning of the dramas played out, diagnosed, and
treated at the hospice. Charcot needed to control not only the iconography of the Salpêtrière, but its complete spatial contextualization and
manifestation—the dramaturgy of illness.

Some commentators sought to maximize the positive aspects of the
Salpêtrière's scenographic allusions by skating over any troubling references
to the role of the King, his ministers and the Church in the foundation
of the *hôpitaux généraux*. Instead they focused upon the somewhat less
fraught precedent set by the enlightened royal scientists at the nearby Jardin
des Plantes.[46] The science practiced at the Jardin des Plantes was not without controversy. The royal scientists based around the Jardin des Plantes had
come to be seen as representing a progressive wing of pre-Revolutionary
discourse, allied to Enlightenment figures like Pinel. Consequently these
institutions were relatively easily later integrated into the history and ideology of Republican Positivism. Vulpian himself later presented lectures in
neurophysiology at the Natural History Museum located within the grounds
of the gardens, whilst a sculpture by Richer depicting a Cro-Magnon man
carving a mammoth was erected outside the Museum in 1890, thereby con-
secrating in bronze the link between the Salpêtrière school of neurology and
the leisure precinct of the nearby Jardin des Plantes.[47]

Guérin capitalized on this by noting the proximity of the Salpêtrière to
the Jardin des Plantes, where the biologists Georges Leclerc de Bouffon,
Jean-Baptiste Lamarck, Georges Cuvier, and others had worked and lec-
tured.[48] Charcot's former student Sigmund Freud likened the spatial
ordering of the specimens in Paris' botanical gardens to Charcot's diagnostic technique, claiming that:

> The pupil who spent many hours with him going round the wards of
> Salpêtrière—that museum of clinical facts, the names and peculiar characteristics
> of which were for the most part derived from him—would be reminded of
> Cuvier, whose statue, standing in front of the Jardin des Plantes, shows that
> great comprehender and describer of the animal world surrounded by a mul-
> titude of animal forms; or else would recall the myth of Adam ... when God
> brought the creatures of Paradise before him to be distinguished and named.[49]

Carl von Linnaeus had famously devised a system of botanical classification, from which the arrangement of the specimens on display at the
Jardin was derived. At the Jardin des Plantes, flowerbeds made manifest
in spatial terms the classification of nature. Freud further related this spatial organization of nature to the sculptural symbology of Paris. Cuvier's
statue reinforced the mastery of nature realized in the overall design of
the Jardin itself, highlighting the role of "that great comprehender and
describer of the animal world" in revealing the underlying patterns which
the landscaping traced. The reference to Cuvier's statue also evoked that
of Pinel before the Salpêtrière gate—where a statue of Charcot himself
was later erected following the neuropathologist's death (later removed
during the German occupation).[50] Charcot performed for the Salpêtrière
the same function that Cuvier and Linnaeus had at the gardens, bringing
order to the disorderly space of the wards through the act of naming.
Charcot was the Adam of the Salpêtrière, categorizing each condition and
assigning it to its proper place. The layout of Charcot's wards echoed this
ideal, separating patients of each type into their own specialist services
(little matter that such niceties were rarely fully realized in practice).

By the mid nineteenth century the Jardin des Plantes had become a
popular leisure precinct. In *The Skin of Sorrow* (1831), Honore de Balzac
waxed lyrical on the wonders identified by Cuvier and which were displayed
in the gardens' museums. Families and friends strolled through the Jardin's
leafy promenades on the weekend, mixing pleasure and relaxation with
an appreciation of science and learning. In addition to the gardens themselves, the grounds of the Jardin des Plantes housed museums of natural
history and anatomy, as well as the former royal menagerie, now formally
described as a zoological garden. These scientific marvels were extremely
popular. Over eleven thousand visitors passed through the new Museum of
Comparative Anatomy on the first Sunday following its opening in 1898.[51]

The popularization and spectacularization of science to which these
institutions catered and which they encouraged was largely seen as beneficial to both science and society. Nevertheless many felt that this kind of
disinterested, *flâneur*-esque promenading through picturesque scientific
marvels was not entirely compatible with the more serious work carried
out at the Salpêtrière and elsewhere. This tension was highlighted in a
later theatrical piece authored in association with Charcot's former student Alfred Binet, entitled *A Lesson at the Salpêtrière* (1908; see Chap. 9).
One of the interns in the play mocked the fictional successor to Charcot
for constantly dropping in at the hospice before abruptly departing in his

carriage again. "The Salpêtrière isn't the Jardin des Plantes!" the intern complained.[52] If the Salpêtrière was to be seen as lying at the forefront of experimental medicine, one could not draw too closely together the medical investigation carried out at the hospice and the spectacular practices popular at the Jardin des Plantes. Here, too, space proved to be a difficult yet crucial factor which both practitioners and commentators negotiated, with the sensuous pleasures of spectacle or the pathos of suffering as threats to keep at bay.

Charcot's identification of hysterioepilepsy as a neuropathological condition itself resulted from his attempt to separate the hysterics treated by the alienist Louis-Jean-François Delasiauvre and Delasiauvre's assistant Bourneville, from the epileptics and others with whom the women shared mixed wards in the condemned Saint Laure building, who were to be placed under the charge of the neurological section. Charcot responded with a tripartite definition. There was hysteria proper, which was a functional disorder of an otherwise healthy neuromotor system. Such a condition could exist either independently of, or as a complication of, actual structural neuromotor illness. Hysteria minor, as this was sometimes termed, typically had relatively benign or small scale symptoms such as localized paralysis. Versus this, there was global neuromotor epilepsy itself, with its primary symptoms of seizure and fugue. Epilepsy was deemed to be caused by actual tissue damage, which prompted the functional short-circuiting of the nervous system characteristic of the condition. Finally, there was the fully-evolved functional illness, what Charcot christened hysterioepilepsy, which mimicked many of the symptoms of other conditions with somatic, structural causes (such as epilepsy and paralysis agitans or Parkinson's disease; see Chaps. 6 and 7). Hysterioepilepsy often developed from hysteria minor, but was more debilitating, and was signalled by full blown seizures, or at least partial versions of these, depending on the patient. Significantly, Charcot's novel classification failed to actually divide the patient population between groups best treated by neurologists versus those best treated by psychiatric alienists. Charcot's nosology rather constituted an appropriation of psychiatric subjects, space, and personnel.[53] Bourneville and Delasiauvre's patients were transferred to Charcot's service, where Bourneville became one of Charcot's most energetic advocates, his publisher, and collaborator. Classification enabled Charcot to accrue both spatial and administrative power with the theatre of the Salpêtrière.

The space of the Salpêtrière and other settings before which the drama of neuropathology was played out in the nineteenth century was not simply an inert collection of signifiers which physicians and writers could harness for their needs. Space exerted definite and sometimes disconcerting effects upon the bodies and individuals which moved through it, transforming them and affecting their perceptual fields—a point to which I return in Chaps. 7, 8 and 9. Space constituted not only the venue or context for Charcot's dramaturgy, but it could also serve, in a manner of speaking, as the subject. Performance not only occurred within space, but subjects performed the spaces they inhabited. It was this process which Charcot strove to master.

Charcot's interest in the mutability of the diseased, fungible body was, therefore, consonant with the realm within which he practiced. It was this concatenation of the decaying, disorientating environment of the Salpêtrière with Charcot's own studies in polymorphous hysterioepileptic seizures, hypnotic phenomena, tremulous subjects, and dying women that led former Salpêtrière physician Peugniez to introduce his readers to the neuropathologist using a scenario which resembled the visitation of old Hamlet's ghost. The younger doctor, his mind full of thoughts brought on by his patron's funeral, was overwhelmed by visions of the past. Memory replaced reality as Peugniez was transported back to the Salpêtrière:

> Thrown into the room of a silent and empty hotel by the express train which brought me to Paris for the funeral ceremony, I evoke the image of my former master, that most venerated friend who is no more!

> Memories appear all around me: they surround me: little by little they replace the banal, cold décor which surrounds me and then all at once I see again, in that immense hospice of the Salpêtrière, the modest office lined with red and black panels with its single, wide window opening onto the courtyard, its photographs, its engravings, its designs relating the history of hysteria in arts, where, for the first time, nearly thirteen years ago, Charcot first appeared to me.

> Gently and without noise, the door glided open.[54]

Whilst illustrations "relating the history of hysteria in arts" swam before Peugniez's eyes, the door silently swings open. Peugniez's phrasing is deliberately ambiguous here, so the reader cannot be sure if this is the door to Peugniez's hotel room or that of Charcot's office. In effect, the two spaces bleed into each other, and then Charcot's own profile appeared to Peugniez again. Moving though this passage is, it bears a striking resemblance to a nervous hallucination. Indeed, Peugniez's note regarding the tiring train journey which had brought him to Paris suggests that his own nerves may have been jolted and excited to the point of fraying, "railway spine" being a common cause of neuropathology. The passage thus potentially undermined his status as an objective medical biographer upon which the rest of the text in fact depends. It would seem that Peugniez shared Charcot's conviction that his status as a doctor was sufficient in itself to distinguish between the *products* of psychoneural disorder from medical commentary *upon them*, even as these emotive engagements with the space of the Salpêtrière and his journey towards it undermined this. Many of Charcot's contemporaries did not share this opinion, however.

In setting hysterioepilepsy and other diseases free from their chains, Charcot unleashed a range of discourses which proved difficult to control. These practices made it increasingly difficult to differentiate between physicians like Peugniez, and their patients, who were said to be in the thrall of their disordered nerves or febrile imaginings. The Salpêtrière continued to be a compelling, contradictory site of performance throughout the nineteenth century. Even today it has the feeling of a haunted space.

NOTES

1. Goetz et al., 231–5; Platel [Ignotus], "Cabotinage," 1; Louis de Meurville, "Le docteur Charcot," *Gazette de France* (18 August 1893): 1; C.L. Dana, "Charcot," *Medical Record* (9 September 1893): 351.
2. For Charcot's biography, see Goetz et al., 3–62; Simon-Dhouailly, ed., 31–43.
3. OC, vol. 7, pp. 302–353.
4. Goetz et al, p. 32; Jean-Martin Charcot and Paul Richer, *"Les démoniaques dans l'art" suivi de "La foi qui guérit,"* facsimile reproduction; ed. and commentary Georges Didi-Huberman and Pierre Fédida (Paris: Macula, 1984), 111–123.
5. F. Clifford Rose and W.F. Bynum, eds, *Historical Abstracts of the Neurosciences* (NY: Raven, 1980), 383–396.
6. On the relationship between Republicanism and the medical establishment, see Jack Ellis, *The Physician-Legislators of France* (Cambridge: Cambridge University Press, 1990); Goldstein, *Console*, 329–374.

7. Charles Sowerwine, *France Since 1870* (Houndmills: Palgrave, 2001).
8. Micale, *Approaching*, 207–8. On these widespread social anxieties, see Daniel Pick, *Faces of Degeneration* (Cambridge: Cambridge University Press, 1989); Robert Nye, *Crime, Madness, and Politics in Modern France* (Princeton: Princeton University Press 1984).
9. *OC*, vol. 1, p. 183.
10. Henry Meige, "Charcot artiste," *NIPS*, 11 (1898), esp. pp. 500–2; Sigrid Schade, "Charcot and the Spectacle of the Hysterical Body," *Art History*, 18.4 (December 1995): 499–517; Debora Silverman, *Art nouveau in fin-de-siècle France* (Berkeley: California University Press, 1989); James Parker, "The Hotel de Varengeville Room and the Room from the Palais Paar," *Metropolitan Museum of Art Bulletin* (November 1969): 129–146.
11. Jan Goldstein, "The Wandering Jew and the Problem of Psychiatric Anti-Semitism in Fin-de-Siècle France," *Journal of Contemporary History*, 20 (1985): 547.
12. Robert Hillman, "A Scientific Study of Mystery: The Role of the Medical and Popular Press in the Nancy-Salpêtrière Controversy on Hypnotism," *Bulletin of the History of Medicine*, 39.2 (1965): 163–183; Anne Harrington, "Metals and Magnets in Medicine: Hysteria, Hypnosis and Medical Culture in *fin de siècle* Paris," *Psychological Medicine*, 18 (1988): 21–38; Marshall, "Kleist," 261–281.
13. Edouard Brissaud and Pierre Marie, "Nécrologie: J.-M. Charcot," *Revue neurologique*, 1.16 (31 August 1893): 30–31.
14. Goldstein, *Console*, 69–72, 85–101, 130–196; Caroline Hannaway and Ann La Berge, eds, *Constructing Paris Medicine* (Amsterdam: Rodopi, 1998), 1–70.
15. Charcot, *Charcot*, xvi.
16. Peugniez, 4.
17. Guillain, 51–52; C.F. Withington, "A Last Glimpse of Charcot at the Salpêtrière," *Boston Medical and Surgical Journal*, CXXIX.8 (1893): 207.
18. Paul Richer, Georges Gilles de la Tourette and Albert Londe, "Avertissement," in *NIPS*, 1 (1888): II.
19. See Michel Frizot, *Étienne-Jules Marey* (Paris: Nathan, 2004); Denis Bernard and André Gunthert, *L'instant rêvé Albert Londe* (Nîmes: Chambon, 1993); Lisa Cartwright, *Screening the Body* (Minneapolis: Minnesota University Press, 1995); Stephen Herbert, ed., *A History of Pre-Cinema* (London: Routledge, 2001); Laurent Mannoni, *The Great Art of Light and Shadow*, trans. Richard Crangle (Exeter: Exeter University Press, 2000).
20. The collection of the Musée d'histoire de la médecine de Paris includes several of these devices, whilst original traces are held in the Bibliothèque Charcot and the Bakken Museum of Electricity in Life, Minneapolis.

21. Paul Richer, *Physiologie artistique de l'homme en mouvement* (Paris: Octave Doin, 1895), 15–16.
22. *OC*, vol. 5, p. 5, vol. 6, pp. 2–3.
23. *OC*, vol. 6, pp. 3–4.
24. *OC*, vol. 5, p. 6.
25. Walter Benjamin, *The Arcades Project*, trans Howard Eiland and Kevin McLaughlin (Cambridge, MA: Belknap, 1999). Vanessa Schwartz's superb *Spectacular Realities* (LA: California University Press, 1998) offers an insightful analysis of how visual pleasure and *flânerie* was associated with such morbid para-medical sites as the Paris morgue and the Musée Grévin.
26. Désiré Bourneville, "J.-M. Charcot," *Archives de neurologie*, 26.79 (September 1893): 194; *OC*, vol. 1, p. 2.
27. Jules Claretie, *La vie à Paris* (Paris: Victor Harvard, 1881), 125.
28. Jules Claretie, "Charcot, le consolateur," *Annales politiques et littéraires*, 21 (1903): 180.
29. Mark Micale, "The Salpêtrière in the Age of Charcot," *Journal of Contemporary History*, 20 (1985): 703–731.
30. Claretie, *Vie*, 125.
31. Maximilien Vessier, *La Pitié-Salpêtrière* (Paris: Groupe hospitalier Pitié-Salpêtrière, 1999).
32. Michel Foucault, *Madness and Civilization*, trans. Richard Howard (NY: Vintage, 1988).
33. Maurice Guillemot, "À la Salpêtrière," *Paris illustré*, 5.22 (24 September 1887): 354–5.
34. Jules Claretie, *Les amours d'un interne* (Paris: Ollendorf, 1902), 69.
35. Victor Hugo, *Les misérables*, trans. Isabel Hapgood (Adelaide: Adelaide University Press, 2014), book IV, chapt. I, reproduced on <https://ebooks.adelaide.edu.au/h/hugo/victor/lesmis/book2.4.html.>
36. Alexandre Guérin, "Une visite à la Salpêtrière," *Revue illustrée*, 4.40 (1 August 1887): 97.
37. Claretie, "Charcot," 179–180.
38. Ibid., 179–180.
39. Guérin, 57.
40. Georges Guillain and Pierre Mathieu, *La Salpêtrière* (Paris: Masson, 1925), 25.
41. Guérin, 97, 175.
42. Moses Allen Starr et al. [23 November 1925], minutes of Boston Medical History Club centenary meeting, *Boston Medical and Surgical Association*, 194 (1926): 10.
43. Louis Boucher, *La Salpêtrière* (Paris: Progrès médical, 1883), 11–12.
44. Fulgence Raymond, *Leçons sur les maladies de système nerveux* (Paris: Octave Don, 1896), 6.
45. Didi-Huberman, *Invention*, 13.

46. On the history of the Jardin de Plantes, see Yves Laissus, *Le musée national d'histoire naturelle* (Paris: Gallimard, 1995).
47. Philippe Dagen, "Le 'Premier artiste,'" *Romantisme*, 84 (1994): 69–78.
48. Guérin, 97.
49. Sigmund Freud, *The Standard Edition of the Complete Psychological Works of Sigmund Freud*, ed. and trans. James Strachey (London: Hogarth Press, 1973), vol. 3, p. 13.
50. François Helme, *Les jardins de la médecine* (Paris: Vigot, 1907), 307–8.
51. Laissus, 68.
52. André de Latour de Lorde with Alfred Binet et al., *Théâtre d'Épouvante* (Paris: Charpentier et Fasquelle, 1909), 6.
53. Goetz et al., 177–181, 213. It remains difficult even today to establish medical consensus regarding the nature, causes, and treatment of what is now classified as "non-epileptic seizure"; see John Gates, "Non-Epileptic Seizures," *Epilepsy and Behavior*, 3 (2002): 28–33.
54. Peugniez, 3.

CHAPTER 3

Building the Stage and Materializing the Archetype

1 FRAMING THE THEATRE

Charcot was reported to have mused to his students: "When I am dead, per-haps they will erect a statue of me. I would like it placed near that of Pinel. We will talk through the night."[1] In 1898, his wish was realized through the placement of a bronze by Alexandre Falguière, famous for his scientifically precise works at the Jardin des Planets and other locations. Falguière was known to Charcot, having attended salons at the Charcots' house. Ludovic Durand's earlier sculpture of Pinel had been erected in front of the entrance to the Salpêtrière in 1880, during Charcot's tenure. The neuropathologist also presided over the laying of a monument to Guillaume Duchenne de Boulogne, Charcot proclaiming at the dedication ceremony that Duchenne was "the greatest promoter of modern neurology."[2]

Charcot's role in commissioning these additions to the material ico-nography of the Salpêtrière demonstrated his awareness of the impor-tance of controlling and managing the space he worked within. The Salpêtrière functioned as a physical and institutional manifestation of Charcot's model of neuropathology—a "Neuro-Pathological Institute" or "museum of living pathology"—within which diseases were staged and performed. Despite his interest in concrete spatial dramaturgy, Charcot's work reflected a distrust of performative phenomena as made manifest in space and time. Charcot was an enthusiastic proponent of Plato's model of classification, a theorization which Jonas Barish and others have shown

© The Editor(s) (if applicable) and The Author(s) 2016
J.W. Marshall, *Performing Neurology*,
DOI 10.1057/978-1-137-51762-3_3

to be inimical to the variability of theatrical action.[3] Plato argued that human perception is inherently deceptive, and that the best way to consider entities was to imagine their perfect "archetypal" manifestation. Such a version did not, however, exist in real space and so could not be materially performed in its totality. It was rather an idealized realization which transcended space, time, and performance. Diseases were, therefore, classified not so much according to the imperfect, fragmentary actions of the actual patients themselves (important though this source data was), but rather according to this offstage performance. This archetypal model was a major reason for Charcot's ambivalence towards theatricality. Charcot's conceptualization of the diagnostic theatre was two-fold, dependent on the material presence of the diseased body—the actual patient in the lecture theatre—but always referring beyond itself to another, more fully realized staging. The possibility that a body could be constructed in the moment, radically changing with each performed iteration, such that the archetype became untenable, was countered by reference to this idealized staging. Charcot might be considered then to have constructed a dramaturgical framework against the concept of performativity itself.

Perhaps the most well known of the commemoratives to the history of the Salpêtrière acquired during Charcot's stay at the hospice were the paintings. Nineteenth century French medical theatres were often decorated with paintings of figures from medical history. After ordering the construction of a new lecture theatre at the Salpêtrière, Charcot adorned it with a particularly fine painting by Robert Fleury, namely *Pinel Delivering the Salpêtrière's Madwomen from Their Chains* (1876).[4] Insane patients had often been chained during the seventeenth century in order to counter their rages. Pinel proposed that rather than restraining the mad, one should listen to them and treat their symptomatic delusions in a reasoned fashion. This famous act of liberation was also the topic of Durand's sculpture in front of the gate. Commentators frequently associated Charcot's practice with this literally iconographic act of Pinel. Peugniez, for example, likened Charcot's "oeuvre as a liberator and a humanitarian" to that of Pinel, claiming that "under Charcot's words the last chains fell" from the women of the Salpêtrière.[5] Doctor François Helme later reiterated this symmetry between the work of Pinel and Charcot. The author extolled the justice in placing Charcot's likeness beside that of Pinel on the grounds that just as the alienist had liberated the mad, so "Charcot, himself, emancipated hysteria" from its fearful status as a vexing, ill-defined disease.[6] Fleury's painting visibly brought the architectural hagiography manifest beyond the walls of the amphitheatre into the space of the lecture presentations themselves, establishing a continuity between Charcot's pedagogy and Pinel's reforms; between Charcot's commission of a new, modern amphitheatre and the striking of the chains of ignorance. This at once iconographic and architectural project came full circle when a painting of Charcot's morning lecture was itself produced in 1887.[7]

André Brouillet's *A Clinical Lesson at the Salpêtrière* was exhibited in the Paris salon of 1887 (Fig. 3.1). From 1882, Charcot performed the majority of his lectures on the stage above which Fleury's image hung in the new amphitheatre. Brouillet however portrayed a more informal gathering in a room lacking the raised platform of the amphitheatre itself—either another space or a different part of the venue.[8] *A Clinical Lesson at the Salpêtrière* was presented to the public at the same salon exhibition which included Henri Gervex's more dynamic portrait of the prominent surgeon Émile Péan, *Before the Operation* (1887). Comparison between the pieces detracted from

Fig. 3.1   Brouillet, *A Clinical Lesson at the Salpêtrière* (1887); collection of the Musée d'Assistance publique des hôpitaux de Paris. Photograph by the author

the initial critical reception of Brouillet's work, and *A Clinical Lesson* failed to secure a prize. Brouillet's painting was nevertheless well received, especially by physicians such as Norech, who was also a critic for *La gazette des beaux-arts.*[9] Lithographic reproductions of Brouillet's tableau were widely distributed amongst Parisian medics and interested parties, one even adorning Freud's office in Vienna. The original painting was acquired for the Nice Museum by Dr Jean Lépine, the son of Charcot's former student René Lépine. A full-sized copy has been in the possession of the Salpêtrière neurology department since 1890, and today resides in the staircase leading to the Museum of Medical History located within the old Paris medical school.

Brouillet's painting echoed the conventions of Naturalistic salon art upon which Fleury drew. Brouillet's specific choice of subject and setting was revealing though. Fleury had promoted Pinel as an enlightened reformer in the field of alienism or psychiatry. Brouillet's image could itself claim a degree of scientific accuracy, as the image of Charcot was taken directly from a photograph supplied to the painter.[10] Charcot was here depicted as the head of a new school or approach to the body whose followers could be recognized in the audience. *Pinel Delivering the Salpêtrière's Madwomen* was a hypostatized act of liberation showing Pinel in a sentimental, almost saintly light. A grateful woman knelt by his side, confirming his wisdom in recognizing her humanity. *A Clinical Lesson at the Salpêtrière*, however, showed Charcot as a scientific figure even more indifferent than Pinel to the emotions that whirled about his presence. Many found Brouillet's style detached. Whilst Gervex employed dramatic shadows and directional lighting, Brouillet's work is characterized by a diffuse glow which permeates the space evenly. The spectators' faces appear cool and rational, whilst even the gestures of surveillant Marguerite Bottard seem stiff as she reaches out to catch the falling patient. *L'illustration*'s reporter commented that "the execution seems cold, as is the technique, and the purplish background is of a poor tone ... But a certain reality seizes you."[11] The flat, statuesque pose of the medical figures eloquently evoked the aura of unemotional, scientific materialism which Charcot advocated.

Indeed, *A Clinical Lesson at the Salpêtrière* offers what might be considered a kind of embodied *deus ex machina*: the indifferent unfolding of rational truth through a cool, rational dramaturgy. All three paintings exhibited a theatricality in the posing and arrangement of figures. Only Brouillet, however, presented the viewer with an event which was specifically conceived of as theatrical, staged before an audience, prior to its visual recreation. Brouillet's setting was, therefore, eminently logical. Brouillet avoided painting Charcot in the new amphitheatre, with Fleury's painting on the wall behind. Such a depiction would have called attention to the iconographic and theatrical framing, suggesting a *mise en abyme* or hall of mirrors in which the source of unmediated truth became hard to identify. Brouillet's relatively restrained treatment helped to situate the scene within *reality*, even though the lecture itself remained a self-conscious theatrical event. Charcot's supporters such as Brouillet strove to minimize or de-theatricalize the neuropathologist's work, placing it more firmly within the realm of rationalist medicine.

Though Charcot took an active part in the growing hagiographic iconography of French medicine, his most significant interventions in the organization of space at the Salpêtrière were in the form of clinics, laboratories, and libraries. Charcot's legacy was closely associated with the revolution in spatial design and departmental specialization which he instigated at the Salpêtrière. Glosses on Charcot's career published during his lifetime as well as the many eulogies attest to the importance of his building programme to his reputation. Charcot himself emphasized this aspect of his career. Dr Morton Prince recorded that when he spoke to the neuropathologist "in complimentary terms of his contribution to neurology ... with a gesture of his hand he waved this aside and pointing to the Salpêtrière he deprecatingly said, 'This is my monument.'"[12]

Charcot began his 1889 course in neurology by reflecting that his lessons were only possible because of the spatial innovations he had inaugurated. He explained that he had established "within the hospital walls" a service for the temporary admission of patients (the policlinique), as well as "an anatomopathologic museum to which is attached a casting studio and a photographic studio; a fully equipped laboratory of anatomy and pathological physiology."[13]

Charcot's spatial reforms were consistent with the overall development of museology during the nineteenth century. The mixed collections or cabinets of curiosities commonplace in the eighteenth century had become increasingly systematized. The museums of the nearby Jardin des Plantes, for example, gave nosological relationships a physical form through the ordered display of animals, plants, and minerals. Faculties and hospitals routinely housed materials related to studies conducted on the premises. Bourneville, for instance, gathered casts of various deformations at the museum which he later founded at the Bicêtre, and similar materials were used by Mathias Duval and his peers at the École Nationale Supérieure des Beaux-Arts (ENSBA) in teaching artistic anatomy.[14] Pinel himself had used a hinged-top, papier-mâché skull for lecture demonstrations in the 1790s.

These displays and stage properties were largely promoted as aids to the objective contemplation of reality as exemplified by rationalist science. The largest nineteenth century museums were nevertheless often characterized by a riotous profusion of materials, a superabundance of wonders barely contained by the extravagant architecture within which they rested. Living human oddities and medical freaks were moreover commonly displayed even within the most proper of museums and pedagogic institutions.

The other new services sponsored by Charcot at the Salpêtrière itself included a library, an ophthalmological unit (run by Henry Parinaud), a refurbished autopsy room, a nursing school, a histological laboratory, an electrotherapy unit, hydrotherapy baths, a gymnasium, and a physiotherapy unit, as well as Charcot's new amphitheatre, which he proudly noted was "equipped, as you can see, with all of the modern devices for demonstration."[15] Charcot's former student Charles Féré was one of many commentators who reflected: "This ensemble currently constitutes a neuropathological Institute."[16] Charcot's transformation of the buildings into a series of specialist departments—each under a *chef de clinique* answerable to Charcot—paralleled the neuropathologist's project to order both the pathological body and the regimes to which it was subject. A formal organization of disciplines, therapies, diagnostic techniques, and types of knowledge was established at a discursive, spatial, and institutional level. In short, the spatial design of the Salpêtrière performed knowledge itself.

The impressive multiplication of specialist diagnostic and therapeutic divisions which Charcot promoted at the Salpêtrière nevertheless concealed a high degree of functional equivalence between the methodologies described above. The spatio-technological reform over which Charcot presided was governed by a two-way imperative, moving towards a fragmentation of the body and its discursive description (specialization), whilst Charcot attempted to compensate for this by uniting these approaches under the single, master discourse of neurology. Charcot's 1889 lecture included the warning that the multiplication of spatial and technological realms could lead to the individual components of "the territory of neuropathology" becoming too "narrow" or walled in. The new departments had to remain both physically and philosophically part of a territory navigated through the use of directives and landmarks derived from neuropathology itself. The growth of sub-disciplines like electrodiagnosis was, therefore, accompanied by an even stronger drive to knit these various discourses together. The chefs de clinique remained under the guidance of the *maître* of the Salpêtrière.

Charcot's attempt to contain, master, and harness the forces produced by advances in different medical specialties helped explain the terminological cross-fertilization found within the texts of the Salpêtrière
school. Although the creation of the Salpêtrière museum was one of
Charcot's most well-known achievements, it was difficult to establish
any clear distinction between the role the museum played and that
assigned to practices conducted in the wards or lectures. The original
Salpêtrière library for instance was located within the museum, whilst
Albert Londe—in addition to succeeding Régnard as head of photography—also took over from M. Loreau as curator of the Salpêtrière
museum, thereby fusing these nominally distinct departments.[17] Indeed,
Brouillet's painting demonstrates how unstable the use of Charcot's
specialist venues could be, as the lecture depicted did not occur within
the lecture theatre itself, but rather a general ward—even though the
entire Salpêtrière school of neurologists crowded around to observe the
scene enacted in this space.

Charcot's 1889 lesson included his celebrated description of the
Salpêtrière as a museum of living pathology:

> The clinical types [are] ... represented by numerous examples which permit
> one to consider the course of the affection at the same time in one glance,
> in a continuous fashion ... the gaps which arise ... are thus filled. We are,
> in other words, in possession of a sort of *museum of living pathology*, whose
> resources are considerable.[18]

This equivalence between museum and ward was further extended to the
amphitheatre. The museum acted as a vivified staging of the pathological body, a striking virtual performance in which all movement had been
reduced to a minimum. Peugniez offered the following description:

> the museum ... consisted of a large quantity of natural anatomical prepara-
> tions, pieces of skeleton, arthropathies or bone deformations, the tabetic
> ossuary; as well as other artificial pieces, molds in wax by Loreau ... an old
> tabetic from the hospice presenting in nearly all of her joints the alterations
> so well described by Charcot, cast whole and with a frightening realism:
> she is referred to as the ataxic Venus: there are diseased brains, hemispheres
> affected by classic lesions ... pathological anatomy no longer dead as it is in
> the books, but resuscitated, animated, living, in other words, putting into
> relief the fundamental characters of the lesions, teaching us, leaving memo-
> ries which will no longer fade.[19]

The pedagogic function of the lectures was, therefore, replicated in the display of the museum, a realm of inanimate objects which nevertheless facilitated an "animated, living … pathological anatomy." As Foucault observes, early nineteenth century French medicine saw the birth of "*la clinique*": a collection of discourses and disciplines which united pedagogy, research, and treatment within one institution.[20] This ideal of an animate, living yet dissected clinique was realized by Charcot.

Although the same principles active in the ward, museum, and amphitheatre served to reinforce each other, it was only in the theatre itself that Charcot could fully combine the total visibility and control over the body, with its dynamic investigation. The "modern devices for demonstration" of the amphitheatre to which Charcot referred included one of the finest selections of anatomical specimens in nineteenth century Europe. One of Charcot's chief aims in accumulating display materials was as an aid for his lectures. He was rightly proud of his collection, reading out an approving letter from James Paget during a Tuesday lesson of 1888.[21] Materials from the hospital museum were frequently shown in Charcot's amphitheatre alongside living patients, whilst illustrations of these items were included in the subsequent published lectures. Charcot considered these anatomical preparations to be of such importance that he took them with him for his lectures at international conferences.[22] Specimens prepared at the Salpêtrière were, moreover, distributed throughout European medical museums, including a copy of the ataxic Venus described above. The neuropathologist integrated the presentation of these stage properties into his lectures to produce what Henry Meige called the "panoramic descriptions" of the amphitheatre.[23]

Charcot employed the same term he had used to describe the wards when outlining how his nosological teaching functioned within the amphitheatre itself, making no significant distinction between activities carried out in these spaces. On the contrary, the living museum of the wards reinforced, and was in turn supported by, the spatial and performative logic of the Salpêtrière as a whole. "To complete our current demonstration" in the amphitheatre on the different forms of chorea, Charcot explained that he would now also:

> use what is called the method of contrasts with the aim of representing several hemiathetosis cases, which I will borrow from my *living museum*, beside our cases of symptomatic hemichorea. You will then be able to recognize not only the unquestionable analogies, but also the radical differences which, from a descriptive point of view, exist between these two states.[24]

Charcot dramatized his nosological method through the synchronic display of examples taken from the wards and the museum of disease species—living and dead—and offered these up within the lecture theatre. Patients and specimens were, in Charcot's words, opposed "one against the other, fixing them more definitively in the mind ... by passing before your eyes, beside several examples of the condition."[25] This enabled Charcot to produce a complete description of pathological entities, distinguished from their literally close semiological neighbours. Comparative illustrations of these physical forms were frequently published alongside transcripts of Charcot's lectures.

Charcot was, nevertheless, adamant that comparative diagnosis and classification was most effective when carried out in a *theatrical* fashion, using living patient material. The virtual comparison of examples within the mind was a poor alternative to the methods available to Charcot in the wards and the amphitheatre. Charcot's ground-breaking work in distinguishing rheumatism and arthritis from gout, for example, had only been made possible by the wide range of clinical cases available at the Salpêtrière. He insisted that it was "indispensable, in effect ... to have before one's eyes a large number of patients, in order to better be able to compare between the diverse types which affect chronic rheumatism."[26] The discursive practices carried out in the different contexts of the ward, amphitheatre, and museum were fundamentally the same, conforming to an overall performative or theatrical spatio-temporal logic.

Charcot legitimized his extensive architectonic programme by extolling the historic role played by the specialties housed in the new departments and by former Salpêtrière physicians such as Pinel. Charcot's own specialty lay between anatomy proper (the description and classification of structures visible on the exterior of the body and in post-mortem) and pure semiology (the description and classification of disease entities on the basis of clinically observed symptoms in living subjects). Charcot carried out a particularly rigorous and successful integration of these two practices, correlating lesions, infectious necrosis, and other physical phenomena identified through autopsy, with disease behaviour observed in living patients. Charcot's physical observations dealt particularly with motor coordination and other dynamic or sensory functions controlled by nervous tissue. Locomotor ataxia (also known as tabes dorsalis) and other conditions that produced complications of the gait (myopathies, sclerosis in plaques, now known as multiple sclerosis, amyotrophic lateral sclerosis) provided Charcot's classic examples of the progress of modern science in mastering disease.[27] Charcot refined the piecemeal work of Salpêtrière practitioners such as Duchenne and Jean Cruveilhier, as well as anatomist Pierre Paul Broca, to produce nuanced distinctions between various clinical neuropathologies and their associated signs.

Charcot's aim was to map human behaviour and its pathology onto the material structure and function of the body:

> *In pathological anatomy*, to localize is to identify in the organs, in the tissues, the seat, the spread, the configuration, the material and palpable alterations; *in pathological physiology*, it is taking into account the data provided by the clinical observation and the insights offered by experimental data, to establish the relationship between the functional notes taken during life and the lesions revealed by the autopsy.[28]

Charcot's method was to record the symptoms living patients exhibited and then upon their death to examine the bodies for more "palpable" signs of disease. Where an isolated deformation of the nervous tissue was perceptible, this was related to what Meige called the *"habitus humain"* of specific patient behaviour.[29] For example, anatomoclinical investigation suggested that spinal amyotrophic degeneration was "circumscribed within the anterior columns" of the spinal cord, constituting an "exclusive lesion … imprisoned in the region, without the participation … of the nearby regions."[30] Charcot similarly determined that widespread destruction of tissue in Broca's cerebral circumlocutions engendered hemiplegia, whilst "irritative lesions" in the same area of the brain caused partial-epilepsy.[31] Once these initial cartographies were developed, this categorical method was employed in a more intricate fashion, inverting or layering it. Charcot endeavoured to identify the consequences of multiple lesions or disease entities complicated by secondary illnesses, as well as to successfully recognize the underlying material pathologies from externally visible traits.

Post-mortem investigation was not an ideal tool. Charcot's studies were only possible due to the high mortality and morbidity amongst the aged population of the Salpêtrière. It was because the vast majority of the patients were destitute that physicians at the Salpêtrière were able to routinely perform dissections without the intervention of the families. Charcot could only proceed slowly using this methodology, nor was it compatible with experimentation proper. More significantly, a temporal and phenomenological separation remained between the disease process active within the living body and its subsequent interpretation through autopsy. This rendered already opaque bodies even more difficult to access and read. Only Charcot's theatrical display brought these morbid signs— *"anatomie morte"* as he called it—in combination with the living body.[32] Charcot made it clear that in the final analysis both knowledge of the body, and the truthful dissemination of that knowledge, revolved around the problem of reading and representation. Like Richer after him, Charcot compared his own project to that of the Ancient Greeks, whose anatomically insightful sculpture he admired. There were:

> nuances, contrasts, which even the most evocative language can only depict with difficulty. The anatomopathologist also has on several occasions felt the need to be an artist himself ... It was natural that art intervened where figurative qualities had such a great importance.[33]

Where speech, writing, and iconography failed, one was left with theatre, a form of representation which encompassed all of these devices, employing the very stuff of the body itself—flesh, literally present before the audience, unifying the referent (the diseased body of diagnosis) with its signifier (the performing patient). In the amphitheatre Charcot fulfilled his "need to be an artist" and was able to dramaturgically sculpt the forms of disease.

As discussed in Chap. 2, physicians such as Charcot, Marey, Londe, and Richer attempted to bring together the anatomized corpse with the living body by marshalling an array of analytic tools. Charcot insisted that anatomy involved not only "the scalpel" but also "relationships ... volume ... consistency ... density ... color ... general aspect ... texture" and even microscopic examination.[34] He claimed: *"The analyst must penetrate into the profundity of the organism right down to the irreducible anatomical elements or parts,"* employing histological advances to "penetrate further into the intimacy of the tissue" in "an incessant molecular task."[35] The body was flayed—literally and metaphorically—through an ever more intensive visual investigation. Duchenne de Boulogne's pioneering use of electrostimulation on patients at the Salpêtrière provided another useful technique for carrying out a comparable examination in living subjects, whereby small electric charges placed on the skin enabled doctor to selectively move different muscle groups below the surface and hence identify how and if they still functioned. In the meantime, Charcot exhorted his audience to "think anatomically" whilst observing patients in the clinic. "From the beginning we looked forward to the day when all the lesions which the naked eye can recognize would be definitively described, classified, catalogued."[36] The multiplication of departments and techniques within the Salpêtrière was, therefore, paralleled by the

anatomical dissection of the body itself. The project of neurological interpretation and pedagogy was to render these phenomena whole again. This
in turn enabled the interiority and dynamic function of the living, theatrical, phenomenologically-present body to become visible to "the naked eye"
of the properly trained medical spectator. Charcot's dramaturgical project
constituted a form of reverse-dissection, a reconstruction of the anatomized
body within the lecture theatre, drawing physiological conclusions from the
fragmentary anatomical data arrayed within its space. Here patient and specimen confronted each other. The demonstrator's task was to integrate this
material within a composite, virtual, nosological body.

Charcot did concede that many conditions did not present clear post-
mortem signs that could be tied to clinical behaviour. He noted, for example, that for subjects afflicted by apoplectic attacks: "in the present state of
science, the absence of true lesions is, anatomically speaking, a common
feature of such fits."[37] For the "large number of morbid states ... which
leave no appreciable material trace upon the cadaver" one could, however,
apply "an analogy to the anatomical attack, and, *mutatis mutandis*, local-
ize the dynamic lesion."[38] The corpses of these subjects themselves did not
proffer unambiguous physical signs. One could, nevertheless, conclude that
this special class of illnesses—"*les névroses*"—involved a dysfunction in the
nervous tissues associated with the same symptomatic behaviour observed
in other, better described, conditions. In this manner the mysterious conditions of chorea, hysterioepilepsy and paralysis agitans were rendered more
comprehensible. The anatomoclinical approach was not, therefore, a simple "contemplative" task, but rather a creative one. Charcot's gaze was
not passive, but active, functioning in a fashion at once akin to a scalpel
(anatomy), a needle and thread (nosology), and a pen or brush (interpretation and presentation). As Meige explained, Charcot exhorted his students
to "Look, look always: it is only then that one manages to *see*."[39]

Although Charcot assumed that all illness had discernible material
causes, his diagnostic method ultimately elevated the clinical performance
of the living body above the imperatives of post-mortem visibility. Charcot
employed the term "dynamic lesion" to describe an *invisible* condition
that existed only in the performance of the living body; an ephemeral
or performative phenomenon, described using a fundamentally dramaturgical approach. Internal visibility was imputed from external signs even
where these signs were known to be invisible.

Charcot's attempt to unify clinical practice with the theatrical dissemination of nosological principles presented significant problems. Clinical

practice did not deal with categoric entities. It was rather focused on the quiddity of the body itself:

> the task of the clinician and that of nosography are very different. The latter principally concerns the *abstract tableau* of illnesses; it intentionally neglects or voluntarily consigns to the background, the anomalies, the deviations of type.

> The clinician, on the contrary, looks especially at individual cases which, nearly always, offer particularities which move more or less away from the *common type*.[40]

Charcot did not, however, conclude that categorization and clinical practice were distinct exercises. There would be little value in a system of classification which one could not relate to clinically observed cases. The two activities were joined by the identification of *essential* behaviours that characterized the underlying diagnostic archetype.

Charcot demonstrated the relationship between clinically observed behaviour and nosography in an 1887 Tuesday morning lecture. He employed various performative clinical tests (asking the patient to attempt to drink a glass of water, move her toes, or raise her arms) to distinguish between the multiple, overlapping conditions she exhibited. Charcot concluded that although she seemed to be suffering from paralytic hypertrophy of the arm (an excess of neuromuscular tissue), her lack of muscle strength identified her condition as pseudohypertrophic:

> the apparent hypertrophy is in sum but an accident in the history of the pseudohypertrophic paralysis. It is not an essential character of the malady. The characteristic of the malady is muscular impotence.[41]

Superficial resemblances were unrelated to the essential nature of the illness. The crucial identifying mark of pseudohypertrophy was a reduction in the ability of the subject to fully flex muscle tissue. The fact that the patient's muscular atrophy was hidden by the presence of fatty tissue within the affected region was not a determining factor in identification. In both clinical and nosological practice the task was, therefore, to identify these essential features or characteristics that correlated with the main causes and functional effects of disease process.

Charcot's theatre was designed to stage and reveal these essential, invariant types. He asserted that Plato's doctrine regarding the essential unity and stability of the material universe remained true, at least as far as disease was concerned. In a discussion of the ability of physicians to know or imaginatively grasp the nature of illness when it was presented to them, the neuropathologist proclaimed: "Myself, I maintain the unity of things, the fixity of the species"—species here meaning not only a type of animal or plant, but also of diseases such as Parkinson's or locomotor ataxia.[42] Charcot did not reject the commonly held scientific contention that environmentally acquired illnesses or morphological changes could be transmitted across the generations. Indeed, Charcot's writings on the sympathetic relationship between the environment and the development of hereditary degeneracy were consistent with the Lamarckist evolutionary theories as promoted by peers such as Duval. Charcot appears to have accepted the assertion of naturalist Jean-Baptiste Lamarck that lived experience could alter the germ plasma. Darwin himself concurred on this point, using Lamarck's theory of "transformism" to bolster his own thesis.

Charcot, however, did reject the suggestion that the basic patterns which underlay the diversity of life or disease could change in a significant fashion:

the doctrine of the fixity of morbid species must be considered true. Morbid species, fortunately, when presented, do not vary as greatly as one might expect. One must not be Darwinian without reason. The principal factor, in evolutionary doctrine, is time and we must consider the fixity of morbid species from the point of view of the time in which we live.[43]

Epidemiology or typical disease progression could alter over time, but the rate of change was too slight to be of nosological significance. Clinical diagnosis and categorization, therefore, dealt with essential, invariant types.

Charcot's commitment to this Platonic vision of the universe was greater than that of many of his peers, a fact which he lamented in his lectures. Following the classification system developed by Carl Linnaeus, it had become standard museological practice to collect and house archetypal examples of biological and geological specimens which were used to define the species. In Charcot's opinion, this "*method of types*" was "often greatly undervalued" in medicine.[44] He insisted that: "Studying types is a fundamental task in nosography," in which one must "dissect the archetype and analyze its parts." This would enable one to learn "how to recognize the imperfect cases, the *formes frustes*" or "crude" and imperfect forms. Charcot did not consider the imperfection of clinical pathological phenomena a major problem. Here as elsewhere, the practice advocated by Charcot was driven by a two-way imperative, moving between the disease in its full, perfect expression (the archetype), and the incomplete, partial or rudimentary *formes frustes* which he routinely encountered. Charcot claimed, for example, that his description of *la grande hypnose* as exhibited by hysterics was "the most perfect form, the typical [or typological] form of hypnosis, and it is this which must serve as the point of departure for the study of the subject."[45] This was because:

> The type contains that which is most complete in the species. Then, as ... with all the other nervous maladies, one must divide up the type ... There are twenty or more varieties, but if you have the key, you straight away reduce it down to the type, which you reconstitute in your mind, and after a certain period you tell yourself: despite the apparently immense variety of phenomena, it [the type] is always the same thing.[46]

It was the discovery and identification of these archetypes that enabled one to separate illnesses which were often combined with each other in patients (e.g., spinal amyotrophy found alongside lateral sclerosis).

Charcot frequently explained in his lectures the difference between the archetype and its *forme fruste*:

> *Fruste* is from the Latin '*frustum*'; it means a strip, a fragment, or as one finds in Plato the expression '*frustum pueri*' to mean a fragment of a child, an abortion ... we can use the word '*fruste*' to characterize an illness in its embryonic state, aborted, undeveloped, that which one cannot grasp because it does not have the character of a type.[47]

Following Platonic theory, the archetype encapsulated within its pathology all of the essential characteristics of the entity in question. It combined within it all of the less perfect representations of the illness. The type was, in this respect, not simply an ideal, but an amalgam or synthesized reconstruction of the numerous separate varieties as found in reality. The archetype was a veritable Frankenstein monster, birthed from those abortive fragments which were found dispersed throughout the patient population.

Charcot's discussion of the gradations between the various difficult to grasp *formes frustes* and the archetype suggested a certain circularity to Charcot's logic. Charcot explained, for instance, the existence of "incomplete" or "flawed" attacks amongst the hysterical patients which he presented by claiming: "One understands now many varieties can result from such combinations; but it will always be easy to those who possess the formula to reduce them to their fundamental type."[48] The *forme fruste* and the archetype were mutually dependent concepts. Once one was familiar with the perfect type, one possessed "the formula" or "key" to identifying the *formes frustes*—forms which could in turn be virtually assembled to make the archetype itself. That which the nosologist could not understand or "grasp" in such a creative fashion was consigned to the epiphenomena of the *forme fruste*, rather than being employed as a possible identifying characteristic for another, distinctive illness. Charcot's *teknos* of knowledge necessarily excluded that which did not conform to its own internal rules of legibility.

Charcot's methodology rested on the assumption that it was at least possible to encounter perfect archetypal entities within the material universe of clinical practice. Charcot exhorted his listeners to commence their nosological description with a case of "the complete type" wherever possible.[49] Once one had identified such a perfectly formed pathological example, one could break it down into the various isolated elements that one encountered amongst the *formes frustes* more commonly found within the actual patient population itself. Pierre Janet—who was head of the Salpêtrière laboratory of experimental psychology under Charcot—observed that Charcot tended to concentrate on these more representative cases, rather than upon the varieties which one most often encountered in the wards.[50] Meige similarly reflected that although Charcot's method of types was the basis of good clinical practice, it led some critics to "reproach him for possessing an excess tendency for schematization."[51]

Janet noted that Charcot's belief in the perfectibility of essential nosological types meant that:

> Most of the patients who presented themselves at the consultation service are considered as exceptions, irregularities, complications; the types, when they present themselves, are singled out as remarkable and retained as curious examples. Often the same types which Charcot chooses are ... exceptional and rare cases of the disease, as occurs, for example, in those used to represent hysterical attacks.[52]

Charcot's typological approach could, therefore, lead him to misrepresent diseases, especially with regard to their clinical expression. The lecture theatre thereby became a veritable freak show of outlandish pathologies, with little correspondence to the reality of clinical practice. Janet reversed Charcot's distinction between the archetype and the *forme fruste*, implying that it was the more *common* forms which should have been presented in the lecture theatre—even though these were less complete instances of illness. Charcot, however, lavished his attention upon the more exotic, archetypically-expressive varieties. It was, moreover, significant that it was in the context of hysterioepilepsy and its theatrical presentation that this issue offered the greatest problem—despite the fact that the method of types was employed throughout Charcot's practice. Meige explicitly rejected the suggestion that Charcot developed his "theatrical exhibitions" of the amphitheatre so as to be consistent with the equally theatrical:

> convulsive manifestations of *la grande hystérie*. An erroneous insinuation ... Charcot indiscriminately presented in his clinical lessons all of the illnesses which were their object. Paralytics, vertiginouses, myopathics, Basedowians [thyrotoxics], myxoedemics, tremblers or neurasthenics, [all] appeared in turn for the benefit of demonstration. Should he have created a[n arbitrary] rule excluding hysterics?[53]

The criticisms which Charcot brought upon himself through the theatrical display and understanding of hysterioepilepsy would, however, suggest that the answer to Meige's question was yes.

Charcot himself conceded that the frequency with which one encountered the various *formes frustes* made the diagnosis and classification of archetypes difficult. One response was to draw up comprehensive tables showing the daunting variety of related types and their common deformations, visibly arraying for his audience and readers the material from which he constructed his diagnostic species.[54] Many such tableaux appeared in Charcot's demonstrations within the amphitheatre.

Charcot indicated that he saw these issues as but a minor impediment to normal clinical practice. He employed one of his favourite Shakespearean quotations in this context:

> The anomalies of the type, the combination of strange elements ... that growing complexity which begins to say along with Hamlet, "There are more things in heaven and earth [Horatio,] than are dreamt of in your philosophy." But you should not be discouraged in this; because patient, clinical analysis very nearly always disperses without mutilation the diverse elements of such a nosographic complex.[55]

Charcot maintained that his hierarchy of essential relationships and causes enabled him to disperse the vaporous complexities offered by the abortive "anomalies of type," just as the light of day caused old Hamlet's ghost to melt away. If one followed Charcot's former student Freud in reading the ghost of Hamlet's father as representing the "return of the repressed," however, then the *formes frustes*—unacknowledged children clamouring at the margins of Charcot's nosological project—came to represent the incompletely repressed unconscious of Charcot's own methodology. As in *Hamlet*, the stage of the lecture theatre became a place where repressed energies moved through the audience's consciousness in an only partially veiled fashion.

2   PLATO'S CAVE

Ten years after Charcot's death, Richer opened his lecture on artistic anatomy at the ENSBA with the following observation on how the ancient Assyrians represented the living body:

> By accentuating the contours of the nude … the furrows and depressions which separate them, the Assyrians came to render the impression of muscular force by an extremely curious sort of anatomical *trompe-l'oeil*, but also with a truthful strength.[56]

Richer conceded that Assyrian art did not represent anatomical form in a literal fashion. The "*trompe-l'oeil*" of the Assyrians nevertheless had a certain truth to it. It effectively conveyed an "impression" of the functional "strength" and the design of the musculature. This aestheticization of the nude, therefore, enabled the spectator to grasp its true anatomical form. Meige (Richer's successor at the École) employed a similar model in his eulogy to his former teacher in "Charcot the Artist" (1898). Meige characterized Charcot as a "caricaturist":

> to discover a comic anomaly and to cast it into relief, that is the very principle of the art of caricature. But is not the object of the clinician's art, like that of the comic, to identify corporeal anomalies and to render them perceptible to others?

> That is why it is not too audacious to consider that Charcot's aptitude for caricature was often profitable for him in his *métier* as a clinician.[57]

The construction of anatomical mimesis by Richer and Meige was not transparent, but opaque. The objects of representation were subjected to distortion in order for their truth to become visible. Caricature and Assyrian sculpture might exaggerate certain features, but if these features represented what Meige described as "the essential contours" of a disease and the "elements necessary for its expression," then such a form of representational distortion aided in the construction and display of truth.[58] Reality, therefore, was neither self-evident nor readily accessible to conventional representation. On the contrary, anatomical form had to be approached via a degree of abstraction, such as the caricature and the archetype.

The explanation for this surprising combination of aesthetic mediation with rationalist science lay in the Platonic theory upon which Charcot's ideas were based. Plato's original discussion of the archetype described a hypothetical scenario in which prisoners, fixed to the spot by chains, were unable to turn their heads towards the performers whose shadows they were condemned to observe.[59] This tortuous theatre was proffered as a model for a universe in which human perception was flawed. The spectators had to strive to see beyond the silhouettes moving before them and to imaginatively reconstruct the transcendental forms that lay behind their heads—even though these forms (the only real actors) forever eluded the spectators' direct gaze. Reality was a degraded theatre. Plato, therefore, singled the theatre out as a particularly deceptive representational forum. It was a second order representation: a reflection of an already unreliable material universe (a simulacra). Immaterial representations such as poetry, philosophy, or nosology could, however, grope towards the archetype, which rested in the virtual space beyond the material universe.

Charcot's aim was not to bring before his audience the degraded, imperfect forms commonly encountered in the wards. He strove to evoke the universal, transcendent forms which underlay clinical experience, using the imperfect, fragmentary material available to him. The infrequency with which one encountered perfect types paradoxically made the theatre an ideal space for the synthesis of examples otherwise difficult to access in normal space. The true drama of the presentations did not lie with the actors proffered to the audience's view, nor with the images and specimens presented alongside them. The drama lay rather in *archetypal space itself,* sitting beside, in and under the forms Charcot manipulated within the literal, material amphitheatre.

Later chronophotographic studies of the body in motion by Marey, Londe, and Richer offered a visual parallel to Charcot's method. Marey managed to photograph the archetypal body in motion by dressing the subject in black, with only white lines running down the major articulations being visible in the final images. This costume erased the quiddity of the subject's body, which lay hidden under the fabric and hence invisible to the photographic gaze. The photograph presented pure, abstracted lines, which Marey, Richer, and Londe reproduced in their publications.[60] Richer and Londe, moreover, employed a similar technique when photographing healthy subjects so as to draw up a table of normal proportions. The individual was placed in front of a black screen, on a neutral wooden stage, and the positions regularized to remove any other variations.

Charcot's gaze functioned here in a fashion akin to the photographic abstracting which Richer, Londe, and Marey conducted. In Meige's words: "The particular cases fuse themselves together before one's eyes into a unique type, a living expression of a nosographic entity."[61] This "unique type" remained curiously unfixed, however, "living" before the listener's eyes, but not within the actual patients sitting on the stage. Charcot effected a kind of truthful, scientific-rationalist mirage—much like Marey's rippling lines of mobility—producing a translucent template which Charcot superimposed over the multiple subjects onstage, melding them together. Although Charcot placed great emphasis on the role of the living body in the amphitheatre, the patient was no more the real subject of his performances than the individual was in Marey's photography. Charcot's patients acted as little more than particularly expressive stage properties within the neuropathologist's dramaturgy. Charcot was, therefore, ambivalent regarding theatre, employing a dramaturgical method to minimalize and annihilate the performative epiphenomenon of the individuated, moving, clinical body.

It is to the staging practices conducted within the amphitheatre itself that we must now turn, to see how these patterns of spatial and material authority (painting, monuments, specialist departments) acted as a setting for the performative generation and dissection of archetypal form in Charcot's lectures.

NOTES

1. François Helme, *Les jardins de la médecine* (Paris: Vigot, 1907), 306.
2. Viggo Christiansen, *Centenaire de J.-M. Charcot* (Paris: Masson, 1925), 6.
3. Jonas Barish, *The Antitheatrical Prejudice* (Berkley: California University Press, 1981); Jonathan W. Marshall, "Performing Hysteria," *Proceedings of the Western Society of French History*, 28 (2002): 19–26; Timothy Murray, ed., *Mimesis, Masochism, and Mime* (Ann Arbor: Michigan University Press, 1997), 63–86. Auerbach (*Private Theatricals*) also makes a similar point.
4. *Simon*-Dhouailly, ed., 17–21.

5. Peugniez, 19–20. It should be noted that particularly troublesome patients remained in chains at the Salpêtrière throughout Pinel's tenure. By Charcot's time, the camisole or straight jacket had replaced chains.
6. Helme, 306.
7. Sander Gilman, *Seeing the Insane* (NY: John Wiley and Sons, 1982), 212–3.
8. See Charcot, *Charcot*, xxviii–xxx.
9. Norech, "Le dr Charcot à la Salpêtrière," *Paris illustré*, 5.1 (30 April 1887): 14, 70, 76.
10. Fernand Levillain, "Charcot et l'école de la Salpêtrière," *Revue encyclopédique*, 4 (1894): 113.
11. Roger Ballu, "Le salon de 1887: Supplément," *Illustration*, 2305 (30 April 1887): unpaginated.
12. Starr et al., 14.
13. *OC*, vol. 3, pp. 6–7.
14. Collections and displays of the Musée d'Assistance Publique, Paris; Simon-Dhouailly, ed., 64–65, 109–110; Michael Roth, "Hysterical Remembering," *Modernism/Modernity*, 3.2 (May 1996): 23–25.
15. *OC*, vol. 3, p. 6.
16. Charles Féré, "J.-M. Charcot," *Revue des deux mondes*, 122 (15 March 1893): 414.
17. Charcot, *Charcot*, 181–5.
18. *OC*, vol. 3, p. 4.
19. Peugniez, 5–6.
20. Michel Foucault, *Birth of the Clinic*, trans. A.M. Sheridan Smith (NY: Vintage, 1994).
21. *OC*, vol. 12, p. 464.
22. F. Clifford Rose, ed., *A Short History of Neurology* (Butterworth Heinemann, Oxford: 1999), 229–230.
23. Meige, "Charcot," 494.
24. *OC*, vol. 12, p. 457.
25. *OC*, vol. 10, p. 2.
26. *OC*, vol. 7, p. 44.
27. I largely employ Charcot's own preferred terminology; thus, the use of locomotor ataxia rather than tabes dorsalis.
28. *OC*, vol. 4, p. 190.
29. Meige, "Charcot," 494.
30. *OC*, vol. 4, p. 379.
31. *OC*, vol. 4, p. 379.
32. *OC*, vol. 7, p. XX.
33. *OC*, vol. 7, p. XIX.
34. *OC*, vol. 7, pp. XVIII–XIX.
35. *OC*, vol. 7, pp. XXII–XXIV.

36. *OC*, vol. 7, p. XIX, XXI.
37. *OC*, vol. 1, pp. 182, 252.
38. *OC*, vol. 3, pp. 14–17.
39. Meige, "Charcot," 496.
40. *OC*, vol. 2, pp. 1–2.
41. *OC*, vol. 12, p. 71.
42. *OC*, vol. 12 [BC], p. 177.
43. *OC*, vol. 12 [BC], pp. 178–9.
44. Charcot, *OC*, vol. 12, p. 462, 196, *Charcot*, 24–25.
45. *OC*, vol. 9, p. 511.
46. *OC*, vol. 12 [BC], p. 175.
47. *OC*, vol. 12 [BC], p. 181.
48. *OC*, vol. 3, pp. 15–16.
49. *OC*, vol. 9, p. 299, vol. 12 [BC], p. 182.
50. Pierre Janet, "Charcot: Son oeuvre philosophique," *Revue philosophique de la France et de l'étranger*, XXXIX (June 1895): 575, 602.
51. Henry Meige, *Les possédées noires* (Paris: Schiller, 1894), 80.
52. Janet, 576.
53. See also chapter three. Meige, "Charcot," 493.
54. *OC*, vol. 11, pp. 424–9, vol. 12, p. 299, vol. 12 [BC], pp. 398, 417.
55. *OC*, vol. 12, p. 415; Shakespeare, *Hamlet*, I.v.167–8.
56. Paul Richer, *École nationale et spéciale des beaux-arts: Cours d'anatomie. Leçon d'ouverture (25 novembre 1903)* (Paris: Masson, 1903), 10.
57. Meige, "Charcot," 516.
58. Ibid., 491.
59. Plato, "The Allegory of the Cave," from *Republic*, VII.514.a.2 to VII.517.a.7, trans. Thomas Sheehan, reproduced on <https://web.stanford.edu/class/ihum40/cave.pdf>; Murray, ed., 63–86.
60. See Richer, *Physiologie*; Albert Londe, "Le nouveau laboratoire de la Salpêtrière," *La Nature*, 21.2 (1893), 370–4; Marta Braun, *Picturing Time* (Chicago: Chicago University Press, 1994); Cartwright, 2–70.
61. Meige, "Charcot," 496.

CHAPTER 4

The Theatre of the Lecture Theatre

1   IMPROVISED AND EX CATHEDRA TEACHING

Charcot was one of several Parisian medics who presented public lessons. One of Charcot's former students and eventual successors, Pierre Marie, listed Alfred Vulpian, Alfred Fournier, Jules Parrot, and Félix Guyon as amongst the most popular physicians whose lectures at various locations made up the courses administered by the Medical Faculty, to whom one might add those of Charcot's fellow specialists in hysteria and hypnosis, Charles Lasègue and Jules Luys, as well as general physician Armand Trousseau.[1] In the field of surgery, Jules Péan's publicly performed operations also attracted much attention, the latter also being discussed by journalists such as Charcot's former student Léon Daudet. In many cases, however, the tendency towards impressive theatrics appeared as a weakness in accounts of these presentations. The visiting Scottish doctor George Robertson, for example,

---

An earlier version of this chapter appeared as Jonathan W. Marshall, "Dynamic Medicine and Theatrical Form at the *fin de siècle*: A Formal Analysis of Dr Jean-Martin Charcot's Pedagogy, 1862–1893," *Modernism/Modernity*, 15.1 (January 2008): 131–153, reproduced here by kind permission of Johns Hopkins University Press.

69
J.W. Marshall, *Performing Neurology*,
DOI 10.1057/978-1-137-51762-3_4

found the stage properties Luys used to induce hypnotism—including "a magnetic crown, shaped something like a horseshoe"—ridiculous. Observing how when Luys offered one of his demonstration subjects a bottle of valerian, she reflexively adopted "feline movement and crawling on all fours," Robertson and others concluded that these were little more than "clinical follies," more suited to the stage or *café-concért* than a medical lecture.[2] Pierre Véron from *Le monde illustré* critically observed that Charcot's lessons had become "almost fashionable, giving science an aspect somewhat more theatrical than reason could provide," likening the public's interest in Charcot's work to their equal fascination with the controversial work of Naturalist dramaturg André Antoine.[3] The theatrical quality of fin de siècle medical pedagogy, therefore, presented demonstrators with aesthetic challenges whilst contributing to the social prestige of medicine and spreading new discoveries amongst the public.

Summing up Charcot's ambiguous appeal, the anonymouss author "X" of *Les annales politiques et littéraires* wrote:

> His voice is somewhat dull [*sourde*]; the speech is clear, precise, not meticulously arranged, sometimes slightly hesitant. But the master delays little in choosing words, he speaks simply, the elevation always comes from the subject.

> With a few very short phrases, he poses the problem to be resolved, the question to be studied, and immediately introduced the living examples [the patients] ... one listens only to his voice, monotonous like that of a puppeteer of wax figures.[4]

X's description went to the heart of the aesthetic contradictions which defined Charcot's presentations. An apparently boring speaker whose rhetorical power lay as much in the simplicity of his self-presentation as in his skills as an orator or stage director, Charcot appears here as a puppeteer of the subjects who appeared beside him onstage. The monotony of his delivery and staging acted as a crucial tool in his mastery of the often melodramatic performances by fitting patients which took place alongside him. It is this contradiction, what Didi-Huberman has characterized as a "spectacle without mise en scène" that is the topic of this chapter.[5]

Charcot's public lecture presentations were both stylistically unique and exceptionally popular. Accounts which appeared in the contemporary lay and medical press demonstrate that Charcot was almost as well known for the aesthetic style of his presentations as he was for their specific content. Whilst the transgressive nature of hysterioepileptic symptoms has become a truism of the historical accounts of Charcot, the contradictions embodied within his own demonstrative technique—a technique which he applied to all of the diseases he described, from goitre through to epilepsy—has not been acknowledged. Charcot developed a new multimedia style of teaching whose form echoed that of the living, neurological body with which it dealt. Charcot was an accomplished dramaturg whose refusal to employ elaborate rhetorical flourishes within his personal presentation constituted in itself a highly mannered performance of rationalist, scientific authority.

Charcot's work may in this sense be compared to that of twentieth century dramaturg Bertolt Brecht in that Brecht too formulated a self-conscious theatrical mode the purpose of which was not to move the audience or to tell stories, but to outline causes—to show how and why something happened. Brecht called such demystifying actions or set of scenes *gestus*: a gesture which explains. To support this demystifying approach, Brecht advocated various techniques to remind the audience that they were in a theatre.[6] The descriptor "Brechtian theatre" now refers to theatre which draws attention to its own technical devices, where the mode of staging is visibly presented to the audience, rather than being hidden or obscured as in conventional illusionistic theatre. Lighting sources and costume racks rest onstage, in full view, which was also true at the Salpêtrière. Charcot echoed Brecht in attempting to stage his own thought process and diagnostic method whilst he presented patients and diseases onstage, making visible any devices or tools he used to communicate or express his concepts, and, therefore, hopefully dispelling any sense that what the audience was viewing was a "fiction" rather than simply placing reality under a clarifying spotlight.

Charcot did employ a number of spectacular dramaturgical devices in order to highlight and amplify the performative, diagnostic characteristics of diseases which he identified. His demonstrative technique was often perceived to function as an imagistic theatre of memory or site of audience, in which images and concepts were engraved upon the mind of the audience member. Charcot's teaching represented a well-developed dramaturgical methodology which paradoxically evolved out of a distrust of the theatrical medium itself.

Charcot presented two distinct lecture series. There was the fully-prepared, afternoon, *vendredi* (Friday) lessons, offered as part of the Faculty of Medicine courses. The second was the morning, *mardi* (Tuesday) lessons—in addition to other less formalized presentations. Each lasted for approximately two hours: slightly longer than a short play.

Charcot and others emphasized the improvised nature of the Tuesday stream, in which he interviewed subjects who had ostensibly been chosen that morning from the clinical admissions of the hospice (*la policlinique*). Charcot claimed that:

> Dogmatic teaching, or what we call *ex cathedra* lessons, is something arti-ficial ... My aim is to fool no one, and so, before your eyes, I will plunge right in and proceed just as I do in my own practice. I ... interview patients whom I do not know.[7]

A comparison of the published lectures from both streams, the patients who appeared, and Charcot's detailed notes shows that the "improvised" quality of the Tuesday presentations was exaggerated. In both cases, Charcot's speech closely corresponded with his notes, which he recited from memory, and both covered similar topics and used much the same theatrical machinery (slides, casts, and so on).[8] The distinction between the two streams was, therefore, primarily a matter of their rhetorical fram-ing. In both situations, Charcot consciously strove to manipulate the dramaturgy to best serve his aims. Charcot may not have actually plunged "right in" and proceeded "just as I do in my own practice" before the eyes of the audience at his Tuesday lectures, but he successfully maintained the *illusion* that this was what he did.

Sigmund Freud (who studied at the Salpêtrière 1885–1886) was partic-ularly impressed by this aspect of the neuropathologist's pedagogy.[9] Freud observed that Charcot portrayed the true difficulties of clinical practice in the latter's more informal lessons. This was not the "dogmatic" Charcot of the Friday lessons, but rather a skilled yet humble physician, visible in all his fallibility. If the Friday lectures represented the summit of medical scenography, then the Tuesday demonstrations offered a glimpse into the more problematic, haphazard backstage world of actual diagnostic prac-tice. The Tuesday presentations functioned through a process of deliber-ately crafted Brechtian demystification. Just as the patients' neuromotor disorders were only fully manifest in real time, open to the exigencies of the moment yet nevertheless following a predictable pattern known to the physician, the same was true of how Charcot composed his own discourse and arguments.

The use of curial terms such as "dogmatic" and *"ex cathedra"* by Charcot and Freud gave the lectures an aura akin to a respectful com-munity of shared worship—in this case to the god of rationalist science. As Freud put it, Charcot:

would put aside his authority on occasion and admit—in one case that he could arrive at no diagnosis and in another that he had been deceived by appearances; and he never appeared greater to his audience than when, by giving the most detailed account of his processes of thought and by showing the greatest frankness about his doubts and hesitations, he had thus sought to narrow the gulf between teacher and pupil.[10]

By showing "his doubts and hesitations," the professor transformed both himself and science itself into figures comparable to the heroes of classical tragic theatre: protagonists aware of their own limited, human powers, and hence heroic. Charcot crafted himself as a sympathetic character, narrowing "the gulf between teacher and pupil"; between the papal chair (*cathedra*) and the seated congregation in "his audience."

Charcot's performance style, therefore, effected a double movement: it demonstrated the awesome powers of modern science at mastering the mysteries of the nervous tissues, whilst simultaneously rendering visible the fraught, provisional nature of scientific truth and medical diagnosis. Charcot's theatre was at once seductive in its impressive theatrical display of scientific praxis, whilst simultaneously reminding the spectators that the fundamental principles upon which neurological dramaturgy was based were accessible to all with proper training.

2   MULTI-MODAL MEMORY IN THE AMPHITHEATRE

The lecture theatre provided the ideal site for the dissemination of knowledge about the living, moving body. But public presentations alone were not sufficient to establish an academic career. One of the problems facing Charcot and his fellow neurologists was how to transfer their work into *textual* form.

Salpêtrière *chef de clinique* Joseph Babinski provided the most detailed discussion of the difficulties involved in putting Charcot's lectures onto the page. In his preface to Charcot's published Tuesday lessons, Babinski related that a Viennese student was disappointed by a visit he made to the clinic of a famous German physician. The student in question claimed of his Teutonic master that:

> I worked under him for several months, and I never heard him express a single original idea that was not already contained in one of his published works ... If you have read his book you know as much as I do ... But it is

not the same with your professor. I have read and re-read his books. [But] reading his books is not enough to know him and appreciate him.[11]

The German physician was most likely Ernest Kraepelin, whilst the Viennese student is likely to have been Freud. What is significant here is that the Viennese narrator implied that the medical techniques which Charcot dramatized within the Tuesday lessons defied written documentation. To fully "know" Charcot and his method, one had to personally attend the lectures. Babinski continued that:

> It is for these ... reasons that MM. Blin, Charcot *fils*, and Colin ... have thought ... that publishing these Tuesday lessons would be a significant service ... It will be greeted with the greatest satisfaction by those who have attended the classes and happily can relive them.[12]

Despite having issued this publication, Babinski remained reluctant to concede that a close transcription of Charcot's Tuesday lessons could displace the authorial presence and medical knowledge which Charcot developed through direct theatrical presence. Babinski concluded that: "Without replacing the speech of the professor, the reading of these new lessons permits everyone ... to better know the ideas of the master and to broaden their own [understanding of them], as the Viennese doctor thought."[13] The text did not, therefore, replace the professor's voice; rather it supplemented it, expanding (*"d'élargir"*) both his ideas and the circle of his acolytes. Lecture-scripts remained an imperfect record of pedagogic performance, just as the textual description of the cadaver was an imperfect record of dynamic, living neurophysiology.

The disappointment of the Viennese doctor might be said to echo Jacques Derrida's model of phonological discourse.[14] So long as authority was closely tied to the thoughts and opinions of a single, phenomenologically real author—as was the case during the nineteenth century—the written text served primarily to register traces of an absent authority and an absent body. Only the author could (literally) breathe life into the text by speaking its words. This was particularly true of Charcot's discourse, where the subject of his speech was embodied neurological behaviour. Not only was Charcot's own authority made physically manifest by his presence as a speaker, but so also was the subject of his discourse enacted and performed by patients through movement. There was, therefore, a close parallel between how one gained access to the topic of Charcot's discourse itself (watching the patient perform), and how one gained access to Charcot's own discourse (listening to the author speak).

In the words of Charcot's immediate successor to the chair of neurology, Fulgence Raymond, Charcot first carried out his own "mnemonic exercise" in learning the text of what he was to say. "That which was engraved in his mind, he set himself the task of penetrating into the minds of his listeners and engraving it there also."[15] Ultimately, it was not the illustrated pages of Charcot's published texts that served as the primary site for the re-transcription of Charcot's lectures. Rather the minds of those present in the amphitheatre acted as the primary slate or site of audience for Charcot's medical pedagogy. As Charcot's former student Moses Allen Starr observed:

> It has been said that the whole clinic was arranged for theatrical effect. I believe that was the only manner in which it was possible to demonstrate in a clear light ... all of the features, clinical and pathological, of the subject. But grant that it was theatrical; it left on the mind of the students a series of mental pictures of patients and of lessons which no amount of private study could possibly produce. It taught men so that they could not fail to remember.[16]

The arrangement of images and forms in space constituted a spectacular, mnemonic system similar to the theatre of memory advocated by Cicero and other classical rhetoricians.[17] One recalled concepts through the logical placement of visual keys located within specific spaces found within a virtual, mental theatre like the Salpêtrière. Starr and others felt that Charcot transposed the manifest dramaturgy of the physical demonstrations onto the immaterial architecture of the audience's psyche—"it left on the mind of the students a series of mental pictures" such that "they could not fail to remember." Starr and Janet, moreover, recognized the importance of the multi-modal quality of Charcot's lectures for this act of memory. Janet noted that not only were the demonstrations "animated and lively like a show [*un spectacle*]" but that "Everything in his lessons was calculated and disposed to strike one's attention ... through the eyes as through the ears."[18] Memory and learning was fostered through the simultaneous stimulation of neuroperceptual pathways, a process consistent with Charcot's construction of kinesthetic memory (see Chap. 7).

The venue within which lectures of both streams were eventually held was designed to meet Charcot's needs. A theatre was built at the

Salpêtrière for Charcot's lectures and it was in use by 1880. Audience members entered at the rear and descended from the back row, filling the seating from the front. Grand, lavishly decorated structures in the style of Renaissance dissection theatres were still employed at institutions such as the Paris Medical Faculty building.[19] Charcot's venue, though, was not in fact a true amphitheatre, nor did it feature any superfluous adornments. It was rather a long rectangular hall, more akin to a spartan performing arts building than a conventional anatomy theatre (Fig. 4.1). If one removed the proscenium arch found at sites such as Antoine's modest Théâtre Libre—a venue regularly attended by Charcot's former student Léon Daudet, and located close to the Théâtre du Grand Guignol later visited by these students—one would have had a comparable space. X from *Les annales politiques et littéraires* somewhat melodramatically described the auditorium as follows:

> The amphitheatre is a long room, of which perhaps one half is occupied by tiers. All of the windows are hermetically sealed and locked. Not a ray of daylight comes in to pierce ... the dark light of the gas lamps with

Fig. 4.1   Salpêtrière amphitheatre, early to mid twentieth century. Photograph © Assistance publique des hôpitaux de Paris, Photothèque. Original archival reference: Centre d'image de l'Assistance publique des hôpitaux de Paris (CMT d'AP), *Hôpital de la Salpêtrière. Service personel**, 48.XII, réf. 48 1050B

their frosted globes. The high walls painted in red give this light a special quality ... in the other part of the room [on the stage itself], several rows of chairs face in upon themselves [i.e. in a semi-circle], surrounding a modest space, reserved for the professor, his subjects and his aides; two little tables with a few instruments for electricization, demonstration illustrations, a large blackboard, this is the entire mise en scène.[20]

Although the space had a claustrophobic air, it was not entirely "sealed," as X put it. Heavy coverings were fitted to the windows. Starr noted that it was only "After the audience had gathered" that the "dark shutters were closed at the windows, the footlights were turned up, and the clinic began." He added that "sometimes, when a particular feature had to be demonstrated, a calcium light"—or limelight—"was turned on the patient, whose figure" became "the chief point of light in the darkness" and consequently "could always be perfectly seen by all."[21]

Many commentators echoed Starr in extolling the modernity of the amphitheatre's stage machinery. The venue was fitted with various equipment not uncommon at theatre venues and popular magic lantern displays since the 1850s. Charcot's main innovation was the introduction of these mechanisms within the specific context of university medical teaching. The lighting, for example, was controlled by a central dimmer which enabled Charcot to darken the foyer, a convention which Antoine later pioneered at the Théâtre de l'Odéon. Electrical slide projections and limelight spots could then be deployed to full effect. As Starr explained, this rendered the demonstration subject the chief focus within the darkened space. Comparison of illustrations showing the lectures with those of technologies of his day suggests that Charcot probably employed Léon Laurent's relatively novel design for an electrically-powered "megascope," or slide projector as a light source, as well as to show images.[22] This also added a visible level of modernity to Charcot's otherwise piecemeal use of theatrical tools and new technologies.

The descriptions of journalists such as Pont-Calé and Starr indicated that the lighting of the space overall had a dismal, high-relief, almost Gothic tone. Even when natural light was allowed into the room, the dark colour of the walls tended to absorb it, rather than diffusing it throughout the venue. Pont-Calé opined that: "The high walls painted in red lend their own gloomy note to that obscurity."[23] When the directional lighting of the floor lamps and spots was deployed, however, the objects captured by the glare took on a harsh, bleached aspect, leaping forward within the

viewer's depth of field. Félix Platel of *Le Figaro* similarly found the lighting extremely bright and consistent with the anatomical style of the lecture
presentations themselves: "The smallest details of the scene are beaten into
tiny fragments [*découpés à l'emporte-pièces*], under the bluish steam and
rawness of the gas."[24] Charcot's stage machinery tended, therefore, to cast
the body into a stark, high-contrast relief, vividly demarcating the shadows
from illuminated clarity. Light took on a poetic function, rendering the
nature of illness visible and banishing darkness to the margins of the space.

One notable concession to decoration within this harsh, gloomy ambience ("the only adornment in the room," as one author put it) was located
on the wall behind the stage.[25] This was Robert Fleury's salon painting *Pinel
Delivering the Salpêtrière's Madwomen From Their Chains* (1876)—an iconographic model which André Brouillet paraphrased in his own, later salon
painting of Charcot: *A Clinical Lesson at the Salpêtrière* (1887; Fig. 3.1).[26] As
noted in the previous chapter, the presence of Fleury's painting in the amphitheatre helped to establish a metaphoric link between the pioneering work
carried out at the Salpêtrière by the alienist Philippe Pinel, and Charcot's
later, more anatomically-based discourse. Excepting this iconographic set-
piece, the unadorned aesthetic of Charcot's theatre was consistent with the
project of rationalism itself, being stripped back of superfluous details so as
to reveal fundamental truths caught in the bright light of science. This was
notably different from the ambience created by the neoclassical ornamentation at the Faculty of Medicine amphitheatre and other locales.

As noted above, long wooden benches rested on tiered seating banks
extending from the rear wall of the Salpêtrière amphitheatre, which
tapered off at the front with an extended apron one step above the floor
itself, before which sat the stage. The seating at the front consisted of
nine or more rows of approximately ten to twelve unfixed chairs, which
could be added to, subtracted from or moved as circumstances dictated
(Fig. 4.1). The seats furthest forward were often used by the *chefs de clinique*. On some occasions: "On the slightly raised stage with the *chef de
clinique* appeared some favoured spectators, placed near the actors as in
the past were the great nobles at the theatre."[27] Charcot often delivered
his text from a seated position—literally *"ex cathedra"*—or stood side-on,
his much commented upon likeness to Napoleon clearly visible in profile.
The patients sat slightly behind him on the stage, illuminated by foot
lights or adjustable spots.[28]

Charcot's audience was typically mixed, with students and physicians
joined by foreign guests, figures from the School of Fine Arts (ENSBA),

artists, actors, authors, socialites, journalists, and politicians.[29] Notable spectators included Freud, Claretie, Duval, Gambetta, Waldeck-Rosseau, writers and dramaturgs such as Léon and Alphonse Daudet, Émile Zola, Paul Arène, Guy de Maupassant, Edmond de Goncourt, and other intellectuals such as Hippolyte Taine, Emile Durkheim, and Henri Bergson. The lectures were not completely open to the public. Most observers obtained an introduction of some kind, though visiting Glasgow physician Jane Henderson simply walked in off the street after asking for directions.[30] The audience was nevertheless drawn predominantly from the same well-to-do society within which the Salpêtrière physicians themselves circulated. Female medical students, *mondaines* and actresses such as Sarah Bernhardt (who toured the wards of the Salpêtrière) also constituted a highly visible minority, with several commentators disparagingly drawing attention to their presence—notably Charcot's disgruntled former student Axel Munthe. For Munthe, Pierre Véron, and others, the very audience at Charcot's lectures caused the neurologist's work to closely approximate a disreputable theatrical performance, a point to which I return in later chapters.

Charcot was a creature of habit in both his personal and professional life. The lessons began punctually and conserved a high degree of standardization in general format. Anticipating a prompt commencement—as well as competition for seating—spectators often arrived over thirty minutes early. Charcot's famed indifference to elaborate expressions of politeness and his cultivated "mask" of objectivity gave the proceedings a powerfully ritualized character—akin to a religious or Masonic ceremony—which reporters commented upon. X, for example, noted that expectant audience members would talk amongst themselves, when "a door is brusquely opened, the murmur ceases, all eyes turn towards the master."[31] Pont-Calé recorded that after this: "The master moves forward with a slightly heavy step, followed by a cortege of students, the legendary aprons"—part of the physicians' uniform—"tied about their waists."[32] Senior medics like Charcot or the head of the Salpêtrière electrotherapy unit, Romain Vigouroux, often further reinforced their institutional standing by wearing their academic caps. This opening procession was arrayed according to medical seniority. First came Charcot, then the heads of the specialist departments at the Salpêtrière (ophthalmology, photography, histology, hydrotherapy, electrotherapy), any special guests, the general *chefs de clinique*, interns, and then the undergraduate externs and those who tended to the patients on a day-to-day basis.[33] This opening display

of medical hierarchy constituted a mutually supportive, physical reitera-
tion of authority. The credentials visible in the entrance helped authorize
the lecture series, which in turn bolstered the power and hierarchy of the
medics themselves. The procession rendered in moving flesh the status of
the Salpêtrière as a "Neuro-Pathological Institute," made up of various
specialist facilities.

The diseased subjects were the last to enter. Henderson observed that
the "patients who are to form the text of the clinical lecture" waited in an
anteroom offstage, or "behind screens till the time comes for them to come
forward," at which point they shuffled out or were "carried and deposited
on chairs."[34] Illustrations show that decorated Chinese screens such as
were common in fashionable Parisian homes were used for this purpose,
with these stage elements doubtless brought in from one of the doctors'
offices near the amphitheatre (most likely Charcot's).[35] Like the screens
behind which they were sequestered, the patients remained essentially
inactive sculptural elements (or wax puppets, as X said) within Charcot's
dramaturgy, worked upon rather than constituting active participants. As
historian Christopher Goetz observes: "Charcot treated the patient like an
inert object in the laboratory," frequently speaking "in front of the patients
as though he was speaking in front of cadavers."[36] Charcot's presentations
were, therefore, theatrically closer to monologues, such as was the typical form of address for contemporary magic lantern demonstrations, than
they were to the conversational or dialogic form of most theatre.

Through such methods, the performing body was ordered and contained, its theatrical possibilities rendered according to Charcot's model
of rationalist *gestus*. The content and form of Charcot's lectures resembled
in this sense what Tom Gunning and André Gaudreault have described in
the case of the first showings of the Lumière brothers' filmic *actualités* as
a "spectacle of attractions."[37] At the Salpêtrière, the role of the lecturer-
demonstrator—or the Brechtian *monstrator* in Gaudreault's terms—was
to de-sensationalize, rationalize, and discursively master the often shocking physical deformations and diseases which were placed upon display in
slides or onstage. As we shall see in later chapters, this distinction between
the scientist-who-shows (the monstrator), and the actors whom the monstrator ushered onto the platform, was not always clear. Various commentators found Charcot to be subsumed within those presentations which
he attempted to frame; more of a dramatic thaumaturg than a rational
demystifier.

3   SPEECH VERSUS SPECTACLE

Few commentators praised Charcot's vocal delivery or use of gesture. Charcot's former student Paul Peugniez noted that Charcot shared:

> Neither the rounded tones, nor the sonority, nor the beautiful cadences, all of the attractive qualities which Lasègue and Trousseau possessed to such a high degree. But how many of them had his color and above all such clarity![38]

Charcot's speech was not however without its flourishes. The German neurologist Ernst von Leyden commended Charcot's use of "such sharp, striking, living expressions, for example: accentuated speech, stepping walk."[39] Even more notable was what medical biographer A. Lubimoff called "the singular aptitude of M. Charcot" at "reproducing" illnesses through "gestures and general appearance [*allure*]. In the pathetic moments, his voice had a timbre as attractive as a baritone making grave intonations."[40] Other commentators went so far as to describe the neuropathologist as a "skilled scientific actor" on the basis of his ability "to show the gait characteristic of various nervous disorders, or describe with his hands different forms of choreiform movements."[41]

Nevertheless, these moments of accomplished physical and vocal mimicry constituted rare dynamic interjections within an overall sedate aesthetic in which such dramatic materials as hysterioepilepsy and gross deformity were calmly monstrated to the audience—diseases were simply shown and then verbally emplotted within Charcot's scientific discourse. To achieve this effect, Charcot largely eschewed dramatic or oratorical demonstrations of authority in his own deportment and speech. Charcot's leading student Georges Gilles de la Tourette, for example, reflected that as an undergraduate Charcot had initially performed poorly in oral examinations: "Nothing was less suited to Charcot's temperament than such oratorical jousting where high-sounding words replace arguments of a scientific order."[42] Tourette for his part was renowned for his aggressively loud speech and vigorous rhetorical manner, acting as a more forthright proponent for Charcot within various oratorical environments, notably medicolegal debates.[43]

Tourette's assessment of Charcot was echoed by Georges Guillain, who claimed that the neurologist had a "horror of" exaggerated "emphasis," just as he despised: "commonplaces. His language was slow, his diction impeccable; he did not use gestures and sat as much as he stood. His exposé was always remarkably clear."[44] As with X from *Les annales politiques et littéraires*, contemporary journalists found Charcot's oratory modest. X concluded that "the professor is self-effacing," tending to subside into the background and let the subject matter speak for itself: "he contents himself with being a great demonstrator."[45] This meant that spectators rarely kept their eyes upon the neuropathologist, or even upon such attractions as his patients, but instead "one listens only to his voice," gazing about distractedly as one attended to this plain, disembodied monologue suffusing the space.

The importance of Charcot's *speech* over his physical *performance* or even his use of *images* was particularly emphasized in Henderson's account:

> Charcot's voice was not at all strong, so that the raised seats were too far away [for it] to be appreciated, and the majority of the students came as near as possible to the front, even although [*sic*] the view of the platform was apt to be obscured by the heads of those before them.[46]

For these audience members, Charcot's slides, sketches, and specimens were less significant than his vocal text. Accounts such as these show that, despite Charcot's famous innovations in spectacular presentation, his monstration was often judged to be primarily *aural* and *conceptual*, strongly in keeping with his uncompromisingly rationalist, Positivist stance, and in opposition to the more extravagant aesthetics of both the popular and the *beaux arts* entertainments of the period.[47]

Charcot's authority was, therefore, not attributable to the "attractive" qualities of either his vocal or linguistic expression itself. Charcot was in fact a slightly boring and banal presenter—his style echoing the unremitting, unalloyed truth he revealed. As Raymond noted, Charcot:

> appealed primarily by means of a language stripped of all useless research, but with a clarity of expression, in harmony with the clarity of the thinking ... a language seductive in its simplicity, and where each word had its proper value.[48]

Echoing both Raymond and Tourette, Platel ungenerously (but accurately) observed that: "He goes over his descriptions [*épithètes*] with his dull voice and drives the argument into the brain of his listeners, heavily and dully,—as one drives in a nail with a large block of wood."[49]

As X observed, the "elevation" came "from the subject," and not from Charcot's performance. Charcot's rhetorical power, therefore, seemed to derive as much from a stoic absence of activity or flourishes, a tendency towards stasis and imperturbability, more than anything else.

For these and other commentators, Charcot's presentation style was deemed superior to those of Lasègue and Trousseau because of its *lack* of rhetorical enhancements. Charcot's personal presentation constituted a form of deliberate non-performance—Didi-Huberman's "spectacle without mise en scène"—a performative technique which (ironically) established the very mastery which Charcot refused to overtly display. This created a clear dramaturgical distinction between Charcot and his more extroverted, mumbling, staggering, or fitting patients. Charcot's theatrical framing was simultaneously spectacular yet banal, effecting a contradictory balance between artifice and science.

Charcot's most famous theatrical demonstration involved the differential identification of illnesses exhibiting symptomatic trembling. Charcot brought onstage patients suffering from paralysis agitans (Parkinson's disease), locomotor ataxia (tabes), and chorea. Raymond observed that:

> By various ingenious artifices, he sometimes amplified a symptom to produce specific characteristics … [including a] bizarre but instructive collection of trembling patients, provided with head gear terminating in long rods, and which Charcot presented … to demonstrate the oscillatory characteristics of the diverse varieties of tremors.[50]

Feathers at the tip of each rod wavered distinctively according to the illness in question. Charcot demonstrated the "specific character" of Parkinson's by having assistants hold the subjects about the trunk. When the upper body of a Parkinson's sufferer was stabilized, the feather remained still—which was not true of the patients afflicted with other illnesses. The apparent head tremor of Parkinson's was, therefore, a secondary consequence of vibrations which originated in the trunk, showing Parkinson's to be a distinct disease entity associated with a loss of neuromuscular control centred in the torso.

These feather-topped hats constituted merely the most flamboyant device Charcot employed in these contexts. Another commonly rehearsed identifying mark involved the separation of intention tremor (loss of precise control over transitory voluntary actions) from persistent, involuntary tremor. The standard test was to have the patient attempt to drink a glass of water. Otherwise coordinated subjects often exhibited a marked tremor during such an action. The intention tremor of those afflicted with sclerosis in plaques (multiple sclerosis) helped distinguish them from sufferers of paralysis agitans, who exhibited a tremor whilst at rest.[51] Other physical examinations performed in the amphitheatre included walking, writing, holding one's arms horizontally, or attempting to balance with the eyes closed (Romberg's sign). Charcot's presentations conformed in this sense to a tautological pattern of orally telling, then visually showing through the directed actions of the patient, and then further explication in words.

These diagnostic tests constituted, in Raymond's words above, a form of performative amplification and reinforcement. As in a sketched caricature (a form of illustration at which, as we have seen, Charcot excelled), the neuropathologist exaggerated the apparent scale of, or relative focus upon, various physical signs in order to make them more visible to the viewer. To manipulate the audience's attention, the physician utilized hand drawn illustrations, theatrical lighting, commentary, and the direction of onstage action to dramaturgically change the apparent proportions of the body in such a way as to enhance his pedagogic demonstration and diagnosis.

Charcot's most influential contribution to medical display was his enthusiastic use of projections. Commentators were quick to proclaim his skilful manipulation of slides as a particularly impressive innovation in scientific pedagogy. After reading out case notes and having the patient perform basic diagnostic actions such as those described above, Starr notes that Charcot would move on to causes:

> Dismissing the patient, he would begin to describe the lesion, and at once on the screen on the opposite side of the stage the magic lantern would flash out the picture he wished to show, either in the form of a sketch made from nature, or an actual slide of a section of the spinal cord, or part of the brain magnified by the microscope, or a photograph of some unusual clinical type.[52]

It is unclear whether Charcot was the first to use photographic slides in an anatomical context. Slides were nevertheless relatively uncommon formal pedagogical tools at this time. The sheer quantity of photographic materials associated with the Salpêtrière during Charcot's tenure was without precedent. The photographic laboratory at the hospice produced a vast quantity of images, which were widely disseminated throughout the publications of the Salpêtrière school. Contemporary commentators made frequent mention of the impressive slide presentations which Charcot gave and this practice continued at the Salpêtrière under Pierre Marie (professor of neurology 1917–1925), whose talent for audiovisual display was said to surpass even Charcot's.[53]

Slides from the Salpêtrière photography clinic made up the most overtly modern, rational element within Charcot's iconography. There does not appear to have been a set location from which the slides were cast. Fully-enclosed, modern projection booths were not common until sometime in the twentieth century, following conventions first established in the cinema, phantasmagoria (moving magic lantern shows), and other forms like Charles-Émile Reynaud's idiosyncratic Théâtre Optique. The Faculty of Medicine amphitheatre had a bio-box added after Charcot's death, for example. The projector at the Salpêtrière, however, was visibly present to the audience, being typically directed onto movable stands resting on the stage, to one side of Charcot and the subjects.[54] The distance of throw was short and so images would have been bright and sharp, but relatively small. The theatre could also be fitted with a translucent cyclorama for more impressive displays, but there is no indication that Charcot took advantage of this possibility. Charcot's presentations were, therefore, notable not so much for the integrated scale of their effects, as for the number of slides, their flow, and what Guillain described as the "luminous clarity" which they permitted.

Even more than the literal body which had been "beaten into tiny fragments" by intense light, the projected photographic image enabled a transmutation—a transfiguration—of the body into its immaterial, nosological characteristics. These elements constituted a veritable inverse panopticon, beaming out images with which Charcot enabled his audience to see through the eyes of observers past and present, arraying historic art works depicting deformities and seizures alongside his own representations of modern patients. Images lifted from the retina of this unblinking, all-seeing composite eye were distributed throughout the space of the amphitheatre.

The body-made-fleshless through projection—a body of pure light—was arrayed beside these numerous other iconographic representations, reifying the body even as Charcot established his mastery of it. As Starr's account above suggests, slides not only enabled one to compare different physical fragments, but also to metaphorically look within the body of the patient in question, revealing the causes of these dynamic diseases of movement in tissue damage and other anatomical phenomena. The subject was dismissed from the theatre and the interiority of the pathological body displayed. No sooner was the body of the living patient presented onstage than it was replaced by its iconographic representation in the form of photographs, post-mortem preparations, verbal explications, and other materials. Charcot's methodology thereby minimized—but did not altogether disallow—the possibility that the live performance of the subject could destabilize his *gestic* presentation of this material.

4   The Perils of the Stage

Charcot emerged from these and other accounts as a highly adept multimedia dramaturg and monstrator who nevertheless, either by choice or from necessity, presented himself in a modest, theatrically uninteresting light—even during his *ex cathedra* lessons. Charcot attempted to forge a reconciliation between theatrical aesthetics and the new science of neurology. However, the rhetorical devices which Charcot brought together were not always compatible, highlighting conflicts which existed between different discursive forms and genres. Charcot's demonstrations constituted an evolved theatrical form which was nonetheless characterized by absences and contradictions. His dramaturgical methodology remained an incomplete one. Neither the lectures themselves nor the published clinical lessons could fulfil their function without the other. These discursive forms existed as part of a performative dialectic, each sustaining (whilst also undermining) Charcot's neurological discourse. As Charcot himself conceded, one had to constantly return to the living body in the amphitheatre. The dynamic, "theatrical" subject of his discourse often seemed to subvert Charcot's methodology and transform the lecturer himself into a subject within his own mise en scène, as we shall see.

No commentator better expressed the ambivalence felt for the theatre than Maurice de Fleury. In his *Introduction to Medicine of the Mind and Spirit,* he observed that Charcot "strongly loved truth, unlike those minds which preferred mystery."[55] Charcot could, however, be accused of inciting such misguided thinkers through his exhibition of hysteria, hypnosis, and somnambulism (a point to which I shall return in Chap. 7). Fleury claimed that Charcot had for this reason considered closing the amphitheatre to the public altogether—although no other biographer records this. Even lay commentator Thomas Grimm of *Le petit journal* had felt it necessary to stress to his readership that "This is not a spectacle ... Science is making an investigation."[56] It is worth recalling here that the French word *la spectacle* translates as both "stage performance" and "spectacle." Fleury and Grimm, therefore, sought to clearly delineate between the visually striking but unscientific performances of the popular magnetizers who toured the public theatres of France, versus Charcot's more restrained work carried out at a formal medical institution. Fleury, for example, suggested that "if it is perilous to see, it is less perilous to read."[57]

The issue here was not merely one of popularization, nor of debates around hypnotism, but one of theatrical, performative "spectacle." Reading was imputed to generate a more reflective, conceptual, or rational relationship between author and receiver—a relationship which closely paralleled that which commentators attributed to Charcot's plain, oral presentation. Charcot's demystifying, *gestic* approach helped ensure that the neuropathologist's lectures remained stylistically close to such textual forms of knowledge. Theatrical diagnosis and presentation nevertheless continued to invoke questions of appearance, kinesthesia, of identification with the diseased subject, and of what Fleury called "offensive" displays of "lubricity" by some patients. That an otherwise vigorous advocate of Charcot's like Fleury ventured such an opinion was indicative of the controversies engendered by the use of theatrical methods, tropes, and topics within the context of medical pedagogy. The devices which Charcot drew upon nevertheless accorded with both the ideal form of neurological documentation and of Charcot's construction of the neurological body itself.

NOTES

1. Pierre Marie, "Éloge de J.-M. Charcot," *Bulletin de l'Académie de médecine*, 93 (1925): 579.

2. George Robertson, "Hypnotism at Paris and Nancy," *British Medical Journal* (Oct 1892): 527.

3. Pierre Véron, untitled eulogy of J.-M. Charcot, *Monde illustré* (26 August 1893): 130–1.

4. X, "M. Charcot à la Salpêtrière," *Annales politiques et littéraires* (5 July 1885): 12–13; Pont-Calé, "Le professeur Charcot," *Hommes d'aujourd'hui* no. 7.343 (1890): 1–3. Much of X's account reappeared in Pont-Calé's later article, so it seems likely Pont-Calé in fact authored both.

5. Didi-Huberman, *Invention*, 23.

6. Bertolt Brecht, *Brecht on Theatre* (London: Methuen, 1957).

7. *OC*, vol. 12 [BC], p. 1.

8. The folders at the Bibliothèque Charcot contain Charcot's case notes, related notes from the Salpêtrière and other doctors, histories, patient exams (ophthalmological reports, descriptions of skin sensitivity, and so on), sketches, and medical and literary quotations. Examples of specimens, tables, and advanced visual aids used in the Tuesday lectures appear throughout *OC*, vol. vol. 12 [BC], and other publications.

9. Freud, *Standard*, vol. 3, pp. 7–23.

10. Freud, vol. 3, p. 18.

11. *OC*, vol. 12, p. III.

12. *OC*, vol. 12, p. III.

13. *OC*, vol. 12, p. III.

14. Jacques Derrida, *Writing and Difference* (London: Routledge, 1978).

15. Raymond, 14.

16. Moses Allen Starr, "The Neurological Clinic at the Salpêtrière: Jean-Martin Charcot," in Arthur Selwyn-Brown, ed., *The Physician Throughout the Ages* (New York: Capehart-Brown, 1928), vol. 1, p. 653.

17. Frances Yates, *The Art of Memory* (London: Routledge, 1966).

18. Janet, 577.

19. See various, *Musée de l'assistance publique des hôpitaux de Paris*, catalogue d'exposition (Paris: Musée de l'assistance publique des hôpitaux de Paris, 1998), 94–95, 117–8.

20. X, 12–13.

21. Starr et al, 11–12.

22. Gilles de la Tourette "Jean-Martin Charcot," *NIPS*, 6 (1893): 248, specifies that Charcot's projector was fitted with an electric light, presumably a carbon arc device. This is substantiated by the illustration in A. Cartaz, "Du somnambulisme et du magnétisme: À propos du cours du Dr Charcot à la Salpêtrière," *La Nature*, 7.1 (1879): 104 and Léon Laurent, "Lanterne de projection et mégascope," *La Nature*, 6.2 (1878): 69–70; see also cover image of this book.

23. Pont-Calé, 1–3.

24. Ignotus [Platel], 386.

25. Jane Henderson, "Personal Reminiscences of M. Charcot," *Glasgow Medical Journal*, 40 (1893): 293.

26. Simon-Dhouailly, ed., 17–21.

27. Léon Dequillebecq, "Une matinée à la Salpêtrière," *Annales politiques et littéraires*, 21.531 (27 August 1893): 135–6.

28. Starr, "Neurological," 653.

29. See Goetz et al, 243–250.

30. Henderson, 292–8.

31. X, 12.

32. Pont-Calé, 1–3.

33. Goetz et al, xvii–xviii.
34. Henderson, 293.
35. Foveau de Courmelles, *Hypnotism* (London: Routledge, 1895), 33.
36. Christopher Goetz, "Charcot: Scientifique bifrons," *Revue neurologique* 150.10 (1994): 488.
37. Thomas Elsaesser and Adam Barker, eds, *Early Cinema* (London: BFI, 1990), 56–75.
38. Peugniez, 22.
39. Ernst von Leyden, "Éloge de J.-M. Charcot," *Archives de médecine experimentale*, 6 (1894): 151.
40. A. Lubimoff, *Professeur Charcot*, trans. Lydie Rostopchine (Paris: 1894), 37–38.
41. Levillain, 110.
42. Gilles de la Tourette, "Jean-Martin Charcot," 242.
43. A.J. Lees, "Georges Gilles de la Tourette," *Revue Neurologique*, 142.11 (1986): 808–16. Léon Daudet unkindly but accurately observed that Tourette "had a husky and worn out voice, abrupt gestures, a strange gait. He passed for an eccentric, starting an interesting subject but leaving it for another, disconcerting his masters by his queer ways which got worse and worse and became less and less amusing." Léon Daudet, *Devant la douleur: Souvenirs des milieux littéraires, politiques, artistiques et médicaux de 1880 à 1905* (Paris: Nouvelle librairie nationale, 1915), 35.
44. Guillain, *J.-M. Charcot*, 53.
45. X, 12.
46. Henderson, 293.
47. Klestinec (434–463) makes a similar claim about Fabrici's anatomical lessons.
48. Raymond, 14.
49. Ignotus [Platel], 385.
50. Raymond, 15; *OC*, vol. 3, pp. 213–227.
51. A. Lellouch, "Charcot, découvreur de maladies," *Revue neurologique* 150.8–9 (1994): 508.
52. Starr et al, 12.
53. Raymond, 20–24.
54. Simon-Dhouailly, ed., 53–55; Goetz et al, 85–86; Cartaz, 104.
55. Maurice de Fleury, *Introduction à la médecine de l'esprit* (Paris: Baillière, 1898), 3.
56. Thomas Grimm, "Le magnétisme," *Petit journal* (15 February 1882): 1.
57. Fleury, 4.

CHAPTER 5

The Grotesque Body and the Living Nude

1   PHOTOGRAPHY, PAINTING AND SCIENTIFIC MIMESIS

Charcot's lesson of October 1888 included a promotion for his second book with Paul Richer, *Deformed and Ill in Art*. In the lesson, Charcot argued that there was a close relationship between the expertise of painter and that of the physician:

> we … doctors must know *the nude* as well, better even than painters know it. A defect in drawing by the painter and the sculptor is doubtless serious from the point of view of art, but overall from a practical perspective it is not of any major consequence. But what would you say if it were a physician or a surgeon, who mistook … a normal bulge for a pathological deformation or vice versa? … this digression will perhaps be enough to bring out … the great necessity for the physician as for the surgeon to attach a greater importance to the medicosurgical study of the NUDE. Soon, I hope, we will be in

Some of the material from this chapter has appeared in Jonathan W. Marshall, "The Theatre of the Athletic Nude," *Being There: ADSA Proceedings* (June 2008), <http://ses.library.usyd.edu.au /bitstream/2123/2511/1/ ADSA2006_ Marshall.pdf> and "The Priestesses of Apollo and the Heirs of Aesculapius: Medical Art-Historical Approaches to Ancient Choreography After Charcot," *Forum for Modern Language Studies*, 43.4 (Oct 2007): 410–426, reproduced here by kind permission of Australasian Drama Studies Association, and Oxford University Press.

© The Editor(s) (if applicable) and The Author(s) 2016
J.W. Marshall, *Performing Neurology*,
DOI 10.1057/978-1-137-51762-3_5

possession of a grand work adorned with admirable plates, made after nature, in which you will find this part of our science dealt with in all the details of which it is comprised. It is to Dr Richer, the head of my laboratory and more than once my collaborator, that this monument will be due, and in which we will see, for the great profit of all, art and science marching together.[1]

In the years leading up to Charcot's death, Richer and Henry Meige would help to develop this aesthetic project of "art and science marching together," through numerous publications on the topic. Indeed, Richer quoted the passage above in his own early teaching text *Artistic Anatomy: Description of the Exterior Forms of the Body in Repose and in Its Principal Movements* (1890).[2] Richer and Meige later consolidated this approach whilst lecturing at the National School of Fine Art (ENSBA)—though both continued to author more strictly medical texts throughout this period. Each in turn succeeded Mathias Duval as lecturers in anatomy, 1903–1922, and 1922–1940, respectively.[3] Indeed, Marcel Duchamp's Futurist painting of *Nude Descending a Staircase* (1912) explicitly references the lectures on the body in movement which Richer delivered at ENSBA, with Duchamp echoing the stop-motion photographic studies of gait which Richer published in his *Artistic Physiology of Man in Movement* (1894) and *New Artistic Anatomy* (1906–1950).[4]

The work of Richer, Meige, and Duval on the healthy moving body acted as an instructive complement to Charcot's own focus on diseased movement. Considered alongside Charcot's work, their writings clarify the aesthetic values which underpinned Charcot's distinction of health versus disease. Scenes of disorder, the grotesque, carnival, sadomasochism, and the macabre, were set against the rhythmic and performative symmetry of the neoclassical athletic body. Through the medical classification of the living nude in movement, the disruptive spectacle of the sexualized or carnivalesque body was contained. In theatrical terms, if, as Gordon has argued, illness was reflected in the performances of the *café-concért* and the fairground, then healthy, unadorned performance evoked the spectacle of the Ancient Olympic games. This construction of the body was explicitly performative, rather than simply sculptural or visual. As Richer observed, it was above all the "music" or "rhythm" of the body, its uniquely sequential or choreographic action, which defined the body as healthy or diseased. Even so, the separation between the neurophysiological observation of topics such as death, plague, and hermaphrodism, versus a more Bacchanalian communion with such objects of the gaze, was difficult to establish.

Debates regarding the relative status of photography as an artistic form versus its construction as a purely objective, scientific, or technological tool constituted an important part of late nineteenth century discourse. The camera was becoming an essential component in the apparatus of the asylums and prisons located throughout Europe and America. Even Salpêtrière physician Charles Féré felt compelled to point out in his review of the *Iconographie photographique de la Salpêtrière* that "the considerable value of the artistic aspect of this work"—namely the photographs, sketches, and narrative case histories—"should in no way cause one to forget that the scientific aspect remains important."[5]

It was Charcot's sometime mentor Duchenne de Boulogne who first advocated the use of photography at the Salpêtrière during the 1860s, enlisting the assistance of leading photographers Félix Nadar and Adrien Tournachon.[6] His use of the camera for research into physiology and general medicine was continued by A. de Montméja and P. Jules Rengade, who launched *The Photographic Review of the Hospitals of Paris* (*La revue photographique des hôpitaux de Paris*) in 1869. Bourneville largely directed *The Photographique Review* from 1870 onwards, drawing upon cases he encountered at the Salpêtrière.[7] The founders of *The Photographique Review* described it as an innovative "medical bulletin" devoted to publishing superior images of "the most interesting and most rare pathology." These reproductions were accompanied by minimal commentary consisting of a digest of the relevant case history, leaving the images largely to speak for themselves. The editors felt that medical knowledge was self evident in these representations. By today's standards the texts appear rhetorically thin if not naive. The first edition covered examples of teratology such as severe facial necrosis from cancer (cancroide), elephantiasis of the scrotum and vagina, or incomplete genital differentiation and miss-positioning of the urethra (hypospadias). Charcot and Bourneville oversaw the introduction of photography to Charcot's service, with Paul Régnard acting as the hospital's expert from 1875, initially using wet collodion exposure and photolithography, before this was replaced with gelatino bromure stock in 1880.[8] This was rapidly followed by the appointment of Albert Londe, initially as a chemist in 1882, and later as chief of a new specialist photographic laboratory in 1884. Photographs of medical oddities appeared in the lay press as well, although a journalist from *Le monde illustré* stressed that such images should serve to reinforce medical diagnoses and scientific understanding, rather than to inflame popular passion.[9]

Although photographs were expensive to print, lithographs and gravures were relatively easy to reproduce. Given the often nebulous nature of wet collodion exposures, it was common to use film as an immediate record from which more refined sketches were produced. Prints "drawn from nature" or "from a photograph" appeared throughout both the lay and the medical press as a form of authoritative, first-hand evidence, freezing and disseminating such dramatic sights as the charge of cavalry or the opening of a new theatrical production. As photographic techniques improved, Salpêtrière physicians such as Richer increasingly commended the camera for its superiority over the physical eye, enabling one to capture the "most fugitive" or subtle of bodily expressions for further investigation.[10] The spectacle of the Salpêtrière itself was, moreover, frequently represented through photographs and detailed sketches in these journals, with gravures of the gate or the *cour d'honneur* printed alongside journalistic accounts in newspapers.

The phrase "made after nature" which Charcot evoked in his lecture above was crucial here. Charcot was a fair illustrator, and several of his schematic drawings adorned his published lectures. As Charcot's secretary of 1889–1893, George Guinon, observed:

> He himself drew like a true artist, and this talent often served him well in fixing on paper a patient's attitude, a deformation, which he immediately [then] knew how to define with a characteristic word.[11]

Charcot recognized in Richer, however, a superior gift. As a young intern, Richer stayed overnight in the wards so as to capture the transitory fits and seizures of hysterics and other patients.[12] Charcot used these charcoal drawings in his lectures and they became the basis of Richer's own monumental study of hysteria (see Chap. 6), which won the Academy of Sciences' Montyon prize in 1881.

Exposure times for wet collodion stock could be up to a minute, depending on light conditions. Patients were often carried on their beds into the Salpêtrière gardens to facilitate better images, imparting a somewhat improvised quality to the events staged. Although photography was typically characterized as a process involving little to no subjective human intervention—the "pencil of nature" as Fox Talbot put it—most images required extensive touching up, or served as a model for a later hand-drawn rendering or etching. Régnard, for example, provided the publishers of the *Iconographie photographique de la Salpêtrière* with instructions such as: "Lighten a little the bottom of the clothes and the hands; accentuate the eyes in the sentiment of the gaze; put a few creases in the blouse."[13] The same process of a rapid, initially caricatural capture of the image, followed by subsequent clarification and refinement, also applied to the process of preparing drawings for publication, some of Richer's illustrations bearing the credit "after a sketch by M. Charcot."[14] As Phillip Prodger observes, during the fin de siècle, photographs and other published images were judged on "how real they looked, not on how ... they had been produced."[15] Building on and supporting Charcot's work, Richer was particularly adept at this process of reworking photographs and first hand impressions, and many of the exposures taken at the Salpêtrière were converted by him into abstracted line drawings. M. Loreau, who was the first director of the Salpêtrière museum, also performed this role for the *Iconographie photographique* and other publications.

Charcot wrote, with Richer, two major iconographic studies on illness in art, as well as several essays initially published in the *Nouvelle iconographie photographique de la Salpêtrière*. The books were *Demoniacs in Art* (*Les démoniaques dans l'art*) (1886) and *The Deformed and Ill in Art* (*Les difformes et les malades dans l'art*) (1889), the latter of which was referred to in the lecture above. In 1901 Richer drew together this material, as well as Meige's work, to produce *Art and Medicine* (*L'art et la médecine*). These studies received the most comprehensive coverage in Richer's teaching series, *Nouvelle anatomie artistique* (1906–1950). These publications contained innumerable endorsements for the strikingly well-observed realism which the Salpêtrière physicians found in the works of artists from the *beaux-arts* canon such as Eugène Delacroix, Jean Auguste Ingres, Albrecht Dürer, Giotto di Bondone, Raphael Sanzio, Pieter Brueghel, and the ancient Greeks and Romans. The term "drawn from nature" was employed throughout these studies as a synonym for the degree of accuracy promoted in scientific observation.

Even so, there were limits to what the Salpêtrière school considered acceptable in terms of artistic intervention. In a lecture on hysteria, Charcot famously compared himself to a photographer:

It seems that hysterioepilepsy does not exist outside of France ... as if I had forged it by the power of my will. It would be a truly marvelous thing if I were able to create illnesses in this way, by the fancy of my caprice and my fantasy. But in truth, I am nothing but a photographer. I record what

I see and it is too easy to show that it [hysteria] is not found only at the Salpêtrière.[16]

Charcot refuted the accusation that his work on hysteria was capriciously creative by offering his audience reproductions of earlier aesthetic data—specifically paintings by the great masters. Charcot and Richer retrospectively diagnosed within these paintings and sculptures the characteristic gestures and poses of hysterioepilepsy, of glossolabial hemispasm, goitre, and other conditions. The physical signs and actions which patients presented on the stage of the Salpêtrière, therefore, predated Charcot's staging of them.

However, this evidence was only significant if one agreed with Charcot that these artists adhered to a fundamentally realist, or mimetic, approach to representation. As Aristotelian theory would have it, the aim of the poet, dramatist, or painter was to depict reality as if in a mirror. The fact that mimesis was typically conceived in these optical terms further implied that the camera—an optical device designed to fix an image upon a reflective, mirrored plate—was interchangeable with both the eye and a good painting. As Albert Londe put it, the photographic plate is the "savant's true retina."[17] Charcot went so far as to call a sketch then attributed to Paul Rubens as "the most faithful photograph of the contortions of a hysterical attack."[18] Meige concurred, claiming that this illustration constituted "a realistic portrait of one of the patients from the Salpêtrière."[19]

Charcot then constructed himself at once as both a photographer and an artist, and it is significant that he compared himself not with the camera, but with the one who directed its gaze. The scopic identification of significant actions within the moving body was itself an art. As Freud famously recorded, Charcot described himself as a *"visuel"* or "a man who sees"—the term *"visuel"* also referring to Charcot's contention that different individuals developed slightly different neuroperceptual pathways which could be linked together, or disrupted (see Chap. 7). Whilst Charcot placed the patient upon the stage and focused the spotlight, he refused to be seen as a choreographer or conventional stage director. He staged what he saw without intervening.

The Salpêtrière school did not, therefore, reject aesthetic creativity in the identification and description of medical conditions. As Richer explained, individual bodies often varied considerably: "Anatomy is therefore a generalization, it addresses itself to the species; the particularized form [however] is addressed to the individual."[20] Both fine art and medical diagnosis thus depended upon "scientific abstractions" (archetypes), such as Richer's line drawings, which were modelled after the observation of multiple subjects. Painters and physicians produced from their observations a "synthesis ... of the spectacles which incessantly pass before their eyes." The "love of truth," of nature, and of "*exact* imitation," formed the basis for all true art, theatre and science.[21] Indeed, Meige claimed that for Charcot: "the doctor is inseparable from the artist. The one guided the other; they are mutually supportive."[22] Charcot nevertheless "admitted no compromise between the [abstract] dream and reality." He was on the contrary "a fervent lover of the most pure manifestations of Beauty," or as Bourneville said, Charcot put his trust in: "a severe, complete observation, [a] painting which is faithful to reality."[23] Rigorous naturalism as epitomized by Ruben's photographic realism acted as the model for Richer, Charcot, and Meige. Severe visual clarity was to serve as an aid to the enlightened perception and dissemination of truth by modern, civilized science.

Richer provided an especially striking metaphor of how this apparently paradoxical merging of harsh, naturalistic observation and informed, scientific abstraction functioned. He claimed that every age was characterized by a particular art form, which reached its perfection during that period, so as to outshine all others. In ancient Egypt this was "architecture," in Greece "sculpture," and during the Renaissance "painting." In "modern times" however it was "music."[24] Marey and his collaborators such as Londe had indeed experimented with forms of musical and choreographic notation to record movement patterns, heartbeat, and other physiological phenomena, and Richer reproduced illustrations of Marey's semi-musical "notation of movement" throughout his course-books. Scientists had moved from listening for the music of the spheres, to listening to and watching for the rhythms of anatomyological movement.

Richer justified his somewhat unusual teleology by likening the body to an ever-changing musical performance, in which:

It suffices to look at ... [Nature] to see, in the same action, here a contracted muscle, here a distended muscle, and not long after a relaxed muscle ... just like the variety of musical sounds produced by a symphony ... which is the very expression movement.[25]

The body, therefore, defied those static forms of visual representation which existed prior to the invention of cinema in 1894, and even early cinematic depictions barely sufficed to capture the complexity of dynamic relations visible within the moving subject. As Richer observed:

> the volume of the diverse parts of our body are not constantly the same, it [the body] is, on the contrary, in a perpetual state of instability. That is to say that it changes from moment to moment, with our stances, with our actions, our feelings, our emotions, even our thoughts. One of the features of life is the incessant changes in the volume of the limbs and as a result in their form. From this it follows that, in Nature, the form itself is variable, transitory and ever-changing.[26]

Only by careful observation of the performing nude might one fully perceive such changes. The predominantly visual methods of anatomical investigation which Richer championed were, therefore, to be employed to record phenomena which, by definition, *transcended* sight—namely musicality. Like music, the rhythms of the body were only fully manifest within a living, performative context.[27] Demonstrators like Richer and Charcot, therefore, functioned not only as transcribers of musical notation, but also dramaturgical conductors, attempting to carefully manage the orchestral rhythms they presented within their diagnostic mise en scène, with illness signified by rhythmic disarray, and health manifest in a return to rhythmic regularity and beauty.

Meige noted in a lecture addressed to Richer that his former teacher had employed chronophotography to help draw up a detailed, statistical map of "the relations and proportions of the body, to establish your 'canon'" against which "the diverse modalities of human morphology" could be measured.[28] This "heroic" ideal consisted of a visibly muscled, well proportioned man of approximately eight hands in height. Richer developed this model through his collaboration with Londe in the special exercise yard and studio which the photographer established in the gardens of the Salpêtrière, 1893–1903.[29] The statistical mapping of these corporeal variations enabled Richer to objectively identify the perfect, harmonious proportions of physical beauty—in Meige's words "the expression of a natural truth, scientifically established."[30] This act of chronometric, photographic, anthropometric, and statistical mapping rendered corporeal aesthetics quantifiable. The illustrations made by Richer's hand possessed a verifiable, metric accuracy. As in Charcot's multimedia lecture presentations, the body was reified and annihilated through its replacement by such idealized, archetypal representations.

2   THE NAKED GAZE AND SADOMASOCHISM

Charcot's first major collaboration with Richer was their study of hysterical glossolabial hemispasm in 1888. They examined the physiognomy visible within a grotesque from the church of Santa Maria Formosa, Venice. This carving exhibited "all of the characters of a perfectly defined morbid deformation."[31] Charcot noted that true organic facial paralysis was associated with a post-mortem lesion. In most such cases "the labial commissure drops towards the right" whilst the right eye remained open and unaffected. The deformation shown in the grotesque, however, extended across the face, with the glottis, tongue, corner of the mouth, nostril, orbit, and brow all affected as part of a single, unified spasm.[32] Consequently, this sculpture could be diagnosed as reflecting the hysterical or functional version of this disease, rather than that caused by a lesion.

Charcot identified many patients at the Salpêtrière who displayed the features of this disorder. Sketches by Richer of these contemporary hysterical glossolabial hemispastics were placed alongside that of the grotesque to demonstrate the historic continuity of this specific symptomatic complex. Didi-Huberman has since pointed out the circularity of this reasoning, in which modern diagnoses were imposed upon analogous representations taken from art history, which were then in turn proffered as additional evidence of the conditions originally under investigation.[33] In an argument Charcot was to invoke repeatedly, the neuropathologist contended that because the carved hemispasm conformed to an intricate pattern of neuromuscular coordination, it was impossible that the artist had independently conceived of these characteristics himself. The nature of the spasm was too complicated; it was "so grotesque and so hideous" that it was "in no way the result of a simple artistic fantasy."[34] The close likeness of the Santa Formosa grotesque to contemporary patients, moreover, identified it as having necessarily been inspired by the direct observation of actual, living individuals in the past. This sculpture could, therefore, be distinguished from overt caricatures or fanciful exaggerations like centaurs and other monstrous hybrids. Charcot and Richer claimed that these latter representations were, by contrast, unambiguously "inventions" of artistic "caprice," whose existence was contrary to enlightened rationalism. The neuropathologists concluded that although: "We could say much regarding these oeuvres of caricature," they "are not faithful reproductions related to nature" and hence unworthy of detailed discussion. However, when dealing with diseases like glossolabial hemispasm or dwarfism (the latter a consequence of myxedema, goitre, achondroplasty, or rachitis): "it is nature itself which has chosen to break the rules of proportion and to make in dwarfs the caricature of a man ... the artist has nothing to add to its work and it suffices to slavishly copy it." In the case of these illnesses it was not the artist or his interpretive gaze which mocked normal physiology, but "nature itself." Accuracy and complexity was read as a sign of the *hand of nature itself* in the generation of both the disease and its subsequent scientific-aesthetic capture.

Charcot and Richer contended that these artworks were so physiologically insightful that their creators must have used the observation of the nude as their primary data. The totality of the knowledge represented in these works meant that even clothing had not intervened in their genesis. As noted in the lecture quoted at the beginning of this chapter, observation of the nude provided the inspiration for modern medicine also.

Charcot's biographer A. Lubimoff recorded a revealing anecdote in which Charcot further associated his functional, patrician aesthetic tastes with an implicitly gendered exchange of sexual-aesthetic power. Charcot's treatment of patients often appeared insensitive even by nineteenth century standards. He was nevertheless opposed to both vivisection and hunting, the door of his laboratory being adorned with the notice: "You will not find a clinic containing dogs with me."[35] In an interview with A.S. Souvorine from the journal *Nouveau temps*, Charcot compared himself to Leonardo da Vinci, Victor Hugo, and William Shakespeare on the basis that they were all lovers of animals. He went on that:

"I understand only one huntress, that is Diana. Completely nude, the bow in her hand, the quiver full of arrows, she runs in the woods, the branches of the trees flagellate her, her feet hurt her. She thinks neither of her costume nor of the danger."

The assistants laughed amongst themselves, at the remark of one of their guests, that Diana pleased Charcot because of her nudity.

He responded smiling: "Certainly, she pleases me. She is nature herself, the personification of her forces, a symbol. But these Dianas and Venuses, dressed in silk and velvet, rifle in hand, killing pigeons expressly brought before them, they are revolting. Women! ... They do not deserve the name."[36]

According to myth, Actaeon was chasing a stag when he came upon the virgin Huntress, who shunned the company of men.[37] She was bathing and was furious at his voyeuristic intrusion. She splashed water in his eyes, temporarily blinding him, as she angrily challenged him to ever describe what he had seen. Actaeon was transformed into a stag before he could speak and was overcome by his own hounds, led by the other male hunters of his party.

Charcot collapsed beauty, truth, nature, honesty, femininity, and suffering into the dense symbol of the naked, flagellated Diana in pursuit of her prey. Hunting using the simplest of weapons in order to sustain one's existence was functionally equivalent to nudity itself. The nude existed without protection from not only the male gaze, but also the ravages of the elements and disease. It was devoid of deceit, dress, or the unnecessary social comforts and rituals which the French aristocracy in particular still clung to. The "study of the NUDE"—and the data obtained using the "naked eye"—constituted the standard against which veracity was measured. Enlightened *truth* became equivalent to *nakedness*, Charcot's dull oratory itself constituting a form of vocal nudity. Diana's dress metaphoricized her relationship with nature; she was indeed nature personified. The observation of such a figure in her natural state (naked and virginal) constituted the evidence which it was the task of the artist and the physician to reflect, and so bring to fruition. The addition of visual, verbal, or rhetorical flourishes such as feminine "silk and velvet," or technological sophistications like the more masculine "rifle," was, however, a corruption of this naturalistic truth. In Meige's words, "Science, daughter of Truth, may leave behind such frills, like her mother."[38] Moreover, the members of the Salpêtrière school shared this restrained model of aesthetic representation with many of their contemporaries. Maurice Hamel of *La gazette des beaux-arts,* for example, similarly advocated that artists adopt a "simplicity in the face of nature."[39]

Diana maintained her proximity to mother "Truth" through her spartan naturalism. Simply by capturing the Huntress through his gaze, Charcot brought a completeness to the previously virginal woman— though he doubtless did not envisage being blinded, rendered mute, and transformed by Diana before himself falling prey to the other members of his hunting fraternity. In light of the eventual divorce of the arts from science, however, one can conclude that Charcot played Actaeon's role more fully than he anticipated.

To read Charcot's relationship to the object of his gaze as sadomasochistic would be to overextend the Freudian subtext of Charcot's mythical allusion. Not all of his contemporaries were so generous, however.

Prominent female avant-garde poet and mystic Berthe de Courrière compared the neurologist to both the violently repressive Avignonese Pope and Emperor Nero, claiming that Charcot had "invented *scientific Sadism*," whilst an author from the radical feminist *La revue scientifique des femmes* similarly argued that he practiced in the amphitheatre "a form of human vivisection upon women under the pretext of studying an illness [hysteria] of which he knows neither the cause nor the treatment ... this man placed himself amongst the great misogynists."[40] These female critics recognized the strand of cruelty which underlay Charcot's aesthetics. Diana's unforgiving style of life, and the visual exchange it enabled between her and the neuropathologist, was predicated on suffering and pain. In order to achieve her purity, Diana had to be whipped—in Charcot's own words, "flagellated"—and her feet chastised. Although the Huntress had been a common artistic subject since the Renaissance, Charcot's description brought out the violent connotations of this visual aesthetic trope. His statement almost seemed to suggest that Diana had to atone for her threats against the men who gazed upon her. Those who did not conform to Charcot's model of spartan, patrician suffering existed outside of this spectacular relationship. Such figures were neither pleasurable to look upon (they were "revolting") nor did they "deserve the name" of woman. There was therefore a coincidence between Charcot's pleasure in looking at Diana and the pain she was forced to endure, which in turn heightened the empathy between the Huntress and the male viewer (who adopted the role of the soon-to-be dismembered Actaeon). Charcot's medical gaze may therefore be seen to act through a complicitous yet unstable form of masculine aggression. My point is that the possibility that this relationship could be inverted, thereby emasculating or disempowering the male observer, lay dormant *within the very terms Charcot employed*. Here as elsewhere, Charcot's rhetorical expressions served to both reveal and shore up the methodological tensions inherent within his practice.

Although scientists immediately perceived the advantages of photography, this output only constituted one part of what was from the outset a diverse range of material. The erotic and sadomasochistic potential of filmic media became apparent almost as soon as photography was invented, vexing the objective Positivist ideals of figures such as Charcot and Duchenne. Pornographic images made up a notable portion of the booming trade in postcards, titillating *cartes* being sold particularly out of Paris' theatre district of Montmartre.[41] The sometime painter and museum conservator Charles-François Jeandel photographed images of bound, crucified women which bore more than a passing resemblance to Régnard's documentation of the hysterioepileptic pose of crucifixion (see Chap. 6).[42] Performance, the monstrous, and aesthetic voyeurism also came together in the deluxe programmes emanating from Charcot's favourite recreational venue, the Folies Bergère, souvenir programmes containing images of midget acts, criminal melodramas, acrobatic acts, and aesthetically posed female nudes.[43] Richer himself photographed a lithe naked woman executing a number of extreme bodily contortions, her face teasingly hidden behind an Italian-style carnival mask.[44] Although masking medical subjects was a common way to render them anonymous, the theatrical choice of covering tends to have had a more titillating or fetishistic effect here. Quite what justification Richer and Londe might have had for documenting this subject's ability to pull one leg nearly thirty degrees up towards her head, turning her pubis outwards and up, is less than clear. As Michel Foucault noted with respect to the discourse of the Salpêtrière as a whole, Charcot's peers "constructed around and apropos of sex an immense apparatus for producing truth, even if this [sexualized] truth was to be masked at the last moment."[45] The problematic politics of the sexuality and the gaze came into play, with eroticism seeping into the use of the photographic lens and the generation of spectacular tableaux, even as the physicians tried to control and desexualize the medico-aesthetic staging of the gaze.

However, Richer and his associates were far from advocates of an eroticized Theatre of Cruelty such as Antonin Artaud proposed in 1938 when he compared the theatre to the infective body-madness of the plague.[46] For Charcot, pain was part of the natural order which physicians such as he identified and treated. It was not something to be celebrated or extolled. The chaotic potential of the tortured body was rather to be contained by medical science and its visual practices. Charcot may not have been successful in developing any effective new therapies, but he did trial many novel treatments—notably suspension and electrostimulation. Charcot was devoted to the elimination of pain in his subjects, although he acknowledged that it was unlikely he would permanently cure the intractable conditions he commonly dealt with. Artwork which actively revelled in horror, pain, illness, or death had no place in the aesthetics of Charcot and his peers. Meige claimed that Charcot's anatomoclinical approach of relating post-mortem dissection to "the examination of the nude in life" meant that anatomy could now turn away from its former "master: the cadaver" and abandon "this macabre spectacle" which had dominated anatomy in the pre-modern past.[47] However, Charcot's rhetoric suggests these precedents were difficult to entirely disavow in the context of visual analysis of the suffering body—a potentiality later explored by authors such as André de Lorde and Binet.

3   THE THEATRE OF THE ATHLETIC NUDE

Richer's own shift in focus from the diseased to the ideal individual reflected to some his change in position from serving as resident artist at the Salpêtrière to teaching at the École. Moreover, this professional transition coincided with the growth of the sports and athletic movement. Richer's studies were therefore contemporary with the rise of the athletic hygienist movement initiated by scientists such as Marey's collaborator Georges Demenÿ, who founded Circle for Rational Gymnastics in 1880, and with whom both Londe and Richer worked in the lead-up to the 1900 Olympic Games, Paris.[48] However, Richer had begun his comparative chronophotographic studies of movement during Charcot's lifetime, and this model of the healthy body was implicit throughout their earlier work on hemispasm and hysteria.

Étienne Roc of *Les hommes d'aujourd'hui* recorded that Duval had differed from his predecessors in that the professor used "the exterior model or shape" as his "point of departure." Broca and others had excelled in the deep analysis of anatomy as revealed through dissection of the viscera. Duval "on the contrary" turned his attention towards the more superficial science of myology (the study of musculature), focusing:

> upon the actual source of the movements themselves, amongst the muscle groups, applying himself to the reasons for the modelled shape and postures. It is then that, aided in turn by the cadaver and the living model, dissecting the muscle with the scalpel, that he … comes to enable the artist "to analyze through the skin, as if through a transparent veil."[49]

It was Richer, however, who perfected Duval's project of linking anatomical dissection with what Duval had described as "the explication of forms."[50]

Richer proclaimed that truly realistic representation was only possible with the knowledge of internal anatomy as well as that of physiological, muscular anatomy, or in the neurologist's terms, "the *anatomy of forms*" and "the *physiology of forms*."[51] There was therefore a "formal distinction between … anatomy properly speaking, born of the cadaver and of dissection: versus the study of the exterior forms of the human body, born of the examination of the nude alive and in action."[52] It was this study of the living "exterior forms of the human body" which had largely been neglected by physiologists prior to Duval, Charcot, and Duchenne de Boulogne.

Richer added that artists had in some cases been so attentive to the ripples of muscle beneath the skin (gazing "as if through a transparent veil" in Duval's phrase) that this had produced some strikingly accurate representations. The ancients carved their statues by:

> proceeding directly from the observation and interpretation of the nude without troubling themselves over anatomical details, but with a precision so absolute and so perfect that the anatomist himself could find [almost] nothing to alter.

These works were marked by a remarkable degree of "exactitude and truth," with Richer going as far as to favourably compare the stop-motion photographic studies into running, which he and Londe carried out, with the friezes of the Parthenon.

> The representation of movement had been for Greek art a triumph … certain images of running, in particular, are of a truthfulness that have found their justification today in the series produced by instantaneous photography.[53]

Whilst neither the Greeks nor the Romans had conducted anatomical dissections as such, their passion for the theatrical spectatorship of the moving, athletic nude had enabled them to craft representations rivalling those of both their Egyptian predecessors and many eighteenth century French and Italian artists.

The shortcomings of the otherwise accomplished art produced by the ancients were therefore:

> the consequence of the absence of anatomy. They demonstrate to us … that the only guide of the Egyptian artist had been the direct observation of the exterior form without any concern for the profound parts in which that form might hide.

The modern artist was therefore obliged to look not only through the skin at the peripheral musculature, but also deep within the body itself, where the muscles' tendrils and their neurophysiological origin lay hidden. Muscular anatomy or "superficial myology cannot suffice for those who want to penetrate the mechanism of the movements." Knowledge of the exterior forms could aid one in mentally "dissecting" the body. Prior to the invention of soft tissue radiology many years later, however, the external spectacle of the body alone could not substitute for post-mortem investigation itself. By combining the study of the active nude with modern anatomical knowledge, French scientists became the true heirs of the classical tradition, completing and perfecting what the Greeks had started.

Richer dismissed purely anatomical knowledge as being as flawed as that limited knowledge which the ancients themselves had been forced to depend upon. "If ... the flayed corpse is presented to us as a lesson in form," he claimed, "we can say that it is incomplete and misleading." The surgical removal of the skin was insufficient in itself to reveal the mysteries of the body. Both Richer and Meige likened Renaissance *memento mori* effigies to "galvanized cadavers," Meige adding that "Death ... profoundly alters exterior appearances" as well as the quality of the muscles.[54] This was a particularly graphic image given that vivisectionist experiments in electrostimulation on living and recently excised tissue had become a feature of scientific demonstration during this period. Within these *écorchés* or flayed figures, the muscle tone was imperfect, with the muscles of these statues exhibiting the same flaccid state as the dissected corpses on which they were modelled. The engorged and restricted blood vessels such as one would see in a living subject were absent, and the way in which the muscles differentially bulged and compressed was not depicted. In short, no living model had ever marched or danced the way they were depicted in such famous *écorchés* as those which Jean Houdon acquired by the École in the mid eighteenth century. After Duval's appointment in 1873, such materials were used as examples of artistic errors rather than as representations of realistically arranged bodily poses. There was an ineffable quality in the harmony of the organs and physiological elements which even the reconstruction of the flayed corpse could not recapture. One was obliged to relate the two together within the same conceptual space—if not the same *actual space*—as in the lectures of Charcot and Richer. One can indeed see this in the painting by François Sallé of Duval lecturing at ENSBA, *A Course of Anatomy at the School of Fine Arts in Paris* (*Un cours d'anatomie à l'École de beaux arts à Paris*) (1888), which shows Duval beside one of Houdon's sculptures as he demonstrates using a life model.[55] Sallé's canvas was presented at the Salon one year after Brouillet's *Clinical Lesson at the Salpêtrière*, and Sallé echoes the flat tones and unemotional ambience of Brouillet's style. This iconographic parallel in turn reflected the close synergy between the teaching of nude physiology at ENSBA from the 1880s onwards.

The aim in these lessons was to unify external observation with anatomical dissection, heightening the visibility of the body such that its most hidden qualities were represented. Richer described this ideal unity using language which only served to highlight the apparently irreconcilable nature of these two ways of viewing the body. He strove for a "*living* synthesis of the anatomy of *death* [italics added]."[56] Indeed, Richer produced a sculpture depicting quite precisely this: a normal male from whose body the skin had been removed on one side only, thereby showing within the same three-dimensional image the exposed muscles as they are in life, beside the stretched and moulded skin over the living muscles on the other side. This fantastic medico-aesthetic creation was—appropriately enough—known as *L'écorché vivant* (Fig. 5.1).[57] Like Charcot's technique of anatomoclinical

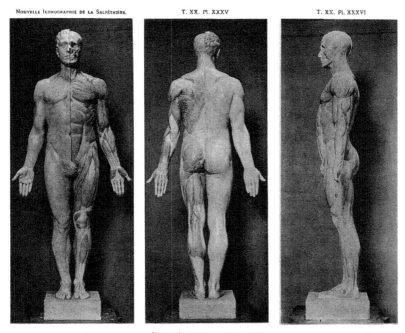

Fig. 5.1   Paul Richer, *L'écorché vivant* (1906), from *Nouvelle iconographie photographique de la Salpêtrière* (1907), plates 35–36. Image courtesy of the Courtesy of the Boston Medical Library in the Francis A. Countway Library of Medicine

analysis, Richer's slightly more specialized approach of physiomyological investigation could only be fully realized in a three-dimensional, theatrical context, producing a "synthesis" which defied reality and representation itself. Richer indeed cited Pygmalion as epitomizing his aesthetic: a celibate artist whose perfect creation was so faithful to reality that his statue of the ideal woman quite literally came to life, sharing the same space as that of the artist himself.[58] The subject of Richer's anatomy theatre was to be melded with the closest thing to this form of physical presence available to Pygmalion's successors: the performance of the life model, moving within the same space as the dissected corpse. Only such a theatrical staging could hope to realize Richer's new "science of the living nude."[59]

The emphasis that Richer and Charcot placed upon anatomoclinical observation of the moving nude led Richer to advise his students to frequent sporting events of all kinds. For the ancients, "the admiration of beautiful forms was in some sense the dogma of a religion, and the science of the nude became the catechism." This devotion was consecrated through attendance at Olympic Games. Richer himself was described as a "constant presence" at gatherings of Paris sporting associations such as the Racing Club and sculpted a number of "statuettes of athletes" which "realized a scientific and artistic synthesis of running" and which were exhibited at the 1900 International Exposition, held in conjunction with the first International Congress of Physical Education and Sport as well as the 1900 Olympic Games.[60] Moreover, Meige's students noted that Richer and Meige organized student excursions to Marey's and Demenÿ's "Stadium at Joinville to study those sporting gestures so favorable to the physiological knowledge of human movement."[61] The theatrical forum most suited to Richer's anatomyological approach and Charcot's anatomoclinical method was not therefore the Naturalistic theatre of Émile Zola or Andre Antoine, nor the flamboyant Romantic melodramas and spectacular events of mainstream theatre. The ideal medical theatre was rather the literally spartan aesthetic of the classical athletic stadium.

Richer and Charcot advocated then the continuation of the harsh, unforgiving naturalism promoted by the Greeks and their Enlightenment successors. The entry on "Dance" from Diderot's *Encyclopedia,* for example, dealt with a female tightrope walker rather than the florid excesses of aristocratic ballet, and one of the first subjects Richer and Londe photographed in the Salpêtrière gardens was a tightrope walker from the Nouveau Cirque.[62] Such athletic spectacles elegantly brought together the otherwise disparate tropes which Charcot and Richer drew upon. Like Charcot's sedate, patrician speech, the athletic body was not artistic in its actual presentation. It was on the contrary aesthetic in its innermost nature, which was nevertheless visible in its exterior form. The medico-athletic body was *metaphorically* (and ideally literally) *naked* and so devoid of any additional rhetorical tropes. Such a body was fundamentally aesthetic without being tainted by artifice. As in the case of the dwarfs described in *The Deformed and Ill in Art*, it was "nature itself" which shaped the body's aesthetic presentation. The only theatrical environment consistent with the unadorned, reflective form of mimetic truth advocated by Charcot, Richer, and Meige was the athletic stadium. Here, a classical and rationalized body proffered its truth in the form of medically sanctioned movement.

4 Taming the Carnival

Whilst Charcot and Richer noted that "The general public itself had its dwarfs, and the mob has always run to exhibitions of this kind at public fêtes, fairs and theatres," the Olympic amphitheatre by contrast presented spectators with the finest examples of myological beauty.[63] Medicine was not, however, addressed purely to idealized perfection. Richer asked his readers if science was not obliged to examine "nature in its entirety?"[64] Consequently Richer recommended his charges also take time to consider other manifestations of physical action:

> Be suspicious of the model in the studio ... with whom one discovers only the immobility of the pose ... But rather go to fairgrounds where 'weight-lifters' re-invent the tasks of Hercules; go to the circus, where acrobats and clowns are often veritable models of well-balanced forms ... You will see at young men's games of football, the most varied and sometimes the most violent movements. Go also to the velodrome; if the attitude of the rider on his machine sometimes shocks you, go there, where he enters the arena, legs entirely nude, the bust covered with a simple cap, and you will soon understand that this exercise is one which endows the body with a fortunate harmony of forms, [with] strength and suppleness.[65]

Richer and Charcot continued in this respect Duchenne de Boulogne's project of mapping human emotion onto the exposed body. Science encompassed the full range of human physiological expression, from violent rage to piteous sorrow, from glossolabial hemispasm to healthy male beauty. Richer endorsed Diderot's proposition that, strictly speaking, Nature "produces nothing incorrect."[66] Physicians and artists were therefore obliged to consider not only "the perfect types," but also "deformities, illnesses, errors, deviations, the aberrations of nature." Since today "Apollo has become a clown or cyclist, [and] Hercules 'works' at the fair in Trône," venues such as the circus, the velodrome, and the sports field offered an ideal environment within which to watch the interaction between animals, athletic human types (gymnasts, strongmen), and aberrant or unusual individuals (dwarfs, clowns, variety acts).[67] Guillain recorded that Charcot himself preferred the circus, or the comic gymnastic performances at the Folies Bergère, to the theatre, a predilection which led the neuropathologist to name one of the poses of hysterioepilepsy "clownism" in recognition of the impressive acrobatic feats commonly performed by clowns during this period.[68]

Richer's statements highlighted how the passion which sports aroused made games of football doubly valuable spectacles for the medical observer. Here one could view not only well-developed human types, but also the inflection of movement by anger, violence, joy, sorrow, and pain. Richer's *Artistic Physiology of Man in Movement*, for example, featured descriptions of the distinction between normal gait and the varieties of emotionally "expressive gaits" like the "enthusiastic gait," such as one might see in "an antique warrior returning from a victory" or even "a man of the people singing" the Republican national anthem of the *Marseillaise* (Fig. 5.2).[69] Richer's medical gaze was not therefore focused solely upon edifying or even objective spectacles. Combat, horror, and suffering also came within the orbit of theatrical-photographic investigation. The unemotional, healthy athlete therefore acted as the standard against which various "deviations" were measured—literally, in the case of Richer's quantitative mapping of these chronophotographic postures. To deal properly with "the pathological subject" it was "necessary," according to Richer, to "know the normal nude thoroughly."[70] Consequently dwarfism, glossolabial hemispasm, and signs of the plague constituted "teratological cases" which were "able to furnish us with useful and precious indications on the object and the goal of the *beaux-arts*" as well as medicine.[71] Nevertheless, Richer insisted that movements "imprinted with an ambience of melodrama mar the most meritorious art works" and were therefore to be avoided in both medical and aesthetic practice.[72] Indeed, *The Deformed and Ill in Art* included a denunciation of the famous waxwork dioramas of heaped plague victims produced by seventeenth century medical sculptor Giulio Gaetano Zumbo. Charcot and Richer described these "*teatrini di morte*" or "little

Fig. 5.2   "Enthusiastic walking," Richer, *Art and Medicine* (Paris: Gaultier, 1901), 215. Courtesy of the Boston Medical Library in the Francis A. Countway Library of Medicine

theatres of death" as having been produced by "the cantor of decomposition, the virtuoso of putrefaction."[73] The separation which Charcot and Richer strove to maintain between the critical spectator and his object was collapsed in such emotionally overwhelming works, the artist desiring an ecstatic union with this Baroque cantata of decomposition. In such works, the danger that Actaeon might indeed become Diana's prey reared its head.

Elsewhere, Richer cited Charcot on the aesthetics of disease, morbidity, and teratology, quoting the latter's contention that viewing such conditions showed that any "irregularity" of pathological morphology was absolutely "circumscribed" by "fixed and necessary rules."[74] Zumbo's works, for example, reflected "a realism more apparent than real." Even unreason, disease, and death conformed to the laws of nature. The observation of the living nude therefore enabled Charcot and Richer to produce a comprehensive description of the living human body in all of its variation: in degeneracy and in health, in aggression and in fear. This goal underlay much of the work carried out at the Salpêtrière. In a lecture addressed to Richer, Meige recalled that he had helped to recruit subjects for the former's photographic investigations, including "fairground fighters, weightlifters, acrobats, boxers, gymnasts; also, one day … a tribe of negroes who exhibited themselves then in Paris."[75] Meige concluded from these studies that:

> We must also compare the artistic expression of the nude across the ages and across peoples … in order … to research the variations of the human type … The nude depending upon sex, the nude depending upon age, the nude of the infant and that of the elderly, the nude depending upon the races.

Meige ended his digression by noting how his own studies complemented those of his former teacher:

> while you [Richer] tirelessly pursued the analysis of normal forms, adding to the knowledge of the male nude with that of the female nude, drafting the study of the infantile nude, I for my part, led by your example, attached myself … to the description of bodily anomalies. … Giants, Dwarfs, Infantilism and *Féminisme* … aberrant human forms.

Richer was an expert in the physiology of beauty and partly acquired illness. It was Meige, though, who proved most adroit at cataloguing teratological subjects, the races, and genital irregularities. Meige's 1893 study of representations of Ahasuerus the "Wandering Jew" provided a more thorough clinical basis to Charcot's contention that the Jews as a race suffered from an elevated rate of neuropathology, particularly the fugue state of "ambulatory automatism."[76] Although the specifically iconographic data Meige amassed was not especially convincing, the parallels he saw between the Ahasuerus myth and case histories from the Salpêtrière caused him to conclude that the Wandering Jew constituted a "sort of prototype of the Israelite neuropaths wandering throughout the world," just as he concluded that for classical sculptors, the recently described condition of "infantism" had acted as the "natural prototype of the antique Hermaphrodite."[77]

Meige also assisted in the identification of several other archetypal deviations from the healthy ideal, including intersexuality, acromegaly, and gigantism. The Salpêtrière physicians as a whole were at the forefront of the diagnosis of glandular conditions popular at freak shows, as well as polydactyly, anencephaly, and hypertrophy.[78] Meige co-authored with Brissaud an account of gigantism in which they argued that:

> The peculiarities of the human body have always provided a pretext for exhibitions.
>
> Alongside giants and dwarfs, which are at all of the fêtes, one sees fish-men, colossal women, dog-men, etc. The description of these monstrosities finds its place in the works of dermatology or teratology. We have good reason to not treat with disdain the curiosity which they inspire; they have sometimes led us to interesting discoveries.[79]

Meige and his peers were not therefore entirely opposed to the public display of human oddities. They rather wished to place such practices within a rationalist, enlightened, medical environment.

Charcot himself had exhibited in one of his lessons a tattooed street-performer or "*saltimbanque*" who "calls himself an 'artist.' The truth is that his art consists in playing 'the savage man' at fairground shacks."[80] After the patient "Lap...sonne" returned from penal transportation to Algeria and New Caledonia, he worked in France as a sword-swallower, fire-breather, and gimp (eater of live animals). The neuropathologist attributed most of Lap...sonne's extravagant behaviour and carnivalesque raging to the latter's hysterioepilepsy—including the patient's proficiency at glottal manoeuvres, which were facilitated by his hysterical anaesthesia. Charcot concluded by recommending that Lap...sonne be hospitalized for his own protection. Charcot had little time for the "art" of the *saltimbanque* and was happy to transform such public performers into (performing) medical patients against their will.

Meige and Brissaud conducted a similar, though less coercive, trans-formation. They described a trip they made to the fairground on the esplanade des Invalides to investigate Jean-Pierre Mazas, the Montastruc Giant. The physicians invited Mazas to the Salpêtrière for further analy-sis. They recorded with some dissatisfaction that he responded haltingly to their questions in language which was "vague or laconic" and "which was translated for us by a woman servant who acted at once as a spruiker [*de barnum*] and a translator."[81] This was problematic, because Charcot and Richer had noted that the information provided by promoters about such diseased individuals was often "necessarily flattering," or as Meige contended, fairground advertisements "chose to pass over in silence the imperfections of their 'subjects.'"[82] The neurologists were particularly annoyed at Mazas' refusal to show them his penis, forcing them to grudg-ingly accept his claim that it was normal.

Overall, Meige and Brissaud found Mazas' "character somber and dif-ficult."[83] They were nevertheless able to conclude that he was "not a *true giant*," but in fact suffered from the recently described illness of acromeg-aly, scoring a victory of sorts over Mazas' difficult character. Meige later concurred with the contention of his peers from the Salpêtrière—Pierre Marie and Georges Guinon—that the relative exaggeration of body parts amongst those popularly described as giants was in some cases confined to the limbs and spine, thus meriting the official scientific designation of "*gigantisme*."[84] However, even this potentially advantageous condition was frequently accompanied by secondary symptoms such as neuromus-cular weakness, cardiovascular complications, and loss of sexual function or desire. Consequently amongst those "'subjects' of great stature of great stature exhibited in public," all acromegalics and most giants offered to the medical gaze signs of "serious infirmities."[85] These men and women were "at once *monsters* and *diseased individuals*." Consequently Meige refuted the eugenic proposition that it would be beneficial to encourage consanguine pairings amongst giants. This would lead not to an increase in height amongst the population, but rather to the "perpetuation of lam-entable defects."

In all of the previous cases, the physicians argued that the final arbi-ter of truth was medicine—and not the aesthetics of the fairground, the waxwork, or the more fanciful representations of classicism. Meige indeed mocked the suggestion that giants could be considered "subjects" of an institution like the sideshow, just as Charcot ridiculed the idea that street performance was an "art." Therefore, the practice of the Salpêtrière physicians constituted an attempt to tame the carnival of its destabilizing potential. The Salpêtrière lectures were not a site for play, nor the free reinterpretation and inversion of social norms, as Mikhail Bakhtin argued was the case with Renaissance carnival. On the contrary, Meige and his associates hoped that by taking Mazas from the esplanade to the hospice, they had defused the reciprocity which the carnivalesque gaze could activate. As with the critique of Zumbo's waxes offered by Charcot and Richer, it was felt that the medical context provided by the Salpêtrière and its associated publications like *The Photographic Review of the Hospitals of Paris* assured a clear distinction between the scientific observer and his medical object. Freak shows were not totally condemned. However, their exhibits were found to be first and foremost the proper subjects of medicine and science, rather than a source of aesthetic entertainment, wonder, or horror for "the mob." It was this tendentious conviction which gave Bourneville the confidence to produce the most well-known work of this genre: the *Iconographie photographique de la Salpêtrière*. In this work, photographic teratology enabled the description and diagnosis of the Salpêtrière's performative illness par excellence: hysterioepilepsy. These various visual, photographic, and performative projects constituted a concerted effort on the part of Charcot and his associates to avoid the pitfalls of both the horrors of anatomical dissection, and the Bakhtinian disorder of the carnival, through the production of a pedagogically useful and clearly demarcated theatre of the living nude.

NOTES

1. *OC*, vol. 13, pp. 20–22; Paul Richer [1890], *Artistic Anatomy*, trans. Robert Hale (NY: Watson-Guptill, 1986), 15.
2. Jean-Martin Charcot and Paul Richer. *"Les démoniaques dans l'art"* suivi de *"La foi qui guérit,"* facsimile reproduction, edited and commentary by Georges Didi-Huberman and Pierre Fédida (Paris: Macula, 1984), *Les difformes et les malades dans l'art*, facsimile ed. (Amsterdam: N.V. Boekhandel et antiquariaat, 1972); Paul Richer, *L'art et la médecine* (Paris: Gaultier, 1901), *Nouvelle anatomie artistique* (Paris: Plon, 1889–1929), 7 vols.
3. See Marshall, "Theatre"; Anthea Callen, "The Body and Difference," *Art History*, 20.1 (1997): 23–60, "Masculinity and Muscularity," *Paragraph*, 26.1–2 (March–July 2003): 17–41; Philippe Comar et al, *Figures du corps* (Paris: ENSBA, 2009).
4. Jonathan Marshall, "The Archaeology of the Abstract Body: Parascientific Discourse and the Legacy of Dr J.-M. Charcot, 1876–1969," *French*

History and Civilization: Papers from the George Rudé Seminar, 3 (2009): 94, reproduced on <http: www.h-france.net rude rudevolumeiiiMarshall-Vol3.pdf>.

5. Charles Féré, review of *Iconographie photographique de la Salpêtrière*, *Archives de neurologie*, 1 (1881): 626.

6. Guillaume-Benjamin Duchenne de Boulogne, *The Mechanism of Human Facial Expression*, ed. and trans. R. Andrew Cuthbertson (Cambridge: Cambridge UP, 1990).

7. *Revue photographique des hôpitaux de Paris*, eds A. de Montméja, P. Jules Rengade, Désiré Bourneville, et al (Paris: Delahaye, 1869–1876), 8 vols.

8. Bernard and Gunthert, 99–143, 206–211.

9. Anon, "La femme 'à la crinière de cheval,'" *Monde illustré* (5 August 1893), back-page (unpaginated).

10. Richer, *Physiologie*, 16.

11. Georges Guinon, "Charcot intimé," *Paris médical*, 56.21 (23 May 1925): 514.

12. H. Richard, "Richer (Paul-Marie-Louis-Pierre)," *Les Biographes médicales*, 4.1 (January 1930): 65–76.

13. Roth, 22.

14. Désiré Bourneville, *Science et Miracle: Louise Lateau ou la stigmatisée belge* (Paris: Progrès médical, 1875), 39.

15. Charles Darwin, *The Expression of the Emotions in Man and Animals*, commentary Paul Ekman and Phillip Prodger (London: HarperCollins, 1998), 409–410.

16. *OC*, vol. 12 [BC], p. 178.

17. Bernard and Gunthert, 65–98.

18. The image recurs throughout works of the Salpêtrière school. *OC*, vol. 9, p. 296.

19. Meige, "Charcot," 495.

20. Richer, *Physiologie*, 14.

21. Ibid., 8–9.

22. Meige, "Charcot," 498–510.

23. Bourneville, "J.-M. Charcot," 202.

24. Richer, *École*, 31.

25. Paul Richer, "L'anatomie et les arts plastiques," *Séance publique annuelle des Cinq Académies* (25 October 1907): 12.

26. Paul Richer, *Dialogues sur l'art et la science* (Paris: Auxerre, 1897), 30.

27. Richer's aesthetic can be considered the rational, scientific antithesis of Futurist "body madness" in this sense. Umbro Apollonio, ed. and trans., *Futurist Manifestoes* (London: Thames and Hudson, 1973), 38–41, 196.

28. Henry Meige, *École nationale supérieure des beaux-arts. Cours d'anatomie. Leçon d'ouverture (18 décembre 1922)* (Paris: Masson, 1923), 5; Paul Richer, *Canon des proportions du corps humain* (Paris: Delgrave, 1919).

29. Londe, "Nouveau," 370–4; Bernard and Gunthert, 99–143, 206–211.
30. Meige, *École*, 15.
31. Jean-Martin Charcot and Paul Richer, "Le mascaron grotesque de l'église Santa Maria Formosa," *NIPS*, 1 (1888): 87–92.
32. *OC*, vol. 13, p. 79; Jean-Martin Charcot and Paul Richer, *Les difformes et les malades dans l'art*, facsimile edn (Amsterdam: N.V. Boekhandel et anti-quariaat, 1972), 1–5; Paul Richer, *L'art et la médecine* (Paris: Gaultier, 1901), 166–9.
33. Jean-Martin Charcot and Paul Richer, *"Les démoniaques dans l'art" suivi de "La foi qui guérit,"* facsimile reproduction; ed. and commentary Georges Didi-Huberman and Pierre Fédida (Paris: Macula, 1984), 166–175.
34. Charcot and Richer, *Difformes*, I, 1–33.
35. Maurice Debove, "Éloge de J.-M. Charcot," *Mémoires de l'Académie de médecine*, 39 (1901): 14.
36. Lubimoff, 59.
37. Thomas Bulfinch, *Bulfinch's Mythology* (NY: Grosset and Dunlap, 1913), 34–36.
38. Meige, *École*, 10.
39. Maurice Hamel, "Le salon de 1887," *Gazette des beaux-arts*, 35–36 (June 1887): 476.
40. Courrière, 144–6; Reenooz, 245.
41. Chrissie Iles and Russell Roberts, eds, *In Visible Light: Photography and Classification* (Oxford: Museum of Modern Art Oxford, 1997), 75–78.
42. Sylvie Aubenas, ed., *L'art du nu au XIXe siècle: Le photographe et son modèle* (Paris: Hazan / BNF, 1997), 104–7.
43. Anon, *La revue d'amour*, souvenir program (Paris: Éditions artistiques de Paris, 1933), possession of author.
44. Collection de photographies anciens, Bibliothèque d'ENSBA, Paris. Reproduced in Aubenas, ed., 124.
45. Foucault, *The History of Sexuality. Volume I. An Introduction*, trans. Robert Hurley (London: Penguin, 1990), 56.
46. Antonin Artaud, *The Theatre and its Double*, trans. Mary Caroline Richards (NY: Weidenfeld, 1958).
47. Meige, *École*, 12–16.
48. Marshall, "Theatre," 16.
49. Note that in the English trans. above, the phrase "s'est-il appliqué" has been moved to clarify its relation to its subject "la source." "s'est-il appliqué, tout au contraire, à partir des régions profondes, à puiser à la source même des mouvements, au milieu des groupes musculaires, les raisons du modelé et des attitudes. C'est ainsi que, s'aidant tout à tour du cadavre et du modèle vivant, que, disséquant avec le scalpel le muscle qu'il ... arrive à rendre l'artiste 'à même d'analyser à travers la peau, comme à travers un

voile transparent.'" Étienne Roc, "Professeur Mathias Duval," *Hommes d'aujourd'hui*, 273 (1886): 1–4; see also Mathias Duval [1891], *Précis d'anatomie à l'usage des artistes* (Paris: L.-H. May, 1900).

50. Aubenas, ed., 155.
51. Richer, *Physiologie*, 15.
52. Richer, *École*, 1–20.
53. Richer, *Nouvelle anatomie artistique* (Paris: Plon, 1889–1929), vol. 5, p. 399.
54. Henry Meige, "Les 'écorchés,'" *Aesculape*, 16 (1926), 1–7, Meige, *École*, 12–13.
55. François Sallé, *Un cours d'anatomie à l'École de beaux arts à Paris* (1888); collection of Art Gallery of New South Wales, Sydney; Callen, "Body," 23–60.
56. Richer, *École*, 21.
57. Henry Meige, "Une révolution anatomique," *NIPS*, vol. 20 (1907), plates 35–36.
58. Richer, *Physiologie*, 10.
59. Richer, *École*, 22–24.
60. Anon, "RICHER (Paul-Marie-Louis-Pierre)," in Maurice Genty and Paul Busquet, eds, *Les biographies médicales* (Paris: Baillière, 1930–36), vol. 5, pp. 65–76; Simon-Dhouailly, ed., 100–101.
61. P. Bellugue, "Henry Meige," *Presse médicale*, 29–30 (2–5 April 1941): 372–4.
62. Chevalier de Jaucourt, "Dance," in Denis Diderot, ed., *Encyclopédie* (Paris: 1751–65); Londe, "Nouveau," 372–4.
63. Charcot and Richer, *Difformes*, 12.
64. Richer, *Art*, 540.
65. Richer, *Dialogues*, 36–37.
66. Richer, *Art*, 6–8.
67. Richer, *Dialogues*, 36. Londe took a series of photographs of clowns, animals, and their trainers at the famous Hippodrome des Champs Elysées on avenue de l'Alma, 1887–88. André Gunthert, *Albert Londe* (Paris: Nathan, 1999), tirages 24–28.
68. Guillain, x.
69. Paul Richer, "Locomotion humaine," in Arsène d'Arsonval, Étienne-Jules Marey, et al, eds, *Traité de physique biologique* (Paris: Masson, 1901–03), vol. 1, p. 215.
70. Richer, *Artistic*, 15.
71. Richer, *Art*, 540.
72. Richer, "L'anatomie," 10.
73. Charcot and Richer, *Difformes*, 144–151; Jane Eade, "The Theatre of Death," *Oxford Art Journal*, 36.1 (2013): 109–125; R. Ballestriero,

"Anatomical Models and Wax Venuses," *Journal of Anatomy*, 216.2 (Feb 2010): 223–234; Petra Lamers-Schütze, ed., *Encyclopaedia anatomica: Museo La Specola, Florence*, commentary Georges Didi-Huberman et al (Köln: Taschen, 2001); Lynne Cooke and Peter Woolen, eds, *Visual Culture* (Seattle: Bay Press, 1995), 178–217.
74. Richer, *Art*, 8.
75. Meige, *École*, 1–20.
76. Henry Meige, *Le juif errant à la Salpêtrière* (Paris: Bataille, 1893); Goldstein, "Wandering," 521–552.
77. Meige, *Juif*, 8, Henry Meige, *L'infantilisme, le féminisme et les hermaphrodites antiques* (Paris: Masson, 1895), 7.
78. Wouter de Herder, "History of Acromegaly," *Neuroendocrinology* (5 Jan 2015): 1–11.
79. Edouard Brissaud and Henry Meige, *Gigantisme et acromégalie* (Paris: A. Coccoz, 1895), 3.
80. *OC*, vol. 13, pp. 392–9.
81. Brissaud and Meige, 4.
82. Charcot and Richer, *Difformes*, 51; Henry Meige, *Sur le gigantisme* (Paris: Albouy, 1903), 10.
83. Brissaud and Meige, 6–22.
84. Meige, *Infantilisme, gigantisme*, 11–20, *Sur le gigantisme*, 4.
85. Meige, *Sur le gigantisme*, 3–7.

CHAPTER 6

The Neurological Theatre
of Hysterioepilepsy

1 BOURNEVILLE AND THE ICONOGRAPHY OF HYSTERIA

Of all the material produced at the Salpêtrière on various topics during Charcot's tenure, two series attracted the most attention. These were Paul Richer's *Clinical Studies on Grand Hysteria or Hysterioepilepsy* (*Études cliniques sur la grande hystérie ou l'hystéro-épilepsie*), issued in 1881 and updated in 1885, together with Désiré-Magloire Bourneville's three-volume *Iconographie photographique de la Salpêtrière* (*Photographic Iconography of the Salpêtrière*) (1875–1880). Both were lavishly illustrated, particularly the *Iconographie*, which consisted largely of photographic prints prepared by Paul Régnard, and which were accompanied by case histories and notes by Bourneville. Richer's *Clinical Studies* also included photographs by Régnard's successor, Albert Londe.

Some of the material from this chapter has appeared in Jonathan W. Marshall, "Beyond the Theatre of Desire: Hysterical Performativity and Perverse Choreography in the Writings of the Salpêtrière School, 1862–1893," in Peter Cryle and Christopher Forth, eds, *Fin de siècle Sexuality: The Making of a Central Problem* (Newark: Delaware University Press, 2008), pp. 42–60, and "The Priestesses of Apollo and the Heirs of Aesculapius: Medical Art-Historical Approaches to Ancient Choreography After Charcot," *Forum for Modern Language Studies*, 43.4 (Oct 2007): 410–426, reproduced here by kind permission of Delaware University Press, and Oxford University Press, respectively.

© The Editor(s) (if applicable) and The Author(s) 2016
J.W. Marshall, *Performing Neurology*,
DOI 10.1057/978-1-137-51762-3_6

Reproductions and sketches from these volumes reappeared throughout the corpus of the Salpêtrière school, and were also disseminated in the lay press.

Hysteria was a controversial and topical illness during Charcot's lifetime. Charcot staked his reputation on his claim that hysteria was an illness of neurosensory function—and not principally a psychological or sexual disease, as others contended. As such, hysteria was closely associated with other altered nervous states such as seizure, paralysis, ticcing, hypnosis, and fugue. Though many competing theories existed in the 1880s, Charcot's influence was such that even his opponents such as Hippolyte Berheim tended to see seizure, temporary paralysis, and fugue as conditions which often occurred amongst hysterics, even if Bernheim disagreed that such behaviours were necessarily symptoms of hysteria itself. Charcot contended—incorrectly—that only hysterics were liable to hypnotic suggestion, whilst Bernheim argued not only that anyone could be hypnotized, but also that suggestion was principally a therapeutic tool for healing patients rather than a sign of latent neuropathology. The extremely public nature of this debate ensured that those works of the Salpêtrière school dealing with hysteria attracted a degree of interest which arguably exceeded their place within Charcot's larger practice.[1] Meanwhile, sensational legal cases such as the 1890 murder trial of Gabrielle Bompard—the Eyraud-Gouffé Affair—provided a stage upon which medico-legal expert Jules Liégeois of the Nancy school squared off against his opposite numbers from the Salpêtrière school, Paul Brouardel and Georges Gilles de la Tourette, to debate the nature of criminal responsibility under hysterical hypnosis.[2] Such trials involving hysteria and fugue had a highly melodramatic flavour throughout the nineteenth century, as defendants and lawyers sought to evoke theatrical and narrative tropes of the wronged lover or the crime of passion in association with medical lore to support their case, often playing to a packed house of public spectators.

Despite the differences between Bernheim and Charcot, hysteria functioned for both as a Matterhorn to be conquered: the most confusing and variable disease of the time. Reading Charcot's model of hysteria in the context of its performative nature and variability, it becomes apparent that it acted as the very essence of neurophysiological disorder itself, closely related to many of the other equally problematic illnesses of the day, such as chorea, epilepsy, and Tourette's syndrome. If the neurological body was fundamentally chaotic and difficult to describe, hysteria then was the ultimate version of this, an illness so polyphonic in its iterations that it all but defied diagnosis itself. The fungible, exaggerated performativity of hysterioepilepsy epitomized the diseased body, constituting a radical challenge to Charcot's discourse, to which he responded by marshalling the tools of theatrical analysis.

The sheer quantity of illustrations in the *Iconographie* and *Études cliniques*, together with narrative details and other information, meant that these works went far beyond offering a visual analysis of disease. Rather, the texts documented a series of complex dramas exhibited by the patients in an attempt on the part of the neurologists to come to grips with the profligacy of their charges. The reader was encouraged to read across the images, and reconstruct patient behaviour in all its chaotic totality. The *Iconographie* resembled in this sense a flip-book of cinematic stills more than it did a collection of self-contained, static images. The performances represented in these texts were pathological because of how such dramas transgressed the rules of classical theatre and Aristotelian drama. Instead of being representations of real events, they acted as corporeal manifestations of a compulsion to perform itself. Hysterioepilepsy was a disease because, in the final analysis, it depicted nothing other than itself; it was pure performance, or as Charcot observed, "art for art's sake." Viewing Régnard's photographs, Surrealist André Breton (who studied under Charcot's senior student Joseph Babinski) declared that hysterical performance offered "the most expressive and the most pure *tableaux vivants*" which reflected the "dialectical movement" between normal life and its most abstracted forms.[3] However, this was also true of a number of other associated illnesses, as we shall see. My contention, then, is that hysteria was not so much atypical in Charcot's practice as it was the most intense manifestation of abnormal neurophysiological performance. As such, hysteria should be read in the context of neuropathological performativity as a whole. Chapters 6 and 7 are devoted to this close corporeal and rhetorical analysis of the practice of Charcot and his associates.

The *Iconographie* was launched as a special edition of *La revue photographique des hôpitaux de Paris*, and featured several of Désiré-Magloire Bourneville's case histories as well as more fragmentary material from his clinical notes, photographs by Régnard, and sketches by Richer and M. Loreau. In 1888 the success of the *Iconographie* led to the *Nouvelle iconographie photographique de la Salpêtrière*, replacing *La revue photographique*, which was to run to nineteen volumes, closing in 1918.

Bourneville was a former Salpêtrière alienist or psychiatrist who had been transferred to Charcot's neurological service in 1870 along with the

ICONOGRAPHIE

PHOTOGRAPHIQUE

DE LA

SALPÉTRIÈRE

SERVICE DE M. CHARCOT

PAR

BOURNEVILLE ET P. REGNARD

PARIS

Aux bureaux du PROGRÈS MÉDICAL   V. ADRIEN DELAHAYE & Cᵉ, Libraires-Éditeurs
6, rue des Écoles, 6.   Place de l'École-de-Médecine

1877

Fig. 6.1   Frontispiece, *Iconographie photographique de la Salpêtrière*, vol. 1. Courtesy of the Boston Medical Library in the Francis A. Countway Library of Medicine

choretics, hemiplegics, and epileptics under his care.[4] Bourneville's alienist training led him to include in the *Iconographie* more expansive case histories than were typical of Charcot's own work, with a greater emphasis on biography as possible threshold events in the course of illness. Bourneville was nevertheless an unswerving supporter of Charcot's neurophysiological approach. He succeeded Montméja at *La revue photographique* in 1870, and three years later founded *Le progrès médical*: a journal under whose auspices almost all of the publications of the Salpêtrière school were issued. In this role, Bourneville functioned as Charcot's main publisher and editor.[5] The textual solidarity promoted under *Le progrès médical* was itself signalled iconographically, with the frontispiece of each book-length study bearing an image of the theatre which they emanated from—the Salpêtrière (Fig. 6.1). Each volume of the *Iconographie photographique* bore two such images. The exterior page was illustrated with a sketch of the dome and main gate from just outside of the hospice. As the reader moved into the text to the title page, a photograph taken from inside the gate echoed this textual progression: in volume one a rear view of the Chapel St Louis, in volume two a perspective of the Chapel's front porch and façade, and in volume three a prospect of one of the roads through the hospice leading past the Chapel gardens.[6] As in the lay reports described in Chap. 2, the medical reader was here guided inside the theatre of the Salpêtrière, moving towards the wards, where one came into the presence of the living clinical bodies photographically documented within the text.

In addition to his medical career, Bourneville sat on both the Paris municipal council and the National Assembly, where he lobbied for the professionalization of medicine and the transfer of authority out of the hands of clerical bodies and into those of state-employed physicians.[7] Moreover, Bourneville was the founding editor of the *Bibliothèque diabolique*, a series devoted to the publication of historic medical data relating to religious ecstatics, witchcraft, and those claiming to be possessed by demons, all of whom were retrospectively diagnosed as suffering from pathological religious delusion in the form of hysterioepilepsy. Bourneville facilitated the construction of Paris' first formal training facility for lay medical nurses on the grounds of the Salpêtrière, which enjoyed the patronage of Jean-Martin's widow Augustine and their daughter Jeanne. The laicization which Bourneville, Charcot, and others promoted reached its apogee in 1908 with the expulsion of the religious sisters of St Augustine from Paris' Hôtel Dieu hospital, located beside Notre Dame cathedral. The Salpêtrière, by contrast, had employed lay *infirmières* since its royal foundation in 1656.

The *Iconographie* dealt primarily with approximately twenty patients from the wards which Bourneville administered on Charcot's behalf. Some of these subjects had first been shown as examples of medical oddities in *La revue photographique*, before being arrayed in a more organized diagnostic fashion within the *Iconographie*.[8] The *Iconographie* offered not only a transcription of the dramaturgy which Charcot and his associates described, but also an attempt to translate this living, performative material from the stages of the Salpêtrière into a published, textual form. Photography was enlisted to aid in this task of bodily transcription. A tension existed between the alogical, pathological body of hysterioepilepsy and its rational, medical description. This conflict between medical diagnosis and its irrationally disordered object was reflected in a similar opposition between performance and its textual documentation. It is significant in this context that Bourneville's project of somatic description was contemporary with not only the work of Marey, Londe, and Richer in finding ways to record and analyse movement, but also with attempts to carefully notate and examine choreography by dance theorists such as Maurice Emmanuel of the Paris Conservatoire, or the founder of Eurhythmics, Émile Jaques-Dalcroze, both of whom drew on advances in chronophotography.[9] Ways of linguistically describing and transcribing both the poetic, and the poetically deranged, medical body were of widespread concern in the arts and science throughout the 1880s through the 1930s.

The *Iconographie* dealt exclusively with female patients, often in detail. The most famous of these included Thérèse ("Th..."); the paradigmatic demoniac Rosalie Leroux ("Ler..."); Madeleine W...; the loquacious ecstatic Geneviève Basile Legrand (whose erotic nocturnal delusions led Bourneville to describe her as a veritable "succubus"); her friend Célina Marc... (who temporarily escaped from the Salpêtrière with Geneviève before succumbing to illness within the hospice walls); the Salpêtrière's own impoverished Madame Bovary, Suzanne N... (or "Ma...," who dreamt of chateaux and a wealthy husband); V.C.; the young, charismatic Augustine Louise Gleize (or "X...," whose first attack occurred after her fiancé Maxime committed suicide and about whom the Surrealists were to wax lyrical; her treatment ceased when she "ran away from the Salpêtrière, disguised as a man"); the equally charismatic rival of Geneviève—B.A.; Blanche Marie Wittman ("W... Marie," cited by Salpêtrière neurologist and faculty professor Alphonse Baudouin as the subject depicted in Brouillet's *A Clinical Lesson*); and Hel... Eudoxie.[10] Although no male patients were featured in the *Iconographie* itself, Charcot and Bourneville insisted that hysteria also afflicted men, endorsing the alienist Pierre Briquet's finding that the ratio of male sufferers to female was one to twenty.[11]

2   CONTRACTING CHOREA, EPILEPSY, AND TOURETTE'S

The first key symptom which the *Iconographie* documented was that of paralysis itself. Bourneville noted that in such cases:

> The arm is typically more or less strongly fixed against the thorax, the fore-arm is flexed onto the arm, in pronation [palm downwards] such that the hand is, often, at a right angle to the wrist.[12]

This was the main corporeal sign associated with not only hemiplegia (asymmetrical paralysis localized to one side of the body), but also astasias (complications of gait) such as sclerosis in plaques, and other degenerative paralyses or pareses (partial paralyses). These conditions were typically accompanied by analgesia (diminution of neuromotor control coupled with loss of sensitivity to touch) and abasia (problems of stance), and in many instances were further complicated or intensified in the form of the more global illness of hysterioepilepsy itself. Such contractures typically constituted a permanent or transitory paralysis of the arm or leg—though in some cases it extended to the tongue or sphincters (larynx, vagina, bladder, rectum). Volume two of the *Iconographie* in particular featured a series of portraits showing patients' arms in contracture. The term itself highlighted the paradoxical aspect of the paralysis with respect to movement. Subjects had little or no control over the affected area, which remained fixed and immobile. This was not a flaccid paralysis, though. The lack of myological movement was solidified within the diseased limb by a corresponding excess of neuromuscular activity. The flexor muscles remained contracted, whilst the extensors were held inactive. The contracture therefore represented a loss of mobility (paralysis) engendered by an excess of movement (muscular contraction). In addition to myological activity generating contractures, it could also erase them. Hysterical contractures, for example, could be distinguished from other types of paralysis by the fact that hysterical contractures disappeared whenever the subject had a seizure.[13] Such conditions were therefore tackled through neuromuscular agents, with Bourneville and Charcot prescribing electrostimulation and muscle-relaxing drugs, as well as other treatments. The contracture then was a common yet paradoxical neuropathological sign, uniting movement with paralysis.

Marguerite-Pauline Gra…, however, exhibited a contracture distinguished by the opposite myological behaviour to that found in the classic contracture.[14] Her left arm rested in a flexed position against her thorax, as was normal. The limb was supple, however, and was constantly in a state of movement, rather than being static. In such cases, the flexed contracture alternated with the relaxation of the muscles, generating clonic spasms (rapid uncontrolled expansion of muscles following tonic contraction), tremors, and other rhythmic phenomena. Charcot defined this condition as athetosis, a term which William Hammond had derived from the Greek for "without fixed position." Bourneville quoted fellow Salpêtrière physician Paul Oulmont on the subject:

> It seems that in the most marked cases, there is a sort of violence; the fingers clench energetically as if to seize an imaginary object, the toes raise themselves at right angles or cling to the ground.[15]

This flexed condition of the feet in athetosis produced the famous "equine" or club-foot pose (*"pied-bot varius"*), which bore an uncanny resemblance to standing en pointe. It had first been identified amongst the alarming ecstatic followers of Saint Medard, incarcerated at the Salpêtrière during the eighteenth century. Illustrations of the *pied-bot*—both modern and historic—appeared throughout the publications of the Salpêtrière school.

The pathological character of even relatively small movements such as athetosis or the *pied-bot* lay in their status as performances devoid of any objective purpose. Gra…'s hand clenched "as if to seize an … object," where no object in fact existed. Charcot noted that in one case of generalized chorea, it was as if "The arms simulated the playing of a tambourine," whilst a Tourette's patient shook his wrists as if "beating eggs."[16] Charcot indeed examined a number of intermediate athetose and choretic cases which were classified as suffering from the disease which now bears Gilles de la Tourette's name.[17] Ticcing was a particularly challenging phenomenon in that it took many forms, ranging from "coprolalia" (vocal expletives) and "echolalia" (repeating of phrases and nonsense) to "illogical movements" such as "salutations" (swipes of the hand over the cranium) and other stochastically occurring poses which lacked any clear, overall choreographic pattern. Charcot noted, moreover, that the distinction between ticcing and chorea was a question of degree, not nature, and a similar shading between disorders existed with respect to chorea, epilepsy, and hysterioepilepsy.

One famous Tourette's suffer named O. who was treated by Meige often found himself taken over by "a veritable debauch of absurd gesticulations, a wild muscular carnival."[18] Just as Charcot characterized dwarfism as a caricature of normal human form, so he described ticcing and related symptoms as a "caricature ... of natural gestures" which became so grossly distorted over the course of the patient's lifetime as to have lost their original function. The tic "is not absurd in itself," he explained: "it is absurd, illogical, because it operates by itself, without any apparent motive." The performance of these and other similarly illogical actions related to an abstract, hallucinatory theatre unconnected with the reality of the situation. As the later theatre theorist Artaud noted in his description of the plague, these states exhibited an imperious "gratuitousness provoking acts without use or profit."[19]

Oulmont's description of athetosis suggested, moreover, that the diseased body was ruled by desires internal to its own "imaginary" psychophysiology, enacting a performance in opposition to not only reality, but also the conscious will of the patient him or herself. O. indeed claimed that during his seizures:

> There seem to be two persons in me ... I am at once the actor and the spectator; and the worst of it is, the exuberance of the one [the pathological actor] is not to be thwarted by the just recriminations of the other.[20]

The body of such a theatrically split subject made visible images which existed beyond both objective existence and the patient's own mind—images coherent only to the pathological body itself.

The textual and verbal language employed by Charcot and his colleagues was not always equal to the task of describing the physical images of athetosis, chorea, hysterioepilepsy, and other illnesses. Bourneville himself conceded that such displays as the ticcer's "wild carnival" were "difficult to clearly describe in an exact manner," drawing instead upon sketches and photographs wherever possible. Visual documentation provided the best way to "pursue the different phases of the convulsive attacks" of these conditions.[21] Commentators supported this proposition, A. de Watteville noting that "We ... must refer the reader once [and] for all to the beautiful illustrations and the myographic tracings with which Dr Richer has enriched his book with no stinted hand."[22] Only such materials could come close to settling the nature of hysterioepilepsy. However, even these documents were not entirely satisfactory.

Here as elsewhere, the writings of the Salpêtrière school reflected the pull of theatrical performance as the primary source and challenge for medical authority over the body. Though eminently valuable, these illustrations remained, in Bourneville's words, "irrefutable witnesses which confirm our descriptions."[23] These secondary representations only carried traces from the images—literally in the case of the myographic tracings which Richer published. The clinical photographer or illustrator merely bore *witness* to this essentially kinesthetic data. The performance of the pathological body continued to lie at the fringes of both medical knowledge and its textual reproduction.

The *Iconographie* included an explanatory drawing by Richer showing Gra...'s fingers spread wide in a motile pose which Bourneville likened to a star.[24] Because the patient was unable to control these illogical, choreiform movements, the permanent agitation of the limb was functionally equivalent to paralysis. More significantly, Gra...'s condition constituted a midpoint between neuromotor paralysis itself and the extravagant movements of hysterioepilepsy, epilepsy proper, or global chorea. Athetosis constituted an active, localized intensification of the same neuromuscular forces which generated both classic contractures and generalized, performative fits.[25]

Like many of her peers, Gra... had initially been diagnosed as suffering from "St Guy's dance"—the same condition which led to Jane Avril being interned at the Salpêtrière, 1882–1884, prior to her career as the Moulin Rouge's most famous dancer.[26] This popular lay term was originally applied to someone under a malign influence and was largely interchangeable with St Vitus' dance and the tarantella (initially said to be caused by a tarantula's bite). "Dancing manias" were indeed associated with numerous saints (John the Baptist, John the Evangelist, Valentin).[27] St Vitus' dance was linked to both the transitory, rheumatic manifestation of Sydenham's chorea and the terminal condition of Huntington's chorea. Popular wisdom had formerly dictated that these conditions receded once their choreographic energy was dispersed in riotous fêtes of dancing, or through religious intervention. Avril offered much the same contention in her biography, claiming that her diagnosis with St Guy's dance was a kind of instinctive "Predestination!" which she eventually learned to control, thus transforming these corporeal urges into a regularized art and thereby becoming cured. Bourneville noted that Suzanne had attempted a similar strategy: "In the country, S... had a preferred dance partner; she never had attacks when she had gone to a fête and danced."[28] Charcot and Richer themselves discussed in *Les démoniaques* a Renaissance engraving "after Pierre Breughel" of a rural saint's festival in which lines of anguished, choretic dancers passed over water or fire, hoping to be cured.[29]

Such intractable diseases had been treated medically since the Renaissance. Charcot adapted the more recent scientific term of athetosis to describe the condition, refining it to refer to a characteristic state of continuous movement of the fingers, toes, feet, or hands in concert with the muscles of the face and neck.[30] Choreiform movements such as athetosis could therefore be distinguished from other fits in that although choretic flexing was generalized, it occurred simultaneously as part of a single, global disturbance. Moreover, choretic movements were often confined to one side of the body (hemichorea), suggesting that their source lay in a problem localized within one of the cerebral hemispheres or the symmetrical division of nervous pathways along the spinal column.

Fully developed, somatic chorea nevertheless remained—like hysterioepilepsy—at the extreme limit of what Charcot could describe in rational, scientific terms. The condition was sufficiently violent to act in opposition to voluntary actions, generating "contradictory movements" or "disorderly and bizarre" physical behaviour.[31] Charcot implicitly conceded that the accurate representation of such phenomena lay more within the purview of the theatre than medicine, noting that "To depict movements of this nature, one would have to be a dance master at the Opera." Another male patient suffering from carbon monoxide poisoning was afflicted with equally regular choretic fits: "abandoning himself to a dance which he … knew well in the past, the polka, it is impossible for him … despite all of his efforts, to respond to our desire." Charcot likened the behaviour of yet another hysteriochoretic patient to the "mazurka." The only consistent character discernible within choretic symptomatology was therefore a repetitive or dance-like "rhythmic" character. Although it was often difficult for Charcot to map the "strange, often highly complex" movements of chorea in terms of their distribution within space, the "music" which Richer had identified in bodily movement—its temporal distribution— could be discerned and measured using Marey's devices.

Charcot in fact presented his lecture audience with a table of quantitative differential diagnoses between seven related degenerative disorders on the basis of tremulous frequency and the distribution of shaking throughout the body (Fig. 6.2).[32] These were intention tremor (sclerosis in plaques, Friedreich's disease); four to five gentle oscillations per minute during repose (paralysis agitans, senility); three and a half to six oscillations

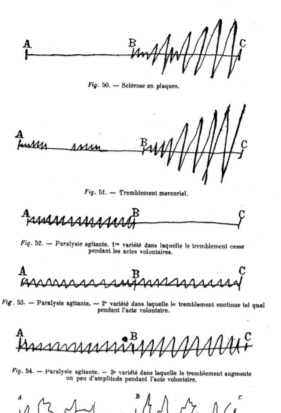

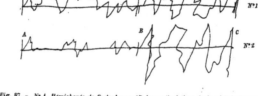

Fig. 6.2 Differential diagnosis on the basis of frequency. A to B is forearm at rest, B to C during voluntary movement. The diseases, top to bottom, are sclerosis in plaques; mercury poisoning; three varieties of paralysis agitans; Sydenham's hemichorea; and post-hemiplegic hemichorea; from Tuesday lessons of 28 May and 24 July 1888 (*OC*, vol. 12, pp. 316, 456). Courtesy of the Boston Medical Library in the Francis A. Countway Library of Medicine

per minute during repose (hysterical); five to six oscillations per minute during repose, exaggerated by both strong emotion and intentional movement (mercury poisoning); and eight or nine oscillations per minute and vibratory tremor during repose, either generalized throughout the body (general paralysis), focused in the individuated fingers (alcoholic degeneration), or localized in body but not in the individual fingers (Basedow's disease or thyrotoxicosis). Charcot claimed that "It was there," in these rhythmic patterns, that one discovered "as is said in *Hamlet*, 'there is *method*, though this be madness.'"[33] Charcot was nevertheless forced to concede that these more methodical varieties of rhythmic chorea (hysteriochorea generating a "motor delirium" in Bourneville's words, or "madness of the leg") constituted only the most common subgroup of chorea, alongside which he placed the "absolutely irregular" arrhythmic *formes frustes*, or "imperfect" manifestations of this diagnostic archetype.[34]

The second volume of the *Iconographie* further drew together these various somatic and hysterical states. Bourneville ordered his text such that the reader moved from the relatively easily described condition of organic partial-epilepsy associated with static contracture to increasingly performative conditions such as partial-epileptic athetosis, and then yet more complex behaviours which blended hysterical phenomena with hemiplegic partial-epilepsy and true chorea.

The partial-epileptic Merl... P..., for example—like Gra...—alternated between a number of conditions, her epileptoid fits generating sympathetic hemicontractures in both her left arm and foot, whilst her neck turned to one side in a choretic spasm.[35] This was sometimes followed by a number of successive poses similar to those which characterized hysterioepilepsy, including tonic positions (those involving muscular contraction) and delirium. Moreover, in her normal state, minor, spontaneous tremors could arise in her otherwise static left arm. Fellow partial-epileptic Br... provided an even more revealing intermediate case. She exhibited no contracture whatsoever in her normal state. Rather, her attacks constituted a kind of dynamic contracture, comparable to athetosis. Bourneville did not classify Br... as suffering from hysterical complications of partial-epilepsy, however, as he did Merl.... Rather, Br...'s condition was entirely somatic. Her symptoms were not, therefore, psychosomatic analogues of true, somatic chorea, as may have been the case with Merl.... At intermittent intervals, Br... guided herself into a seated position, where a light fit would overtake her body whilst she remained conscious (as opposed to fully developed epileptic fitting, which rendered the patient insensible). She ground her jaws and her head dropped as a temporary contracture developed, first with the arm

Fig. 6.3   Sketch by Richer showing partial-epileptic Br... during seizure, progressing *left* to *right*, *IPS*, vol. 2, pp. 65–67. Courtesy of the Boston Medical Library in the Francis A. Countway Library of Medicine

in a straight position and fingers flexed, then with the arm bent as in a classic contracture (Fig. 6.3). These generalized fits began in the contracture itself. Bourneville observed that when such fits commenced, it was as though rhythmic shocks "invade" the body from one site (the left shoulder in Merl...'s case) before radiating throughout the rest of the body.

The wax and wane of such disorderly neuromotor flux generated in the extremities either movement (tremors, fits) or immobility (contractures, tonic poses). Bourneville therefore endorsed L.F. Bravais' conclusion that partial-epilepsy and true chorea were most likely caused by a localized, functional disorder which radiated out along adjacent nerves, although no post-mortem evidence had been found to support this inference. Charcot similarly opined several times in his lectures that along with paralysis agitans:

> Epilepsy, chorea, hysteria ... come to us like so many Sphinxes ... [These] symptomatic combinations deprived of anatomical substratum do not present themselves to the mind of the physician with the appearance of solidity, of objectivity, of affections connected with an appreciable organic lesion.[36]

All of these mysterious, sphinx-like neuropathological conditions were therefore assumed to have a dynamic, functional somatic cause, which did not, however, leave any post-mortem traces yet identified by doctors. It was indeed the *anciens* of the Salpêtrière—namely Paul Brissaud, Paul Oscar Blocq, and Georges Marinesco—who eventually identified the neurological damage which caused paralysis agitans in 1894, whilst Pierre Marie isolated the lesions which generated Huntington's chorea in 1914.[37] Charcot himself found the gaps within pathological knowledge which existed during his own lifetime frustrating, but he remained undaunted. His deductive vivisection of living patients through the clinical observation of performance provided, at this time, the only way to study these diseases. As a writer from *Le progrès médical* observed, "The camera"—and the clinical theatre within which it was active—"was as crucial to the study of hysteria as the microscope to histology."[38] External, visual documentation of live performance such as that described above came to supersede the as yet comparatively unhelpful technique of post-mortem dissection, acting as an essential aid to anatomoclinical investigation proper.

Charcot used this performative information to divide the clinical portraits from the *Iconographie* into four distinct but closely related descriptive categories. Partial-epilepsy "properly so-called" typically developed early within the patient's lifespan. Fitting began in the affected region and was largely confined to that part of the body.[39] Tonic partial-epilepsy followed this pattern also, but was distinguished by the presence of permanent tonic contractures in the adult patient. Mature sufferers from vibratory partial-epilepsy, on the other hand, displayed constant, tremulous athetosis of the affected limb. Moreover, true chorea could be distinguished from such choreiform behaviours by its common manifestation as a highly rhythmic disorder. Therefore, contractures and tremors were often signs of an incipient tendency to fit, an overtly performative aspect of neuromuscular disorder. Neuropathology was highly communicative within the body, spreading from its primary, localized somatic sites via dynamic, periodic eruptions of functional nervous energy—or in visibly organic cases, through tissue sclerosis (pathological hardening), myelitis (gross inflammation of tissue running down the core of nerve bundles), and tubercular growths, which also tended to spread out from a localized source.

Bourneville emphasized the status of the contracture as a hypostatized concretization of more transitory, global neurophysiological pathologies—in a form which was, moreover, particularly amenable to photographic documentation. He noted that the general course of partial-epilepsy was one of childhood convulsions leading to more generalized, long-term hemiplegia or hemiparesis, followed by the development of tonic or athetose contractures, finally evolving into partial-epilepsy itself: a permanent condition displaying characteristic intermittent fits, functional paralyses, and frequent "cerebral atrophy" or idiocy.[40] The contracture evolved out of an initial, generative fit. Subsequent attacks during the patient's lifetime recapitulated this etiology. The contracture was a physiological *idée fixe* which could transform back into the patient's first global event, of which it remained a lasting, somatic memory.

Charcot's practice thus moved between disorders of gait (like paralysis agitans and sclerosis in plaques) into the various fitting disorders. Indeed, Charcot's diagnosis of ambulatory automatism as an unusual, fugue-like manifestation of epileptic attack highlighted the close interconnection between these two symptomatic clusters.[41] Normal epilepsy was a more concentrated eruption of the pathological forces which could set in train dissociated-walking or other complications of gait. British neurologist John Hughlings Jackson had indeed proposed in the 1860s that epilepsy was the "mobile counterpart of hemiplegia."[42] The fits which Charcot's patients exhibited ranged from the "petit mal" or attack of "vertigo" to the "grand mal" of a global fit (nineteenth century medics did not clearly distinguish between vertigo and absence seizures as today's doctors do).[43] In both cases, the disruption of the individual's spatial perception and sense of balance often signalled the onset of a more extensive rupture of his or her spatio-temporal being. Disorders of sensation and visual acuity such as scotomas (abstract patterns of scintillating light impinging upon the visual field), achromatopsia (colour blindness), or tunnel vision also commonly accompanied these states, further attenuating the patient's relation to normal space.

3   HYSTERIOEPILEPSY AND PSYCHOKINETIC MEMORY

Charcot's most spectacular contribution to the diagnosis of fitting illnesses was, however, hysterioepilepsy itself, and it was chiefly this which the case histories of the *Iconographie* documented. Cases of partial-epilepsy, athetosis, and chorea formed both the backdrop and the introduction to this study, Charcot and Bourneville making no significant distinction between the nature of these various functional, performative diseases.

Fulgence Raymond would later proclaim that "Charcot, for the first time, provided us with an analysis of that pathological drama" found in hysterioepilepsy, namely, "He identified four acts."[44] These nominally distinct stages were each characterized by specific psychophysiological behaviours. Attacks were typically preceded by a number of "prodromes" or what was known as the "hysterical aura."[45] Richer observed that these precursors "betray the disorder of the whole [somatic] economy."[46] As with other fitting conditions, hysterical aura was frequently marked by the disruption of the patient's sensorial relation to normal space in the form of vertigo; scotomas, an apparent "fog descending over the eyes"; or other complications.[47]

The most important diagnostic sign of the aura was the "globulus hystericus," or the suffocating sensation of a ball rising through the chest into the throat (like "a small apple").[48] Medieval physicians believed this to be caused by the pathological wandering of the womb throughout the body, but this venerable theory had been definitively rejected by the nineteenth century. Charcot's neurophysiological model reworked this ancient sign as a consequence of neurosensory disturbance, noting that it also occurred in cases of true epilepsy.[49] The globulus hystericus passed through what Bourneville identified as the three main "nodes" around which the long-term somatic symptoms of hysterioepilepsy clustered.[50] These were the ovarian or pelvic region (testes and lower abdomen in men), the epigastric and laryngeal area, and the cephalic region (including the highly focused cerebral pain designated the "hysterical nail"). Ovarian or testicular tenderness, menstrual irregularity, cardiovascular disorders (coughing, palpitations, angina, racing pulse, edema, erythema), hyper-sensitivity, loss of sensation (anaesthesia; analgesia; disorders of taste, smell, and hearing), and sleep disorders and digestive problems (wind, ballooning of the stomach, excretory retention, incontinence, cramps, vomiting, diarrhoea, loss of appetite, anorexia, bulimia, dyspepsia) were also common.

The fit began with the cry (Fig. 6.4).[51] Bourneville reproduced this extraordinary image of Augustine without any accompanying explanation and the photograph crystallized the ambiguity imbedded within hysterioepilepsy. What, if anything, Augustine was crying out for remained unsaid. Indeed, the very absence of explicit meaning behind her wordless vocalization rendered it pathological. Charcot explained that hysterical performance was "a kind of cult of art for art's sake, with a view to producing sensation, exciting pity, etc.," without any appropriate underlying meaning or context.[52] It was a pure sono-physical form, devoid of any real emotional content other than the reflexive response to pain or anguish, existing beyond words—a mute cry in a sense, impervious to further medical description. In the terms of later Artaudian dramaturg

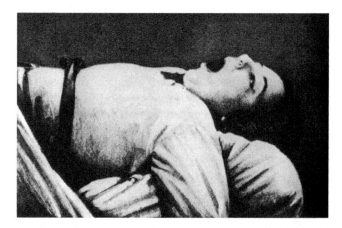

Fig. 6.4   Commencement of seizure: the cry (Augustine); *IPS*, vol. 2, pl. XV. Courtesy of the Boston Medical Library in the Francis A. Countway Library of Medicine

Herbert Blau, theatrical events such as the hysterioepileptic cry consti-tuted a pure "acoustical image ... which signifies nothing, and ... which, out of nothingness, begins to look like a language" which "limins the edge of meaning."[53] Mutism was indeed a common hysterioepileptic symptom itself, patients' inchoate vociferations shading into the linguisti-cally interchangeable state of non-speaking or silence. In describing the hysterical cry, the Salpêtrière physicians depicted hysterioepilepsy as a form of arational, alinguistic, unjustified performativity at the very moment of its commencement. Inasmuch as hysteria could be said to enunciate any-thing specific, it initially spoke, without words, as pure acoustic or embod-ied force. Hysterical communication occurred in the first instance almost entirely through and of the inchoate body.

Stages one and two of the fit itself consisted of generalized *"grands mouvements"* (large or grand movements) which Richer divided into the epileptoid period and the subsequent period of clownism. Typically these movements began with epileptoid poses. The shoulders hunched, the arms rotated so that the palms faced outwards from the body, and the wrists bent. The hands adopted "clawed" or pinching positions. Muscular contraction then spread throughout the body as if the subject were in neuromuscular shock as generated by a tetanus infection (lockjaw) or electrostimulation. Opisthotonos eventually became so extensive as to produce the diagnostically distinctive "*arc de cercle*," in which the entire body was forced into an arched shape. Tetaniform and epileptoid symptoms like these extended, tonic poses were then succeeded by the characteristic clonic spasms of hysterioepilepsy itself. Here, the body often rhythmically rocked back and forth between a hunched, forward position and an arched posture (hysteriochorea) as the patient appeared to hyperventilate (stertor). Patients frequently raged and gnashed their teeth in postures which Bourneville and Richer identified as being closely akin to those which Catholics had formerly designated as being the result of demonic possession.

Some of these acrobatic, "trapeze"-like poses of clownism were so extreme and bizarre as to defy any description which Charcot and his peers envisaged.[54] Attitudes such as patients standing on their heads or twisting their limbs behind and across the body were not strictly speaking tonic, tetaniform, clonic, clown-like, or demoniacal. These radically disordered movements could only be described as "illogical attitudes," a phrase also used to describe Tourette's syndrome (Fig. 6.5). Reviewing Richer's publications, the physician A. Watteville observed that such poses were "illogical" because of "their non-correspondence to any [identifiable] emotional states" or other narrative or contextual justification.[55] This type of choreography was particularly common amongst male, working-class subjects, their highly physical fits tending to eschew the more readable, theatrical scenarios of feminine hysterical delirium.[56]

The choreography of hysterioepilepsy was so violently chaotic as to be not just pathological, but to exist beyond the logical structures of language itself. Hysteria's status as a pre-linguistic, somatic language has since become a truism of feminist psychoanalysis.[57] What is often overlooked, however, is that the alinguistic character of nineteenth century hysteria meant that the disease could only be fully represented through the force of physical performance, and not through written or verbal description, or even the static images of photography. Hysterioepilepsy was manifest in movement, in unpredictable spurts of performative dynamism, and in the scenarios of a delusional theatre. The essence of the disease lay as much between the photographs arrayed with such care inside the *Iconographie* as it did within the actual images themselves. The irony of Régnard photographically representing a cry highlighted how the images could not, in themselves, contain hysterical performance. Hysterioepilepsy represented, therefore, the greatest challenge that neurologists faced. In attempting to textually document hysteria, the

PÉRIODE TERMINALE DE LA GRANDE ATTAQUE HYSTÉRIQUE
Contractures généralisées.

PÉRIODE TERMINALE DE LA GRANDE ATTAQUE HYSTÉRIQUE
Contractures généralisées.

Fig. 6.5   Sketches by Richer of illogical attitudes; Charcot and Richer, *Les démoniaques*, 101. Courtesy of the Boston Medical Library in the Francis A. Countway Library of Medicine

Salpêtrière physicians attempted to return the arational, alinguistic performance of hysteria to the domain of rational medicine and its increasingly textual, tabular forms of knowledge.[58]

The alternating tonic and clonic seizures of the *grands mouvements* and clownism were replaced in the third stage by extended, emotive poses known as "passionate attitudes." These archetypal tableaux condensed into single poses the hallucinatory internal drama experienced by the patient. Some were generalized rhetorical poses, such as "menace," "recognition," "mockery," and "beatitude." Other topics, however, ranged from erotic and religious visitations to horrific encounters with aggressive beasts (snakes, insects, rats, dogs, and more). The patient was relatively quiet and unmoving, conserving emotive, impassioned stances which in many cases prefigured or were drawn from religious iconography. As Didi-Huberman observes, these symptoms were consistent with the eighteenth century Catholic construction of the miraculous as generating living representations of Christ's suffering in the body of the ecstatic, an association Geneviève herself made ("Our Savior also was flagellated").[59] Bourneville went so far as to claim that these statuesque poses were "the most perfect representations of the saints which art has given us."[60] Patients adopted attitudes of prayer and crucifixion (the latter of which Bourneville seemed to see as a physical sign whose resemblance to Christian imagery was largely coincidental). Passionate attitudes were also frequently sexual, many patients closing their arms about their insubstantial, hallucinatory lovers—though even here the performance was disorderly and contradictory, the patient inconsistently failing to make room in her embrace for her phantom companion, whilst at other times leaving a space in her bed for where his body would have been.

Augustine and others staged their sexual encounters whilst under Bourneville's watchful gaze, who recorded that "she seems to see a well-loved, imaginary being":

> She closes her eyes, her physiognomy denotes possession, satisfied desire; the arms are crossed, as if she pressed to her breast the lover of her dreams. Sometimes, one observes gentle rocking movements;—at others she presses upon the pillow. Then, little moans, smiles, pelvic movements; words of desire or encouragement.[61]

Although there are no comparable examples for male hysterics, their illnesses did involve sexual complications such as sexual dysfunction, or in one case, an otherwise virile man was rendered mute and metaphorically impotent by the shock of his wife repeatedly absconding with their rent and by his continual willingness to forgive her.[62] Hysterical performances ranged over a wide variety of topics and contexts, but feminine sexuality was a particularly common subject—even though Bourneville and Charcot stressed that there was no necessary connection between hysteria and sexuality.

Bourneville identified all of these physical actions as "reminiscences … recalling … moral emotions" or "physical pains of events which were the motivating cause of their attacks," including "scenes from the Revolution," sexual violence, industrial accidents (experienced by both men and women), dog attacks, and other traumatic occurrences.[63] Visiting British physician Arthur Gamgee also noted that "the same attitude corresponds to the same hallucination," each remaining "constant" within the performative enunciation of a given patient.[64] Like the choreography of Tourette's, the passionate attitudes exhibited by individual subjects made up an idiosyncratic but nevertheless regular expressive vocabulary within their seizures. As Richer put it, "each one of our patients conserves their eccentricities," right down to which animals they tended to hallucinate.[65]

Bourneville noted that he himself could "see … in her delirium" that the patient herself "saw taking place before her scenes from her existence"—though this required an imaginative act of empathetic identification with the subject on the part of the medical spectator.[66] Augustine claimed to have been:

a spectator at a theatre where a representation of a revolution was being performed: there were negroes with *red eyes* and *blue teeth* fighting with firearms, M… [Augustine's lover] was struck on the head by a bullet, the *blood* flowed, I cried out, and, awakened, I returned at once from my error.[67]

Richer recorded similar fugue states in Geneviève, reflecting that she "often seemed to be in a delirium of a memory which had not finished."[68] As with the contracture, neuropathological fits often functioned as a mnemonic theatre for the traumatized individual who was physically fixated on events from his or her life. Charcot's students Sigmund Freud and Pierre Janet later observed that it was the hysteric's tendency for theatrical repetition that prevented her return to health. Charcot himself implied as much, noting that the patient's delirious conflation of the instigating trauma and her later life meant that hysterical delirium was in actuality "a lot of noise over nothing"—or nothing real, in any case.[69] This was despite the apparent, performative realism of these displays. Watteville noted that events from the patient's life were replayed "with the art of the most consummate actor," whilst even Charcot conceded that during an attack, hysterioepileptics "look quite natural and assume realistic poses."[70]

Like the ticcer Meige described previously, at least some of the Salpêtrière hysterics were aware of how their condition had caused them to become theatrical performers. The histrionic Suzanne N... proposed that:

> I will become an actress ... I will enter the Conservatory, I will spend two years on studies. Then I will arrive on the stage, I will declaim, I will become like Sarah Bernhardt: 'That light which I see again breaks my heart!' (*She delivers this phrase with the emphatic tone of the theatre.*) It is no more difficult than that.[71]

Patients performed in, and in turn became spectators of, performances such as Augustine's re-enactment of the Revolution. In trying to interpret these actions, the physician in turn became a spectator, observing not the event itself, but its refracted, pathological restaging and reimagining by the patient. Doctors were thereby subtly drawn into the dramas they observed.

Richer offered the most detailed discussion of the theatricality phenomenon of hysterioepilepsy. The passionate attitudes were:

> *plastic poses.* And in effect, it is not here simply a delirium of memory or of imagination; the patient is in the throes of hallucinations which ravish or delight her and transport her into an imaginary world. There, she witnesses scenes in which she often plays the principal role; the expression of her physiognomy and her attitudes reproduce the feelings which animate her; she acts as if her dream was a reality. And by the expressive mimicry to which she gives herself over, as well as by the words which she lets escape, it is easy to follow all the peregrinations of the drama which unfolds before her, or in which she takes an active part;—her hallucination, purely subjective, becomes in some fashion objective through the translation which she makes.[72]

Hysterical delusion was not, therefore, primarily a mental condition like a simple "delirium of memory or imagination," which could be accounted using purely alienist, psychiatric methods. On the contrary, hysterioepilepsy was a kinesthetic disease, which acted to "ravish" or "delight" the patient, transporting her both mentally and sensorially to "an imaginary world"—an imaginary theatre. She "gives herself over" to her delusions, body and soul, reflecting her conceits through "her physiognomy" and "expressive mimicry." It was these animated, physical, and neurophysiological signs to which Richer, Bourneville, and Charcot first directed their attention, before they turned to the less important "words which she lets escape."

Richer's most revealing (and problematic) observation was contained in the final passage, however. Physicians ideally observed the subject's "purely subjective" hallucination so as to read her external signs and comprehend from the outside "the peregrinations of the drama which unfolds before her" within her delusional realm. Despite the pathological nature of this performance (which was due to its status as a response to a "dream" which she incorrectly took for "reality"), the translation of this internal delusion into external, clinically observed performance was what rendered it "objective" for the clinician—even if the actor herself was unfamiliar with the true nature of her behaviour. Richer claimed that the clinician could penetrate into the internal performance space of the patient and understand what was being performed, whilst simultaneously maintaining a barrier between the sane medical observer and the internal hallucinatory drama which he watched. The theatre of the hysteric and the theatre of the doctor remained irreconcilable, guaranteeing the accuracy of the physician's observations even if the patients who performed them were themselves delusional.[73] Richer's rather unwise choice of grammar, however, gave the hysteric the agency in ensuring this theatrical distinction—"the translation which *she* makes" (my emphasis)—highlighting the difficulty in maintaining such a delimitation between hysterical performance and its clinical spectatorship. In light of these circumstances, Geneviève's claim, which she "gladly and proudly" shared with visitors, that "I would have invented hysteria [even] if it hadn't already existed!" seemed eminently feasible.[74]

The static deliria of the passionate attitudes gave way to the post-fit delirium proper of the final stage. Patients were often active and loquacious during this period (a veritable "delirium of speech" in the terms of Richer and Bourneville).[75] They cried out for relatives, lovers, or religious figures, cowered in fear from imaginary creatures, and acted out a huge range of imagined scenarios specific to each sufferer. Bourneville noted that Augustine in particular seemed to be "always in conversation with her 'Invisibles,'" including her lovers.[76] Patients also narrated extravagant tales apparently unrelated to any of these topics. Richer described the following delusion experienced by Augustine, for example, as "a pure creation of her mind."[77] She saw:

the *chariot of the dead* drawn by six beasts … accompanied by a dozen men who called out to her, surrounded by flames and crows, and adorned with a tricolour … When the men surrounding her speak, flames leap from their mouths.[78]

The delirious, entirely fabricated scenography which emerged from both the passionate attitudes and delirium-proper was, however, erratic. It flagrantly transgressed Aristotle's concept of the unity of space, time, and character to which conventional Western drama had long adhered. Characters and locations were suddenly replaced in the patient's under-standing, as were the temporal periods from the sufferer's life which were darkly refracted within this hallucinatory theatre. Hysterical actors leapt freely from memories of lovers to Hellish fantasies to saintly delusions. B… Evelina, for example, suddenly ceased her vigorous, silent copula-tory movements to "sing the *Dragoons of Villars*, her favorite romance," without any apparent pause.[79] These delirious performances presented themselves to the clinician as "a mélange of religious ideas and erotic ideas with hallucinations of hearing and vision," a bizarre jumble of scenes which failed to coalesce into a single, coherent drama. Bourneville likened these shifts to a *"coup de théâtre"* which left the clinical spectator "stupe-fied." As with the ticcers whom Charcot and Meige treated, such delirious hysterical performances were not only theatrical in their execution, but they were often partly derived from the theatre. In the case of Célina, for example, "her delirium retraces passages or episodes drawn from the caba-rets or street dances which she frequented."[80] Much the same was true of Suzanne N…, who quoted poems by the playwright Alfred Musset.

Hysterical performance constituted, therefore, a dangerous realm of imperious, self-reflective, avant-garde theatre—"art for art's sake"—in vio-lation of classical unity, dramatic justification, and reason itself. It was this which rendered hysterioepilepsy as the ultimate neurophysiological pathol-ogy, an extravagant collection of behaviours and actions at the limit of what could be encompassed within Charcot's descriptive nosology. Hysteria thereby presented the clinician with an alluring but problematic challenge.

4   THE INFECTIVE PROFLIGACY OF THE PROTEAN BODY

Richer developed the most comprehensive description of both the hys-terical fit and the phases of hysterioepileptic hypnosis (*"la grande hyp-nose"*; see Chap. 7). His *Clinical Studies*, which the historian Étienne

Fig. 6.6 Synoptic table of *la grande hystérie*; Richer, *Études* (1881), pl. V. Courtesy of the Boston Medical Library in the Francis A. Countway Library of Medicine

Table 6.1 Key to synoptic table of *la grande hystérie*

A Prodromes		Precursor signs	
B		Tonic phase	Tonic *grands mouvements*
C First period			Tonic immobility
D		Clonic phase	
E		Phase of resolution	
F Second period, or		Phase of contortions	
G Period of clownism and		Phase of *grands mouvements*	Rhythmic
H illogical movements			Disordered
I Third period, or		Happy passionate attitudes (silent)	
J Period of passionate attitudes		Sad passionate attitudes (silent)	
K Fourth period, or		Delirium, *zoopsie* (hallucination of animals; delirium of speech)	
L Period of delirium		Generalized contractures	

Translation by author

Trillat aptly characterizes as a "totalizing … sort of Vulgate of the Salpêtrière School," included an impressive synoptic table of hysterical movements (Fig. 6.6 and Table 6.1).[81] This chart showed the choreographic palette from which each hysterioepileptic fit was formed. Each column represented a stage in the fit—prodromes, epileptoid, clownism, and delirium—under which were arrayed a series of generalized sketches of hysteria's various physical poses, produced by Richer and derived from photographs by Régnard, Londe, as well as Richer's own observations. Richer noted, however, that even in a complete fit, it was rare that every attitude which he had tabulated was actually performed. Attacks could include any combination of poses drawn from the four columns. Fully evolved hysterical fits which included gestures from every *stage* of seizure—let alone every *posture* of any single stage—were extremely uncommon, occurring only within a small number of demonstration subjects (notably Augustine and Blanche). Bourneville himself conceded that, despite his extensive clinical experience, "we have never been able to see, for ourselves, within a single patient … all of the periods of the fit."[82] An "abortive" or "incomplete attack," such as that Merl… P… or V.C. typically exhibited, was far more frequent. In somewhat more extensive fits, one or more of the hysterical periods tended to dominate—demoniacal in Rosalie, ecstatic in Geneviève. Some patients only exhibited the passionate attitudes, without going through the other stages, whilst other subjects skipped clownism altogether. Such cases constituted the various diagnostic subgroups of hysterioepilepsy, although these descriptions were at best inexact.

Most of the seizures observed in the clinic consisted of what Richer designated as imperfect "entr'actes"—miniature theatrical or balletic scenes which occurred between the main drama; in this case, the purely virtual performance of full archetypal hysterioepileptic fitting itself.[83] Richer's rather poorly chosen term of "entr'actes" took on a distinctly satiric character in the hands of less sympathetic commentators like Platel, however.[84] The hypnotic states of hysterioepilepsy could moreover arise spontaneously, somnambulism replacing post-fit delirium, whilst Richer was at pains to point out that in describing the different phases of *la grande hypnose* itself, "I have no pretensions whatsoever of establishing a definitive classification … in the midst of this immense maze." The distinction between hysterical catalepsy and lethargy, for example, was particularly vexed. Richer stressed, moreover, that although his chart depicted hysterioepilepsy's most common diagnostic "varieties of the classical type," these were "varieties which it would be easy to multiply."[85] Charcot rejected Briquet's earlier claim that hysteria constituted an *"unseizable proteus!"* asserting instead, "The case is quite the contrary, everything is as regular as possible, almost monotonous."[86] This account was not altogether consonant with Richer's admission of the choreographic confusion found within hysterioepileptic and hypnotic symptomatology. Hysterioepilepsy's fungible physical manifestations—"A Proteus which presents itself in a thousand forms and which we cannot seize" in any single patient, as Briquet had it—were indeed so profligate as to be impossible to fully notate even within Richer's exhaustive tabular exegesis, undermining attempts to choreographically map the illness.[87]

As noted in Chap. 3, hysterioepilepsy and its cousins only existed in their complete form within the virtual, Platonic theatre which Charcot constructed using multiple physical demonstration examples and representations. The more fungible, daily, epiphenomenal manifestations of hysterioepilepsy were in turn comprehensible only through the invocation of this distant, intangible ideal. Far from resolving the nature of hysterioepilepsy, Richer's synoptic table brought to light the tenuous nature of its choreographic description, failing to erase the tension between the essentially *non*-Platonic nature of arational illness and hysterioepilepsy's supposedly perfect, archetypal performance in virtual space. Meige and Achilles Souques eloquently summarized the situation by observing that hysterioepilepsy offered "tumultuous manifestations which seemed indescribable and which were to be provisionally catalogued."[88] Even within the Salpêtrière's voluminous studies, the diagnostic portrait of hysterioepilepsy remained fundamentally provisional, subtly changing with each performance.

Richer attempted to limit the disruptive, "indescribable" expansiveness of hysterical choreography by invoking an orderly, mechanical metaphor. He likened his patients to eighteenth century automata—they "resemble those music boxes which possess several different airs, but are disposed" to replay them "in an invariable order."[89] Former Salpêtrière intern Charles Richet concurred, noting of the patients that:

> The regularity of their frenetic deliria cannot fail to surprise. Upon hearing the vociferations, the screams of these demoniacs, upon seeing their furious contortions, it seems that only chance steers this frightful drama. In reality all is foreseen, regulated, determined; all of this disorder proceeds with the mathematical precision of a well-wound clock.[90]

The essential integrity and "regularity" of hysterioepilepsy may have been difficult to discern at first, but it was hidden within its "mathematic" temporal manifestations, which Charcot went so far as to describe as "monotonous." For the trained medical observer, the surprising incompleteness of the individual clinical cases documented within the *Iconographie* and the *Études cliniques* did not seriously detract from hysterioepilepsy's status as a real diagnostic entity. Even if the numerous postures themselves exceeded medical subjugation, their musical arrangement did not. This was, however, a difficult tension to overcome, and many of Charcot's former students such as Janet later rejected the reality of archetypal hysteria.

The profligacy of hysterioepileptic choreography was in turn reflected in the clinical treatment of the illness which Bourneville and Charcot themselves performed. The *Iconographie* was full of statistical data on the patients: the frequency and duration of their fits; the volume and quality of their urinary and faecal excretions, as well as notes on foaming at the mouth, saliva, menstruation, and other "vaginal secretions"; skin and mucosal sensitivity; rectal, vaginal, and skin temperatures before, after, and during fits, as well as across the body; dynamometric measurements of muscular force, the relative weakness and atrophy of limbs; measurements of bodily proportions; transcriptions of patients' delirious ramblings; electrostimulation readings; and more.

Bourneville's laborious documentation graphically conveyed the uncertainty of the clinician in the face of hysterioepileptic performance. Every aspect of the patient's physio-behaviour and anatomy was duly recorded, from diet to physiognomy, in the hope that it might provide a decisive diagnostic clue. Bourneville and Charcot discovered indeed that true epilepsy was typically distinguished from hysterioepilepsy by a rise in body temperature which occurred immediately before epileptic seizures, but not hysterical ones.[91] This obsessive clinical description of the body, all but annihilating the body itself through the reification of its clinical signs, also gave the *Iconographie* its voyeuristic character. Charcot, for example, specifically instructed that a "meticulous surveillance" be made of Geneviève when she was suspected of secretly eating without the surveillants' knowledge, and gave a similar regime for the equally famous patient Justine Etchevery, who was believed to be retaining her excrement.[92] This approach was highly productive, prompting Geneviève—ever the consummate performer—to ingest as much as possible before her medical audience, whilst Etchevery was definitively diagnosed with hysterical ischuria (urinary retention). This form of surveillance thus became the ideal towards which clinical practice was directed (though the vast patient population meant that only a handful of case studies actually received such treatment). Nor indeed was the therapeutic regime directed at hysteria any less expansive. Bourneville and his peers administered a bewildering array of tonics, drugs, and procedures (ether, opium, morphine, chloroform, chloral, amyl nitrate, atropine, iodide, potassium, and bromides—the latter having some effectiveness against epileptoid conditions); hydrotherapy; electrostimulation; magnetotherapy; metallotherapy; diet; physical interventions such as the cauterization of contracted sphincters in the larynx, vagina, and urethra; and more.

Neurology at the Salpêtrière was inescapably theatrical at every level. Although Bourneville and his peers were insistent that hysterioepilepsy was not in itself a sexual disease, the possibility that hysteria's secondary sexual characteristics might be significant could not be ignored. Every physical tic and occurrence had to be witnessed and recorded within the voluminous case notes which Bourneville and his associates produced so that such symptomatic events might be (in Richer's terms) translated into "objective" reality—whether those involved were entirely comfortable with this situation or not. The sexualized theatre of the Salpêtrière was a classic example of what Michel Foucault describes as the "perpetual spirals of power and pleasure" which surveillance engendered.[93] Doctors could not afford to be squeamish. They stared straight into the sexual core of hysteria whilst nevertheless distancing themselves from the reciprocal voyeurism and narcissism that their gaze necessarily activated.

Charcot's practice therefore functioned not only, as Foucault has famously observed, to "hystericize" the patients and their bodies, but also to hystericize medical practice itself.[94] Hysterioepileptic performance and its various cousins (epilepsy, chorea, Tourette's syndrome, hemiplegia) stimulated an ever more thorough theatricalization of the clinic. Hysterical performance forced the physician to adopt the role of spectator, even as Charcot's anatomoclinical approach encouraged patients themselves to perform for his medico-dramatic edification.

Hysterical performance at the Salpêtrière existed, therefore, within a mutually reinforcing regime of techniques and disciplines, performances and symptoms, gazes and treatments, which responded in turn to the forces exerted by hysteria—even as Charcot and his peers attempted to subjugate such diseases. It was, for example, Geneviève herself who first proposed the practice of applying pressure to the area of the belly above the ovaries as a technique to arrest hysterical attacks, and her invention was soon enthusiastically adopted not only for this function, but also to stimulate new seizures for the purposes of pedagogy.[95] Charcot's genius lay partly in his positive response to these pressures—though he nevertheless insisted upon re-establishing his authority over Geneviève by claiming that her self-compression was a merely an instinctive, naive precursor to the now thoroughly medicalized practice of "ovarian compression." Patients nevertheless made constant entreaties in the wards for Charcot ("my doctor," in Geneviève's words) to come and halt their fits or deliver other therapies, undermining this medical hierarchy of power.[96] The contradictory, unresolved nature of hysteria, its dynamic, "indescribable" character meant that the clinic as a whole came to function as a kind of mnemonic theatre in which hysterioepilepsy and the other dynamic diseases were endlessly reperformed because no single performance—textual or otherwise—could fully capture neuropathology's essential totality. Medical practice at the Salpêtrière became itself a somatic *idée fixe*, the clinicians hypnotized by the image of a disease whose performative manifestations seemed to endlessly slip out of their full conceptual grasp.

Whilst the *Iconographie* opened by taking the reader on an orderly tour through the gates of the Salpêtrière and into the wards, Bourneville closed volume three by moving the reader to tracts from the early modern witch trials and demoniacal inquisitions, republishing illustrated descriptions of "Sabbath journeys of witches" featuring accounts of meetings with hideous demons, and of witches mounted on enchanted goats soaring through stormy skies.[97] Far from containing hysterioepilepsy, even the conclusion of the *Iconographie* called forth further performances, exceeding conventional space, time, and logic. Patients and doctors, readers and students, all seemed hypnotized by visions of the imperious hysterioepileptic body and its extraordinary staging.

NOTES

1. Hillman, 163–183.
2. Ruth Harris, *Murders and Madness* (Oxford: Clarendon Press, 1989); Ann-Louise Shapiro, *Breaking the Codes* (Stanford: Stanford University Press, 1996); Katherine Taylor, *In the Theater of Criminal Justice* (Princeton: Princeton University Press, 1993); Georges Gilles de la Tourette, *L'épilogue d'un procès célèbre (affaire Eyraud-Bompard)* (Paris: Progrès médical, 1891).
3. Aragon and Bréton, 22.
4. Goetz et al., 180–1.

5. On the impressive publishing machine behind the Salpêtrière school, see Julien Bogousslavsky, ed., *Following Charcot* (Basel: Karger, 2011), 187–201.

6. This description is based upon the copies held at Assistance publique des hôpitaux de Paris from Bourneville's estate, and those at the Bibliothèque Charcot (available online). The *Iconographie photographique de la Salpêtrière* (Paris: Progrès médical, 1875–1880), 3 vols—hereafter cited as *IPS*—was initially sold by limited subscription so there are minor variations among extant editions.

7. Simon-Dhouailly, ed., 107–112; Goetz et al., 177–184; Goldstein, *Console*, 363–374; Ruth Harris, "The 'Unconscious' and Catholicism in France," *Historical Journal*, 47.2 (2004): 331–54.

8. Désiré Bourneville, "Étude sur les arthropathies," *Revue Photographique des Hôpitaux de Paris* [hereafter *RPHP*], 3 (1871): 9–18, 52–61, 67–77, 120–24, 243–49; Jean-Martin Charcot, "Clinique médicale: De la contracture hystérique," *RPHP*, 3 (1871): 193–203.

9. See Marshall, "Priestesses," 410–426.

10. The likeness to Wittman is not strong and at least one other figure in this painting has been misidentified. Asti Hustvedt's *Medical Muses* (NY: Norton, 2011) provides a useful survey of the lives of these women, though Hustvedt somewhat conflates the actions of her principal subjects with others, including patients treated in August Voisin's psychiatric wards rather than Charcot's own neurological clinic. Alphonse Baudouin, "Quelques souvenirs de la Salpêtrière," *Paris médical*, 56.21 (23 May 1925): 518–519; Francisco Germiniani et al., "Where is Gilles? Or, the Little Mistake in a Copy of Brouillet's painting *A Clinical Lesson at the Salpêtrière*," *Arquivos de Neuro-Psiquiatria*, 71.5 (2013): 327–329.

11. *OC*, vol. 10, pp. 286–291.

12. *IPS*, vol. 2, p. 29.

13. *OC*, vol. 12 [BC], p. 173.

14. *IPS*, vol. 2, pp. 31–41.

15. *IPS*, vol. 2, pp. 40–41.

16. *OC*, vol. 12 [BC], p. 150, vol. 13, pp. 437–483.

17. Charcot, *Charcot*, 56–59, *OC*, vol. 12, pp. 50–51, vol. 13, pp. 15–16, 437–483; Howard Kushner, *A Cursing Brain?* (Cambridge, MA: Harvard University Press, 2000).

18. Henry Meige, "La genèse des tics," *Journal de neurologie* (5 June 1902): 201–6.

19. Artaud, 15–32.

20. Meige, "Genèse," 201–6.

21. *IPS*, vol. 1, p. 16.

22. A. de Watteville, "Critical Digests and Notices of Books: *Études cliniques sur la grande hystérie ou l'hystéro-épilepsie*, par le Dr Paul Richer," *Brain*, IV (1882): 508–9.
23. *IPS*, vol. 1, p. 44.
24. *IPS*, vol. 2, p. 40.
25. Douglas Lanska, "Early Controversies Over Athetosis," *Tremor and Other Hyperkinetic Movement*, 2 (2012) and 3 (2013), <http://www.tremorjournal.org/>.
26. *IPS*, vol. 2, p. 31; Michel Bonduelle and Toby Gelfand, "Hysteria Behind the Scenes: Jane Avril at the Salpêtrière," *Journal of the History of Neurosciences*, 7.1 (1998): 16–42; Jane Avril [1933], *Mes mémoires* (Paris: Association Les Bourlapapey, 2014), <http://www.ebooks-bnr.com/>.
27. John Waller, *A Time to Dance, a Time to Die* (London: Icon, 2009).
28. *IPS*, vol. 3, p. 210.
29. Charcot and Richer, *Démoniaques*, 34–38.
30. *IPS*, vol. 2, pp. 34–41.
31. *OC*, vol. 1, p. 229, 391–2, vol. 12 [BC], p. 130, vol. 13, p. 353–4.
32. *OC*, vol. 12, p. 299–316.
33. *OC*, vol. 13, p. 5; Shakespeare, *Hamlet*, III.i.
34. *IPS*, vol. 1, p. 57, vol. 2, p. 146; *OC*, vol. 12, pp. 170–1.
35. *IPS*, vol. 2, pp. 69–89.
36. *OC*, vol. 4, p. 179.
37. Stanley Finger, *Origins of Neurosciences* (NY: Oxford University Press, 1994), 227–231.
38. F. de Ranse, "*Iconographie photographique de la Salpêtrière* [revue]," *Progrès médical*, 7 (1879): 331.
39. Sufferers included Br...; Madeleine R...; Adéle; Josephine Delet...; Emma St...; Jeanne Til...; Magdeleine Mull.... *IPS*, vol. 2, pp. 7–30, 42–62.
40. *IPS*, vol. 2, pp. 18, 62.
41. Charcot, *OC*, vol. 12, pp. 112–125, *Charcot*, 26–46.
42. Finger, *Origins*, 196–7.
43. Owsei Temkin, *The Falling Sickness* (Baltimore: Johns Hopkins, 1971), 257–259.
44. Raymond, 68.
45. Charcot, *OC*, vol. 1, pp. 325–6.
46. Paul Richer, *Études cliniques sur la grande hystérie ou l'hystéro-épilepsie* (Paris: Delahaye et Lecroisnier, 1881), 1.
47. Ibid., 31.
48. Ibid., 31.
49. *OC*, vol. 11, pp. 390–429.
50. *IPS*, vol. 2, p. 143.
51. *IPS*, vol. 2, pl. XV.

52. *OC*, vol. 3, p. 17.
53. Herbert Blau, "The Audition of Dream and Events," *TDR: The Drama Review*, 31.3 (1987): 62.
54. *IPS*, vol. 1, p. 117.
55. Watteville, 509.
56. Micale, *Approaching*, esp. 164–5, "Hysteria Male," 208–211.
57. Showalter, *Hystories*, 56–67.
58. Jan Goldstein, "Foucault Among the Sociologists," *History and Theory*, 23 (1984): 182–8.
59. Didi-Huberman, in Charcot and Richer, *Démoniaques*, 133–147.
60. *IPS*, vol. 1, pp. 69–70.
61. *IPS*, vol. 2, pp. 135, 162–163.
62. *OC*, vol. 12, pp. 258–260, vol. 12 [BC], pp. 350–1, 361.
63. *IPS*, vol. 1, pp. 97, 123–124, vol. 2, p. 189.
64. Arthur Gamgee, "An Account of a Demonstration on the Phenomena of Hysterio-Epilepsy," *British Medical Journal* (12 Oct 1878): 547.
65. Richer, *Études* (1881), 188.
66. *IPS*, vol. 2, p. 101.
67. *IPS*, vol. 3, pp. 189–190.
68. Richer, *Études* (1881), 94–102, 125–8, 334–7.
69. Charcot, *OC*, vol. 12 [BC], pp. 176–7.
70. Watteville, 510; Charcot, *Charcot*, 106.
71. Richer, *Études* (1881), 162.
72. Ibid., 94.
73. A similar exchange prompted Charcot's former student Freud to explicitly theorize such relations according to transference and countertransference. Freud, *Standard*, Vol. 7, pp. 1–122, Vol. 11, pp. 139–152.
74. Clarétie, "Vie," 130.
75. Richer, *Études* (1881), 128, 336–7; *IPS*, vol. 1, p. 103, vol. 2, p. 100.
76. *IPS*, vol. 2, p. 150.
77. Richer, *Études* (1881), 99.
78. *IPS*, vol. 2, pp. 131–2, 191.
79. *IPS*, vol. 3, p. 81.
80. *IPS*, vol. 1, p. 157; Richer, *Études* (1881), 163.
81. Trillat, 153; Richer, *Études* (1881), pl. V.
82. *IPS*, vol. 1, p. 81, vol. 2, pp. 49, 74, 114–115.
83. Richer, *Études* (1881), 206, 220, 408.
84. Ignotus [Platel], 386.
85. Richer, *Études* (1881), 167.
86. *OC*, vol. 12, p. 219.
87. Briquet qtd in Richer, *Études* (1881), VII.

88. Achilles Souques and Henry Meige, "Jean-Martin Charcot," *Biographies médicales* (May–July 1939): 344.
89. Richer, *Études* (1881), 158.
90. Charles Richet, "Les démoniaques d'aujourd'hui," *Revue des deux mondes*, 1.37 (15 Jan 1880): 358.
91. *OC*, vol. 1, pp. 377–382.
92. *IPS*, vol. 1, pp. 64–65; *OC*, vol. 1, pp. 283–298, 340–354, vol. 9, pp. 289–295, vol. 12, p. 122.
93. Foucault, *History of Sexuality*, 44–45.
94. Ibid., 55–56, 104, 120–2, 146–7.
95. *IPS*, vol. 1, p. 92; *OC*, vol. 1, pp. 332–5, vol. 12 [BC], p. 175, vol. 13, p. 276.
96. *IPS*, vol. 1, p. 59.
97. *IPS*, vol. 3, pp. 231–247.

CHAPTER 7

Hysterical Hypnosis and Infectious Theatre

1 UPSTAGING ART

Historians have generally treated Charcot's work on hypnosis either in isolation from the rest of his practice or collapsed it into his studies on hysteria, or they have characterized hypnosis as an exotic fringe pursuit, unrepresentative of Charcot's thinking as a whole. The multiple ways in which theatre was active throughout Charcot's practice, however, reveal a strong connection—or perhaps a dialectic—between such dichotomies as Charcot's Platonic nosology, the theatre of anatomoclinical diagnosis, pedagogy, and hypnotic performance. Hysterioepilepsy and hypnosis were fields in which the performative tensions within Charcot's discourse over-all were especially pronounced. Even more than hysterioepilepsy itself, hypnosis was a particularly theatrical disease. Through the demonstration

Some of the material from this chapter has appeared in Jonathan W. Marshall, "Beyond the Theatre of Desire: Hysterical Performativity and Perverse Choreography in the Writings of the Salpêtrière School, 1862–1893," in Peter Cryle and Christopher Forth, eds, *Fin de siècle Sexuality: The Making of a Central Problem* (Newark: Delaware University Press, 2008), pp. 42–60, and "The Priestesses of Apollo and the Heirs of Aesculapius: Medical Art-Historical Approaches to Ancient Choreography After Charcot," *Forum for Modern Language Studies,* 43.4 (Oct 2007): 410–426, reproduced here by kind permission of Delaware University Press, and Oxford University Press, respectively.

© The Editor(s) (if applicable) and The Author(s) 2016
J.W. Marshall, *Performing Neurology,*
DOI 10.1057/978-1-137-51762-3_7

of lethargic hyperexcitability, Charcot was able to create something like the unadorned, unreflective athletic theatre which Richer and Meige were later to espouse. The skilled performance of the hypnotized subject threatened, however, to displace artistic hierarchies and to overturn the superiority of healthy performance over diseased behaviour.

This exchange between normality and pathology via performance was possible because Charcot constructed the body as a potentially amorphous entity which acquired its proper neurophysiological behaviour. The healthy performance of movement was not therefore an inherent somatic phenomenon. It was learnt and so could be erased, lost, or sympathetically contaminated. Anatomoclinical investigation revealed hysterioepilepsy to be a form of neuromotor aphasia, a physiological analogue of the linguistic aphasia which Charcot's forerunner at the Salpêtrière, Pierre Paul Broca, had proven was caused by lesions of the cerebral convolutions. Charcot's model of the performative body was therefore a destabilizing one, threatening to render his own performance as a potentially infective form of kinesthetic display.

The Salpêtrière school provided the pre-eminent definition of fin de siècle hysteria. However, it was the issue of hypnosis and magnetism that provided the most controversial, spectacular aspect of Charcot's pedagogy. It was principally Charcot's work on magnetic sleep that prompted Félix Platel to compare Charcot to Wagner in his article "Cabotinage" in the newspaper *Le Figaro* (see Chap. 1). The debate on hypnosis took on a particularly lurid character shortly after Charcot's death in 1893 when Charcot's star acolyte, Georges Gilles de la Tourette, received a non-fatal gunshot to the neck from a former patient of Salpêtrière neuropsychiatrist Joseph Séglas. The weapon was fired by hysterioepileptic hypnotic subject Rose Kamper-Lecoq. Depicted on the cover of the newspaper *Pays illustré*, several journalists characterized this sensational event as a "drama" in its own right, and Tourette himself never fully recovered.[1] At a 1901 lecture on the horror plays authored by his colleague Alfred Binet, Tourette was reported in the newspaper to have shown "nervous impatience" with the audience and had to be shown off stage. He was eventually relieved of his medical post, and was escorted by Jean-Baptiste Charcot to Lausanne Psychiatric Hospital, where he died in 1904 as a result of tertiary syphilis and paralytic dementia. Tourette's spectacular decline all but sealed the posthumous demise of Charcot's theories on hysterioepilepsy, although as we shall see, certain of these concepts continued to circulate well into the twentieth century.

The third volume of Bourneville's *Iconographie photographique* focused upon the remarkable hypnotic behaviours to which Charcot's critics so objected. The most striking patient from the *Iconographie* was Blanche Wittman, known for her virtuosic, somnambulic performances rather than for her delirious hysterical fits, the exemplar for which was Geneviève. The visiting Belgian scientist Joseph Delboeuf compared Wittman to the subjects of David Ferrier's public experiments in the electrostimulation of frogs' legs and chimpanzee brains, which Charcot had observed at the Seventh International Medical Conference in 1881.[2] Indeed, Charcot's student Charles Féré claimed that "the hypnotized hysterical woman is to be regarded as 'the psychological frog,'" or neurological guinea pig in today's parlance.[3]

Charcot's interest in hypnosis stemmed from his appointment to the committee investigating Victor Burq's technique of magnetotherapy. Claude Bernard, the famous professor of experimental medicine at Collège de France, charged Charcot, together with Jules Luys and Amédée Victor Dumontpallier, to prepare a report for the national Biology Society in 1876.[4] Burq was the latest in a long line of physicians who experimented with "animal magnetism." The term originated with Franz Mesmer, who contended that all animate and inanimate bodies have positive and negative poles, much like a planet or a battery, about which "magnetic fluid" flowed. Illness was seen as the product of blockages or interruptions in this electromagnetic flow. Hypnotism, originally termed "magnetic sleep" by Mesmer, was a state induced by physical proximity to skilled human magnets such as Mesmer himself, which facilitated a crisis or seizure in the patient, and in this crisis, normal magnetic flow would be restored. Mesmer's principles had been firmly rejected by the Faculty of Medicine, the Royal Society of Medicine, and the Academy of Sciences in 1784, but popular and lay magnetists continued to practice throughout the eighteenth and nineteenth centuries.[5] Whilst Paris' scientific institutions refused to revisit the topic, Burq's novel contention that non-human agents—magnets and metals—might be able to impersonally produce some of these therapeutic changes prompted Bernard and his peers to reconsider.

Charcot and his colleagues confirmed the original commissions' findings that Mesmer's magnetic fluid did not exist. Charcot nevertheless concluded that the nature of the hyper-responsive psychonervous state which Manchester surgeon James Braid had named "hypnosis" was essentially the same as the exaggerated psychophysiological behaviour found in hysterioepilepsy itself. Hysterical contractures were therefore functionally indistinguishable from those generated through hypnosis. Charcot and Richer would go on to claim that "the hypnotic state" was "nothing else but an artificial, experimental nervous state," an essentially physiological product of the hysterioepileptic nervous disposition.[6] One could reproduce hysterical behaviours under controlled conditions through hypnosis. Subjects were moreover affected by the application of electromagnetic agents such as magnets, electricity, and metals, which redirected electroneural transfers within the body. Only true hysterioepileptics, however, exhibited true hypnosis.

Hypnosis could be brought on by visual fixation—staring into the patient's eyes or having the patient gaze at a bright point of light—or psychosensorial shocks, such as being surprised by what Charcot characterized as an "intense, sudden and unexpected noise," or other vibrating acoustic force which disrupted nervous function. Gongs and large tuning forks were frequently used in this fashion to induce hypnosis during the lectures. Richer noted that this had a weakening effect, as the sound waves were "communicated throughout the body by the vibrations propagated by the resonating box" attached to the tuning fork.[7] Claretie noted that the susceptibility of hysterioepileptics to such disorientating hypnotic agents meant that whilst large-scale musical processions and the like were no longer held at the Salpêtrière, sometimes at the annual balls held for the patients, "A blow upon a great drum has the effect of a gong and the dancers freeze there, in catalepsy, in sudden plastic poses" (see cover image of this book).[8] Under the influence of such provocations, *la grande hystérie* gave way to *la grande hypnose*—an equally circumscribed series of ordered hypnotic states.

Hysteria and hypnosis had been associated with near-miraculous sensory perception since Mesmer's time, and it was his contemporary from Strasbourg, the Marquis Chastenet de Puységur, who discovered the altered state of "somnambulism" in which patients revealed special knowledge and abilities not otherwise available to them. This allegedly included the capacity to diagnose themselves and others through a form of clairvoyance. Puységur also pioneered the use of physical and verbal "suggestion," which was to become the chief method of inducing hypnosis employed by Charcot's rival in Nancy, Hippolyte Bernheim.

Whilst Charcot categorically rejected Bernheim's conviction that hypnosis could be a benign, even therapeutic state closely allied to supersensory perception, Charcot's own findings were hardly any less striking. The Salpêtrière school did accept that the disorders of perception exhibited by hysterics could at times generate extraordinary sensitivity to certain stimuli. Possibly even more remarkable, though, was the ease with which the cerebral hemispheres could be differentially affected under hypnosis, generating bilaterally asymmetrical behaviours which could be transferred from one side of the body to the other using magnets and other agents. As ever more spectacular phenomena emerged within these clinical experiments, Charcot adopted an increasingly paternal role, overseeing work carried out in his name by Féré, Gilles de la Tourette, Alfred Binet, Pierre Janet, Georges Guinon, and August Voisin in the fields of hemicatalepsy; hemilethargy; transfer; and doubling or duplication of the personality ("*dédoublément de la personnalité*," also known as "*vigilambulism*") in which a different persona emerged in the hypnotic subject, independent of the waking state and its memories altogether.[9]

The first stage of *la grande hypnose* was catalepsy (Table 7.1). In this condition the subject was "as if petrified," yet her body remained supple enough to be placed in whatever position the hypnotist desired. Delboeuf claimed that Féré could manipulate Wittman "as if playing a piano."[10] Charcot and Richer noted, moreover, that it was easy to reproduce within the lecture theatre poses which were well known from the plastic arts:

Table 7.1 Synoptic table of *la grande hypnose*[a]

Stage	Induced by	Characteristics of stage
Catalepsy	Neurosensory shock (loud noise, bright light, etc.) Fixation of gaze Application of magnets	Subject silent, immobile, limbs supple and may be manipulated (plastic catalepsy) Anaesthesia (pin test)
Lethargy	Removal of previous agent Closing of eyelids	Neuromotor suggestibility (rubbing of tendons causes contraction)
Somnambulism	Physical or verbal suggestion such as pressure to top of head	Partial imposition of position causes subject to complete larger scenario (imposing gestures of menace causes face to change, etc.) Other sensory stimuli such as coloured light, smells, and so on, may change the hallucination the patient experiences and hence the pose

[a]Translation by author

plastic catalepsy. It permits one to imprint upon the subjects the most varied attitudes, likely even to satisfy aesthetic laws as if the sculptors of antiquity had posed and modelled their work upon cataleptic women.[11]

This was, however, a purely reflexive action on the part of the patient, offering proof of the ancients' excellent knowledge of anatomyology rather than reflecting any familiarity with medical or aesthetic principles which the uneducated, working-class subjects of the Salpêtrière might themselves possess. Charcot claimed it was impossible that either catalepsy or lethargic neuromuscular excitability "could be simulated by our patients, who are assuredly ignorant of all the details of myology."[12] The specifics of neuromuscular embodiment constituted arcane information known only to those trained in its subtleties. Binet's casual observation that one of his patients possessed textbooks on the various forms of paralysis, however, cast serious doubt upon this central tenet of the Salpêtrière school.[13]

Charcot and his peers routinely demonstrated cataleptic anaesthesia by placing a pin into the subject's body—occasionally, though uncharacteristically, causing a large amount of blood to flow. This not only offered a dramatic physical demonstration of the reality of hysterical anaesthesia, but it also allowed Charcot, Richer, and Bourneville to explain the apparent resistance of earlier heretics to this venerable test of demonic possession. The insensibility documented by the Inquisitors was recognized as a hysterioepileptic "stigmata," a term which Charcot and Bourneville retained from their Catholic precursors.[14] The body in performance could not lie—unlike the notoriously unreliable speech of hysterics.

Subsequent removal of the hypnotic agent or closing of the subject's eyes rendered her lethargic. This second state offered even more impressive somatic evidence of the veracity of Charcot's theory, as the patient became highly responsive to the physical excitation of nerves through touch. Any nerve or tendon so stimulated would contract. Delboeuf claimed that this rendered Blanche "a veritable representation or piece [*pièce*] of the living laboratory," enabling one to "perform an exploration of the human body as minute and more demonstrative than that which one can perform using a cadaver."[15] The athletic theatre of living anatomy which Richer was later to propose in his lectures at the École des Beaux-Arts was made flesh through the performance of lethargic neuromotor excitability at the Salpêtrière from 1876 onwards.

Charcot claimed that the neurophysiological responsiveness of lethargy meant that it "became possible" for him "to experimentally intervene in cases of this type," creating "in all its simplicity, the machine man dreamed of" by Enlightenment physician Julien Offray de la Mettrie, which "we [now] have before our eyes."[16] Such comparisons were widespread amongst physicians and commentators, who equated patients with dolls, mannequins, clocks, marionettes, photographic plates, waxes, music boxes, pianos, and more. The hysterioepileptic offered physicians unparalleled access to the mechanisms of physical coordination. The hypnotized subject was both literally and metaphorically an automaton, dramaturgically manipulated by the medical demonstrator for the purposes of research and pedagogy, with doctors often playing the role of platonic Pygmalions to these "expressive statues" and Galateas.[17]

The third phase of somnambulism was hardly less spectacular than its predecessors. Somnambulistic patients became pliable, living, "expressive statues." The hypnotist could manipulate the subject's face or gestures, and she would then alter her total kinesthetic posture so as to be in harmony with the details suggested by the hypnotist. As Richer explained, physiognomic electrostimulation of lethargic individuals caused "the whole body to enter into the action, and to complete through gesture the expression of the face," whilst Charcot observed that the reverse was also true—the expression of "the face ... follows the attitudes which are imprinted throughout the whole body ... putting it into harmony."[18] Janet characterized this form of hypnotic behaviour as "pure mimeticism," representing a "rudimentary form of consciousness" manifest through nervous responses.[19] Here, as with athetosis and the "illogical movements" of hysterical seizure, expressive communication and action was manifest within the harmonic relations of the body itself, independent of the will. As Fulgence Raymond observed, the patient was affected by a profound "clouding of the self" which left the psyche accessible only to subconscious, physical, sensorial stimuli.[20] Charcot noted that although his subjects executed "the most complicated and the most varied automatic acts," they produced only "the illusion" or "appearance of voluntary acts, more or less premeditated."[21] Their reactions were rather dictated by a simple nervous reflex loop akin to the knee-jerk response. As Charcot explained, "The hypnotic experiments thus become the most beautiful demonstration of the automatic function of a part of the brain."[22] For the Salpêtrière physicians, the sensorium of the body constituted the main part of the individual's subconscious, with actual consciousness being a circumscribed function of the higher brain.

Richer's ideal of this "Pygmalion" form of medical representation became a dramaturgically embodied reality in these hypnotic demonstrations. Hypnosis offered, therefore, an ideal model for the theatre of the neurological body which Richer, Charcot, and Meige proposed. Hypnosis was a performance transcendent even of the psychic volition of the performer. The hypnotic subject was the perfect non-reflective actor, her physical and emotional expression being transparently visible—"pure and intense," in the words of visiting doctor George Robertson.[23] As former Salpêtrière intern Charles Richet explained, "The anger of a somnambule is the typical, ideal form of anger, and his expressive physiognomy is such that the sentiment which animates him is forceful and unmixed."[24] The somnambule's lack of self-awareness was also what rendered the patient hysterical. Charcot's construction of hysterioepileptic hypnosis existed therefore in a paradoxical dialectic with true, aesthetic performance, at once superior to it in its visible purity, its physical perfection, and its accuracy, yet fundamentally diseased and so inferior to healthy aesthetic expression. Though historian Jacqueline Carroy has identified a small number of subjects outside of the Salpêtrière whose hypnotic behaviours were treated as actual aesthetic phenomena in their own right—notably the "trance dancers" Madelene Guipert and Lina de Ferkel—these individuals constituted exceptional, avant-garde cases, departing from the dominant aesthetic values of fin de siècle conservatives like Charcot.[25] Richet, for example, stressed that although the hypnotic subjects performing in popular theatres as "divinators" might have resembled those Charcot presented, they were in fact "sick, and their true place is in a hospital for the mad," whilst Gilles de la Tourette published in the *Annals of public hygiene and legal medicine* an account of a diseased, "monomaniacal dancer" who repeatedly returned to the Moulin Rouge's balls and whose chaotic exhibitions constituted a sort of minor seizure.[26]

Charcot's patients enacted a dazzling array of rhetorical tableaux, as well as offering delirious, declamatory demonstrations of somnambulistic suggestibility—though this was a more pronounced feature of Luys' presentations at la Charité than at the Salpêtrière. One Salpêtrière internee, for example, was renowned as "the cat-woman" for her pathological tendency to behave like a cat when in the somnambulic state—a refracted representation of a traumatic incident in which she accidentally crushed a cat in her hand—whilst an ex-soldier under the care of Charcot and Guinon "mimed scenes of military life."[27] Patients responded to medically imposed suggestions such

Fig. 7.1   Sketches by Loreau of hypnotically suggested hallucinations, *IPS*, vol. 3, pp. 182–183. Courtesy of the Boston Medical Library in the Francis A. Countway Library of Medicine.

as that there were snakes at their feet, babies in their arms, and so on, performing extravagant acts for the edification of the audience (Fig. 7.1). Upon their return to consciousness the patients also typically related hallucinations which were in harmony with the expressive dramas through which the physicians had guided them. Green glass held over their eyes often engendered visions of gardens, for example, whilst red slides produced violent, bloody nightmares. Although different manifestations occurred in different patients, hysterioepileptic hypnotic performance was remarkable in its adherence to common, recurrent rhetorical tropes and gestures: suggestions of a kiss caused patients to raise their fingers to their lips, suggestions of a garden caused them to bend to smell flowers, and so on.

Guinon explained that—as with hysterioepilepsy as a whole—these hypnotic performances were so complicated in their total, kinesthetic expression, that they defied written representation:

> This description ... cannot provide a perfect idea of either the [hypnotically] provoked or the spontaneous delirium of this patient. One must see him walk,

gesticulate, painting upon his mobile physiognomy all of the diverse emotions he passes through, one must listen to him speak with that cheeky accent of a Parisian worker, skeptical, a "joker" but a "good fellow" at heart. It is truly an extremely interesting spectacle and one which words alone cannot render.[28]

The most subtle vocal modulations of the hysterical performer, his "accent" and his indefinable aura of good-natured, proletarian comedy, could not be rendered through "words alone." It was on the contrary a form of expression rooted in the neurophysiological body itself, rather than the rational language of the conscious will. It was indeed relatively uncommon for Charcot's own hypnotized patients to give voice to rational language at all. The aural performances of Charcot's demonstration subjects were more generally confined to cries of fear, laughs of merriment, or short exclamations ("Mama!" "Help!" etc.). Guinon's more linguistically expressive patients, by contrast, stretched the definition of hysterioepileptic physiology, rendering Charcot's medical nosology increasingly problematic.

Like Zumbo's waxworks of the plague, the hyperrealism of hypnotic performance threatened to engender a representational crisis. Delboeuf, for example, claimed that:

No actor, no painter, neither Rachel [Félix] nor Sarah Bernhardt, neither Rubens nor Raphael has achieved this power of expression. This young girl realized a suite of tableaux which erased with *éclat* and force the most sublime efforts of art. One could not dream of a more striking model.[29]

Actresses like the famed Rachel were not hysterioepileptics themselves, but such figures were in danger of being upstaged by their ill peers. For Delboeuf, the "force" of the hypnotized subjects' physical expression was such that it threatened to erase ("*effaçaient*") the entire history of art. Existing beyond art, representation, or even rational scientific description, commentators like Delboeuf found the medical theatre of the hypnotized hysterioepileptic to surpass both fiction and the real, engendering a potential rupture in the mimetic relationship between sign (aesthetic performance) and referent (diseased reality, here manifest *as* performance).

2   APHASIA AND THE REHEARSAL OF GESTURE

The disturbing proximity between diseased, hypnotic performance and aesthetic performance was sealed by a highly revealing observation made by Charcot. He noted that in the case of lethargic neuromuscular excitability and other hypnotic behaviour, "by the repetition of these experiments, this phenomenon is likely to acquire a high degree of precision and intensity." Lethargic phenomena were therefore part of one's "reflex nature, the use of which facilitates its development and which perfects it."[30] Richer concurred, observing that lethargic responses were "perfected under the influence of repetition," or in the case of Meige's ticcer O., it was the "force of repetition" which "changes the voluntary act into an automatic habit, the initial motive for which is soon lost." The diseased subject not only performed for his or her medical audience, but he or she became trained in the perfect execution of this performative display through the rehearsal and repetition of reflex actions, as was the case in ballet rehearsal or preparation for dramatic performance. Indeed, Binet would reflect in 1897 that "between the actor and the subject of suggestion there is no radical difference, but only a nuance of difference," noting that both the actor and the hypnotized subject gave him or herself over to their physically prepared psychophysiological other.[31]

This surprising admission was, however, entirely consistent with the construction of neurological function at the Salpêtrière. In 1884 Charcot began what a reporter from *La gazette des hôpitaux* described as "a series of semi-philosophical and semi-medical lectures" on the relation between the idea, its representation as a word, and language as a neurophysiological system: "It is the great problem of the relation between the exterior world with the thinking being, the *not me* with the *me.*"[32] Such topics had previously largely been dealt with from a psychiatric or alienist perspective, but Broca's demonstration in 1861 of the association of language dysfunction with the lesions of the cerebral convolutions had brought the topic under the purview of anatomoclinical neurology.

Charcot identified language as an explicitly kinesthetic process, a term which Henry Bastian had proposed in 1880 to describe how information subconsciously received from the muscles by the central nervous system helped to guide execution of movement. The normal expression of ideas occurred through the harmonious invocation of a series of mnemonic signs or "images," in Charcot's words. Janet observed that Charcot "distinguished within language *sensorial* phenomena, the hearing and sight of the word, and *motor* phenomena, motor images of articulation and writing."[33] These "images" consisted of an "auditive image," derived from the initial stage in the acquisition of language, namely first hearing a word spoken aloud; the "visual image," generated by first seeing the object to which the spoken word referred; and finally a "motor image," produced by the physical sensations of first speaking the word for oneself and so naming the object. The individual became linguistically whole by metaphorically adopting Adam's role in echoing God through naming the beasts of the fields which God had created for him, stepping onto the linguistic stage of which he had previously been an audience member. Language was learnt by individuals themselves performing what they had first witnessed being performed by others—presumably the subject's parents. This essential trilogy of embodied memories was then supplemented by additional, secondary mnemonic images: "graphic" images or a visual image of the written word, and a motor image of producing that sign; "musical images" for those so gifted; and so on. Charcot observed that most individuals were strongest in one or other of these linguistic–mnemonic systems. It was this which lay behind Charcot's famed description of himself as a *"visuel"*—a term which he also used to describe his patients.[34] Charcot rightly concluded that his own kinesthetic memory was strongest in the visual field, his mnemonic system functioning in a way akin to the cameras which he employed throughout his practice.

Charcot's was an explicitly sensorial understanding of language, unlike the earlier, more conceptual linguistic theories proposed by René Descartes and others. It was inconceivable under Charcot's proposals that one could develop language if one did not possess a healthy sensorium. Charcot figured the body and self as a psychosensory ensemble with no fully pre-existing form as such. Instead, corporeality acted as a set of pathways and systemic alliances which tended the organism towards a functional but provisional unity—what the Salpêtrière alienist Joseph Séglas called "coenesthésie," and which he considered the "fundamental basis of the personality."[35] The healthy relationship between the individual and the world was therefore mediated through somatic memories such as those associated with language, thereby effecting a tenuous balance between "diverse kinesthetic sensations."[36] The construction of subjecthood itself, however, was not central to Charcot's own concerns; he was more focused on neuromotor pathologies. These concepts were laid out in more detail after Charcot's death by Séglas and Janet.

Broca had built on the work of the early nineteenth century pathological anatomist Jean-Baptiste Bouilliard, identifying a causative link between lesions of the convolutions and linguistic impairment. It was Broca who first proposed the terms aphemia and verbal amnesia. Charcot went on to propose that this localized syndrome could be further divided into four types, each associated with a particular linguistic "image," which he hoped to eventually trace to specific sites within the convolutions.[37] There was "verbal deafness," corresponding to the loss of the memory of the auditive image of the spoken word; "verbal blindness," or loss of the visual image of the written word; "aphemia," associated with an absence of the motor image of the spoken word; and "agraphia," the loss of the graphic motor image.[38] Linguistic auditive amnesia therefore resulted in an inability to understand, repeat, or write out dictated speech; linguistic visual amnesia led to the loss of written comprehension, the ability to read out loud, or the capability of copying written text; linguistic motor amnesia caused dysfunction of voluntary spoken language, of reading aloud, or of reciting a text whilst writing it; and graphic motor amnesia generated the inability to compose through writing, to write dictation, or to copy out a text.

Charcot observed, however, that patients frequently developed personal habits which aided them in overcoming the loss of one or other linguistic image. An agraphic patient, for example, was able to struggle through reading written text by tracing the words as she read, using her graphic motor memory to supplement and partially re-establish her visual memory of written signs, whilst another individual recited the words aloud to himself, employing his vocal-motor and auditive memories to help re-create his lost graphic visual memory. Charcot explained that the woman was effectively "projecting in some way onto the paper the interior image" of the written word "and fixing it there by the drawing," whilst for the man "the equivalent of the auditive [image] replaces the equivalent visual [image] of the word."[39]

It was not only motor images associated with writing or speaking words which could be forgotten and reacquired. Aphasia at the Salpêtrière typically presented itself as a complication of other, more wide-ranging neurological disorders (astasias, pareses, paralyses, etc.).[40] More significantly, Charcot proposed that it was "the mental motor representation which necessarily precedes the accomplishment of all movement," the representation "of kinesthetic notions" being the first stage in the reproduction of movement as well as communication.[41] One had to be able to recall throughout the sensorium the kinesthetic experience of executing a movement in order to be able to repeat it again. It was therefore no surprise that Charcot's lethargic demonstration subjects had to be hypnotized several times before they exhibited lethargy in all of its kinesthetic fullness, or that the ticcer O. had to enact a movement several times before it took on its true, pathological form. Individuals had to craft an initial motor image of these experiences to fully express them.

A similar reasoning underlay the use of athletic training and "vibratory medicine" at the gymnasium which Charcot had commissioned for the Salpêtrière. Raymond noted that Charcot was an innovator in the use of physiotherapy, following on from the experiments of Bastian and Armand Trousseau in employing various techniques for the "re-education of the muscles."[42] Physical retraining (or what Meige called "psycho-motor discipline") was particularly efficacious for hysterioepileptics because no severe, long-term somatic impairment of muscular potential existed within the patient. The sensorium could therefore readily take up new memories. One consequently used the:

> gymnastic method, in a case of hysterical paralysis, in order to revive, in the cortical motor centers, the motor representation of movements which the patient thinks himself incapable of executing.[43]

As Meige and Edouard Brissaud later put it, one must "replace an absurd and excessive motor action with the same act executed logically and correctly."[44] Electrical devices were developed at the Salpêtrière to further facilitate this end, employing what one journalist described as the "new process of the treatment of certain affections of the nervous system by mechanical vibrations."[45] One such machine consisted of a heavy, four-inch tuning fork attached to a battery which caused it to vibrate and sound. Rationally applied musico-physical force of this kind was another agent for the erasure of pathological kinesthetic memories and paralyses. Several of Charcot's peers also commended the use of dance therapy to encourage physical hygiene. Charcot thus reclaimed the potentially pathological effects of Wagnerian total theatre (*Gesamtkunstwerk*) for therapeutic ends. The Salpêtrière gymnasium acted as an important aid to the recovery of proper sensorial memory, helping to break down the kinesthetic *idées fixes* of hysterioepilepsy and its endless repetition of useless, embodied memories such as those exhibited by Augustine and Geneviève. An embodied tabula rasa was produced, upon which a new, healthy sensorium could be built through gymnastic training.

Charcot thereby constructed the body as an inherently linguistic, performative entity. Charcot's understanding of kinesthetic awareness thus conformed with Judith Butler's concept of performative iteration, in which it is the repetition of original acts which shape and define the body of the subject. Each performance of a healthy or diseased gesture constitutes, in Butler's terms, a "sedimentation, and congealment of the past" which acts as a "citation" of a prior gesture which was either violated or reinforced in each subsequent performance. As Butler cautions:

> In a sense an "act" is always a provisional failure of memory ... every act is to be constructed as a repetition, the repetition of what cannot be recollected, of the irrecoverable, and is thus the haunting specter of the subject's deconstitution.[46]

The neurological body literally reperformed already extant, physical linguistic acts—namely the original motor images. The neurological body's performative repetition of these images ordered and shaped both the body and the sensorium—or disordered and erased it, in the case of hysterioepilepsy and other diseases. The body itself acted as a theatre of memory within Charcot's discourse, a site where neuromuscular coordination was first performed and then mnemonically reinscribed through its replay. Charcot's own multimedia pedagogy in the lecture theatre echoed this construction and was itself composed so as to appeal to all the different aspects of the audience's memory: visual, aural, and kinesthetic (see Chap. 4). Neuromuscular disorder in general, and hysterioepilepsy in particular, constituted a form of neuromotor aphasia—hence the frequent association of hysteria with mutism and agraphia.

The difficulties presented by this understanding of myological coordination are clear from Butler's analysis of performativity. Neuromotor images were not transcendent of their performance by individuals, unlike Charcot's own Platonic nosology of anatomy and disease. Performance did not exist outside time. "On the contrary," each act could generate "a provisional failure of memory," reordering the body and the sensorium. In Butler's terms, the healthy neurological body was always haunted by the "specter" of its performative "deconstitution," in which a new performance had the potential to override pre-existing neuromotor images, re-forming the body from moment to moment. A body which was, to use Butler's phraseology, sedimented and congealed through performance, was also one which was threatened with fragmentation or radical alteration through reperformance, so crossing into the realm of hysterical mimicry, hyperreality, or chaos. This was partly why so soon as 1895—only two years after Charcot's death—Janet noted that few practitioners would still agree with Charcot in placing such an important "role in motor, kinesthetic images" for the healthy development of language.[47] Charcot's formulation was brilliant, but also destabilizing, like performance itself.

3   INFECTIOUS PERFORMANCE

Charcot and his peers warned of the danger of kinesthetic contagion made possible by the performative nature of the body. As noted earlier, many of Charcot's patients suffering from Tourette's syndrome, hysterioepilepsy, and even the wild-man "Lap...sonne" had become ill partly through the observation and repetition of fictional performance. They were contaminated by the acts they had observed in others, uncritically adopting them.

The public interest in magnetism and hypnotism—which Charcot himself had contributed to—meant that, in Tourette's words, "veritable mini-epidemics of that neurosis have been declared."[48] Turin, for example, was struck by an outbreak of hysterioepilepsy caused by "theatrical representations of somnambulism" by travelling magnetists.[49] Although Charcot argued that healthy individuals could not normally be hypnotized, he nevertheless contended that the witnessing of somnambulistic demonstrations could act on an individual's previously concealed latent disposition towards neuropathology—what Charcot called diasthesia—and so cause disease onset. Charcot cited as an example the patient Mme P..., who had submitted to a magnetizer's passes at a fairground.[50] Following a seizure, Mme P... was, in Charcot's words, "tormented by the desire to leave her domicile and go in search of he whom she considered as her master." This was sign enough of her illness for both Charcot and her husband. Monsieur P... complained of this scandalous development to the police and she was eventually hospitalized. Charcot also cited an epidemic in Chaumont-en-Bassigny, Champagne, where a public performance by a magnetizer created "a sort of *active hypnotic mania* which penetrated right into the town college."[51] Local boys began hypnotizing each other, leading one to "promenade almost nude through the square of the Bank of France ... and other provincial jokes of this type."[52]

Perhaps the most famous example of imitative hysterical pathology was the outbreak of demonic possession amongst the Ursuline nuns of Loudon, 1634–1637, which Charcot, Richer, and Bourneville retrospectively diagnosed as hysterioepileptic delirium.[53] This event had become thoroughly imbricated within the popular mythology of hysteria, as evidenced by novelist Gustave Flaubert including within his novel the detail that his classic fictional hysteric Mme Bovary had acquired her unrealistic romanticism during her period with the Ursulines nuns of Rouen (close to the site of another outbreak of hysterical demonism in 1647 at Louviers).[54] Loudon was moreover Geneviève's own home town, Geneviève exhibiting what Charcot described as "rudimentary ... tarantism."[55] Richer claimed that during the Middle Ages, chorea and hysteriochorea were found throughout Europe along the highways leading to saints' sanctuaries such as St Guys' in Ulm because:

> Bands of beggars plunged into vice and into misery took advantage of that illness in order to persist in their vagabondage. They imitated the gestures and the convulsions of the sick, and spread the contagion throughout the country in their search for adventures.[56]

Significantly, Richer made no meaningful distinction between wilfully imitative activity and organic contagion. The beggars in question often did not in fact suffer from true chorea upon the commencement of their travels, but as Richer's statement made clear, their imitation of "the gestures and the convulsions of the sick" spread "the contagion." Hysteriochorea and similar diseases were just as infectious as organic chorea because both types of condition engendered essentially the same kinesthetic feelings and images in the performers themselves, as well as in those observers who were strongly struck by their actions. These sensations were, according to Charcot, "eminently contagious."[57] *Fictional* performance could therefore generate *real* dynamic pathologies.

As a consequence of this, Charcot and his peers sought to limit such abuses by lobbying for a ban on hypnotic displays by non-medical personnel, citing approvingly a recent Italian law to this effect. Charcot claimed that a prohibition against "magnetizers' public representations" would be an "excellent and perfectly opportune thing"—although such legislation was not passed in France until 1900.[58]

Charcot introduced his denunciation of magnetizers' public "theatrical representations" with the observation that one "could easily multiply the examples of this kind." These forms of contagion "have become almost banal in their frequent reproduction during recent times."[59] Charcot nevertheless implied that those most at risk from such ill effects tended to be active participants or demonstration subjects of these public demonstrations, or those with a hereditary predisposition to hysterioepilepsy. This distinction was not entirely tenable in the context of his kinesthetic theory of movement and contagion, however, and was moreover not the case with all of the students from Chaumont-en-Bassigny.

The members of the Salpêtrière school therefore saw imitation as one of the chief propagative agents of hysterioepilepsy—even in the case of relatively commonplace and normative behaviours. This disturbing possibility that merely watching displays of hysterioepilepsy or hypnosis could have pathological effects was implicit within the critique of public hypnotism offered by Charcot, Gilles de la Tourette, Séglas, and others. If—as critics from Aristotle to Diderot had long maintained—spectacular identification with the actors of a drama could have kinesthetic affects, then it followed that even the neuropathologist's own lectures could have infectious consequences upon his own audiences. Charcot himself, however, seemed not to have admitted this possibility, even showing Mme P… herself in a hypnotized state to his spectators without offering any words of caution regarding how to view this performance.

4   ANCIENT THEATRE, DIONYSIAN PATHOLOGY, AND THE AVANT-GARDE

One of the most thorough discussions of the relationship between theatre and illness was provided by Henry Meige in his writings on pre-modern religious practices in pamphlets such as *The Possessed Blacks* (1894) or on the Delphic Oracle in his *The Pythia of Delphi*, the latter being presented at the 1921 Congress of Psychiatrists and Neurologists of France and French Speaking Nations in Luxembourg.[60] Meige continued to author such accounts of hysteria throughout his tenure at ENSBA, long after Charcot's model of hypnosis had otherwise been overturned. Whilst Charcot's contention that susceptibility to somnambulism was confined to hysterical subjects did not outlive him, other aspects of the Salpêtrière model, such as the link between pathological imitation and the theatre, were to endure.

Despite its title, comparatively little of *The Possessed Blacks* was devoted to African women (the title is feminine in the French). On the contrary, Meige collapsed the distinction between European prehistory and contemporary Africa by shifting between examples of Muslim ceremonies, Negro rituals, and those from ancient Greece and Rome, treating all of these phenomena as representing essentially the same level of cultural sophistication. This was indeed a common tenet of European anthropology as it had developed in the wake of Broca—who was also founder of the Paris Anthropological Society—though Meige's inclusion of primitive Mediterranean culture was somewhat atypical. Meige's contention was that "neuropathic manifestations" played a "capital role … in the history of religions and in the practices of all cultures."[61] Meige built here on his collaborations with Charcot, the latter arguing during his own lifetime that not only Catholics, but also the behaviour of America's so-called dancing "Jerkers" at various "Methodist Camp-meetings … offer in their crises the most frightful postures" which closely resembled the hysterio-epileptic pathology of Rosalie Leroux and others.[62]

The evidence which Meige and his peers amassed in support of their Positivist, anti-religious stance illustrated that theatre and dance themselves also had their origins in such "neuropathic manifestations." Meige's discussion dealt with riotous African dances, St Guys' dance and tarantism, ancient Egyptian and Hebrew rites, as well as the worship of Mohamed, Dionysius, Bacchus, Apollo, the Pythi, the Coryphées, and the Maenads, as documented by the playwright Euripides (*The Bacchae*) and others. Meige characterized Bacchic and Delphic rites using almost the same language with which he described Tourette's syndrome:

It was a frenzied dance, with extravagant gesticulations, a debauchery of bizarre postures and attitudes which were convulsive, improbable or indecent, where the equilibrium of the body, like the equilibrium of the mind, seemed to defy the laws of nature.[63]

Similarly, amongst the "strange devotees" of Bacchic dance and Delphic rituals, "numerous also are those who, predisposed to neuropathology, fall under its enervating influence."[64] As with the gongs and tuning forks of Charcot's own demonstrations, within these ancient theatrical rites:

Under the influence of a strong excitation, and by the sound of stunning music or by the whirling of a frenzied dance, man sometimes loses possession of himself.

With the normal subject, this distraction is fugitive or incomplete … But with the neuropath, and above all with hysteria, the loss of consciousness may be total.[65]

Drawing on evidence revealed by the French excavations at Delphi from 1892 onwards,[66] Meige described a situation where acolytes were physically and sensorially shocked by the "discordant music," giving themselves over to these pathological kinesthetic expressions, upsetting their psychokinetic "equilibrium" in a shared, contagious performance. Such barely structured, highly energetic performances agitated all of the senses simultaneously through physical contact, noises, vibrations, and scents (censers, together with volcanic gases rising through the floor of Delphi's Temple of Apollo), overwhelming even a healthy sensorium. Such scenographically intense performances were diagnosed as generating a:

> psychoneuropathic tumult, constituted by an expansive delirium, exteriorized by prophetic words [*paroles ominales*] and rhythmic gestures, with a singular contagiousness, and to which our old alienists justly applied the title choreomania.

> In this way, the dance, which is rightly numbered amongst the arts, can, if it oversteps the mark, tip into gregarious pathology.[67]

Diathesics were the most likely to completely lose both their equilibrium and their conscious control over mind and body, falling into hallucinations of unseen beings, delirious prophecies, and the "convulsive attitudes" of hysterioepilepsy: "The *delirious individual* became a *prophet* ... The *hallucinating individual* became a *clairvoyant* ... The *hysteric* became *possessed.*"[68]

However, Meige did concede that the origins of modern drama and dance lay within such mad rituals, which were often dedicated to the patron of Greek theatre: Dionysius. Meige's German contemporaries Friedrich Nietzsche and Richard Wagner saw such performances as a model for Wagnerian opera, balancing Apollonian and Dionysiac principals within a totalizing theatrical experience. Meige, for his part, noted that over the course of history, these disorganized revels eventually developed into "sumptuous ... processions, theatrical representations."[69] Even within Arabic rituals, Meige found "the elements of a rudimentary theatre" akin to "the dramatic art" which had grown out of the feasts in honour of Bacchus and his peers. The neurologist did not, however, feel that the hysterioepileptic beginnings of theatre and dance meant that all such performance was necessarily pathological:

> It would surely be excessive to attribute a neuropathic origin to all the manifestations of choreography. Dance has been with us throughout the ages; it exists and will always exist amongst all peoples. It is a gymnastic and an aesthetic. On this [hygienic] basis we cannot praise it highly enough.

> But alongside those elegant and balanced dances, there are others in which the disequilibrium of the body seems intimately tied to the disequilibrium of reason.[70]

Meige therefore differentiated between pathological aesthetics and "balanced [*pondérées*]" arts. Dance which contributed to the "disequilibrium" of body, mind, and sensation was "intimately tied" to neuropathology. Any choreography which included the poses identified by Richer as part of the somatic palette of hysterioepilepsy ("convulsive attitudes," the *arc de cercle*, etc.) was similarly suspect. In an earlier essay in the *Nouvelle iconographie* tackling similar subjects, Meige had observed that although the Ancient Greeks were "seduced by harmonious forms," their art only rarely reflected asymmetrical shapes.[71] Léon Roblot, a lecturer at the Joinville military academy with which Richer, Londe, and Marey collaborated, even recommended that physical therapists employ a "sportive eclecticism" so as to avoid asymmetrically overstimulating any single body part or physiological system through dance or other gymnastic methods.[72] Bilateral asymmetry such as was common in hysterioepilepsy, lethargy, and catalepsy was another sign of pathological choreography.

Meige's standard of gymnastic normality echoed therefore the aesthetics of the contemporary French *beaux arts*: classical ballet, opera, and mainstream theatre. The emergent styles of the avant-garde, however— Decadent cabaret, Symbolism, Naturalism, Expressionism, Futurism, and so on—largely coincided with pathological aesthetics. This thesis received its fullest treatment in Max Nordau's *Degeneration,* first published in 1892 shortly before Charcot's death and reviewed in *La revue philosophique de la France et de l'étranger.*[73] Nordau was a former student of Charcot's and went on to become co-founder of the Zionist movement in 1897. In *Degeneration,* he proclaimed that:

> the physician [of] nervous and mental maladies, recognizes at a glance in the fin de siècle ... tendencies of contemporary art and poetry, in the life and conduct of the men who write mystic, symbolic and "decadent" works, in the attitude taken by their admirers in the tastes and aesthetic instincts ... the confluence of two well-defined conditions ... with which he is quite familiar, viz. degeneration (degeneracy) and hysteria, of which the minor stages are designated as neurasthenia.[74]

For Nordau, the work of such an artist was unambiguously a product of his pathology. One did not need to "measure the cranium of an author" to diagnose him; reading his prose was sufficient.[75] Nordau argued therefore that Impressionism, for example, "becomes at once intelligible to us if we keep in view" Charcot's Tuesday lessons on "the visual derangements in degeneration and hysteria," namely nystagmus or "trembling of the eyeball."

The distinction between such psychokinetically contagious practices and Charcot's lectures was, however, unclear. As Robertson commented, "many felt it was impossible to investigate hypnosis without contamination."[76] Platel and others did not accept Charcot's separation of his own ostensibly rational, level-headed discourse from the Dionysian possibilities of hysterioepileptic theatre.

Hysteria had long been considered an inherently mimetic or imitative illness. Long-term hysterical symptoms characteristically closely resembled organic pathologies such as true chorea, paralysis agitans, or sclerosis in plaques, except that there was no discernible somatic damage to the tissues in question. Muscular atrophy rarely occurred and contractures disappeared under the influence of seizures, anaesthesia, electrostimulation, or hypnosis. Charcot described hysterioepilepsy as "that great simulator," noting that an appropriate alternate title for the disease was "neuromimesis."[77] Hysterioepileptics had both "the taste and the aptitude for simulation." Charcot presented the audience to his Tuesday lessons a wealth of differential diagnoses in which he isolated the original organic illness from its hysterical "double," which consisted largely of post-traumatic complications—or as Raymond put it in more theatrical terms, hysterioepilepsy frequently appeared under the "mask" of apparently incurable organic illnesses.[78] It was for this reason that Charcot and his peers placed such emphasis upon such complex or unlikely physical manifestations as lethargy or anaesthesia. These symptoms allegedly could not be simulated.

Richer agreed with Pierre Briquet that in the dormitories, "It suffices for a patient to have seen a gesture once, to have observed an act which has struck her, for her to imitate it involuntarily." Richer weighed up the issue as follows:

What must one make of the influence of imitation on the form of their attacks? ... We are far from contesting the influence of imitation on the production of nervous illnesses ... but ... Its action is only able to exert an effect upon the exterior form, on the phenomenal expression and not upon phenomena's nature itself. If the meeting of several hysterical patients in the same service, in the same room, may, at certain moments, aggravate the illness... the plan has been drawn up in advance by the malady itself, and [the illness itself] has not been able to accept anything but surface modifications as a result of the exterior environment.[79]

According to Richer, psychokinetic echoing produced relatively little more than "surface modifications" or the "ornamentation" of an otherwise invariable "edifice" or patterning of hysterical symptoms. Charcot similarly maintained that the main difficulty which this presented for the clinician was not falsehood per se, but rather a tendency for patients "to amplify" or "exaggerate" their symptoms.[80] Subjects tried to "imprint" their performances with "the cachet of the extraordinary, of the marvelous," in the hope of gaining attention. The solicitude formerly lavished upon ecstatics, demoniacs, and their peers tended to aggravate such behaviour. The medical practitioner was therefore advised to master his subjects and not cater to their whims, placing patients within a quiet, "quasi-monastic" environment. Charcot supported this contention with a case history in which he noted that once a hysterical anorexic he was treating had accepted, in her own words, that "papa and mama had ... gone" and "I saw that you were determined to be master," she then submitted to his therapeutic will, eating again and eventually recovering.[81] However, Charcot was unwilling or unable to draw the conclusion that his own pedagogic use of hysterioepileptic subjects within the amphitheatre violated this principle, encouraging patients' performative exaggerations.

Raymond used the same metaphor to describe the deceptive character of hysterioepilepsy as that which Aristotle had used to describe healthy mimesis—namely the mirror:

> In the case of a mirror the product of the reflection can be the equivalent of a reality, a real image, or a simple fiction, that is to say an optical illusion which one calls a virtual image, it is the same with the hysteric whose auto-suggestion can lead to a paralysis, to a contracture which is real or purely imaginary.

> Which is to say that in the second case there is simulation, but let us impute it to the illness [itself] and not to the conscious, reflective perversion of the patient.[82]

The reality or otherwise of "the reflection" or "virtual image" produced in the body of the hysterioepileptic depended upon one's point of view. A "paralysis" or "contracture" generated by hysterioepilepsy was "real" in that it was an objective quality of the hysterical body. It was nevertheless "purely imaginary" in that "the illness" itself created a convincing simulation of organic paralysis where no actual, underlying damage existed beyond the destabilization of the healthy, harmonious sensorium: a kinesthetic equivalent of an "optical illusion." The hysterioepileptic behaved like a defective camera, turning in upon herself. Optical deformations transformed into somatic simulacra.

Hysterioepilepsy was therefore an inherently paradoxical condition in that it constituted a real illness of psychomotor representation and coordination, yet its very nature was defined by the deceptive performance of organic physical diseases. The hysteric was in a sense trapped within the mirror of representation or upon the stage of Plato's cave, unable to move from empty performance into natural mimesis. As Richet observed, the pathological susceptibility to hypnosis rendered the subject:

> like an actor who, taken over by madness, imagines that the drama he plays is a reality, and not a fiction, and he has been transformed, body and soul, into the character he is expected to play.[83]

Hysterioepileptics were entranced by their own performative skills, yet they lacked a suitable, healthy context for the expression of these acts. In terms of the Platonic construction of representation which Charcot himself drew upon, hysterioepileptic performance constituted a diseased simulacrum which erased purposeful mimesis within the naturalistic body.

Charcot nevertheless claimed that it was relatively easy for trained observers such as himself to distinguish between "real" hysterioepileptic symptoms and pure simulation. Wittman also testified to this effect in a dialogue recorded between her and former Salpêtrière physician Alphonse Baudouin, which he described as the deathbed "confession of a hysteric." Wittman angrily rejected any suggestion that she and her peers had played Charcot false:

> [WITTMAN]: Well then! what do you want to know?

> [BAUDOUIN]: It has been said that all of the crises were simulated, that the patients appeared to sleep, and that, the whole time, the patients were mocking the doctors. What truth is there in this?

> [WITTMAN]: *There is no truth, these are all lies*: if we fell asleep, if we had crises, it is because it was impossible for us to do otherwise. In any case it was not at all pleasant … Do you think that it would be easy to fool M. Charcot? Certainly, there were indeed jokers who tried it out; he threw a simple look at them and said: "Keep quiet."[84]

Despite Blanche's status as the prima donna or "queen of the hysterics"—echoed in the very form of this record as an impassioned deathbed dialogue between doctor and patient—she remained keen to publicly recognize Charcot's masterful perspicacity right up until her death, even if other documents suggested that the relationship between the patients and Charcot was more fluid than she herself conceded.

Charcot therefore possessed a blind spot within his methodology. Although the linguistic nature of the body rendered the presentation of pathological kinesthetic images inherently dangerous, Charcot did not apply this idea to his own pedagogy. The members of the Salpêtrière school appear to have believed that Charcot's own status as one of the foremost physicians of his day—and his placement of his teaching within a specifically medical amphitheatre—necessarily prevented both the possibility of deceptive exaggeration and of kinesthetic contagion. Nordau, for example, saw no contradiction in advocating on the one hand a restriction of sensorial stimulation so harsh that it included rendering dogs mute, the legislation of traffic noise, and the acoustic insulation of musical colleges, whilst at the same time championing Charcot's tireless work in spreading his findings "to the mass of cultivated persons" who frequented his presentations in the amphitheatre.[85] Charcot and his associates identified the neuropathological body as kinesthetically aphasic, whilst denying that this presented a problem for Charcot's own *"visuel"* diagnosis and pedagogy. Charcot's critics would not be so kind.

NOTES

1. Anon, "Un drame de l'hypnotisme," *Pays illustré* (8 December1893): 1ff; M.D., "La suggestion criminelle: À propos d'un drame," *Petite république* (9 December 1893): 1; Lees, 808–16; Julien Bogousslavsky et al., "Crime, Hysteria and *Belle Époque* Hypnotism," *European Neurology*, 62 (2009): 193–199; Olivier Walusinski, "Georges Gilles de la Tourette," *Histoire des sciences médicales* (2015), reproduced on <www.baillement.com/recherche/gdt_sfhm.pdf>; Pierre Chenivesse, "Grand Guignol et aliénisme," in Jacques Arveiller, ed., *Psychiatries dans l'histoire* (Caen: Presses Universitaires de Caen, 2008), 436–437.
2. Joseph Delboeuf, "Une visite à la Salpêtrière," *Revue de Belgique*, 54 (15 October 1886): 143.
3. Robertson, 506.

Charcot, Jean-Martin, and Jules Luys, Amédée Victor Dumontpallier, et al, "Rapport fait à la Société de Biologie sur la métalloscopie du docteur Burq," *Comptes-rendus des séances et mémoires de la Société de Biologie* 6.4 (1877): 1–24 and 6.5 (1878): 1–22.

4. See Adam Crabtree, *From Mesmer to Freud* (New Haven: Yale University Press, 1993), 1–82; Robert Darnton, *Mesmerism and the End of the Enlightenment* (Cambridge, MA: Harvard University Press, 1968); Eric Dingwell, ed., *Abnormal Hypnotic Phenomena* (London: Churchill, 1967), 3 vols; Alan Gauld, *A History of Hypnosis* (Cambridge: Cambridge University Press, 1992); Jonathan W. Marshall, "The Archaeology of the Abstract Body: Parascientific Discourse and the Legacy of Dr J.-M. Charcot, 1876–1969," *French History and Civilization: Papers from the George Rudé Seminar*, 3 (2009): 92–111, reproduced on <http://www.h-france.net/rude/rudevolumeiii/MarshallVol3.pdf>. Alison Winter in *Mesmerized* (Chicago: Chicago University Press, 1998) notes how hypnotic and mesmeric practice in nineteenth century Britain tended to be highly theatrical.

5. *OC*, vol. 9, pp. 305–310.

6. Richer, *Études* (1881), 375.

7. Claretie, *Vie*, 128–9.

8. *OC*, vol. 11, passim.

9. Delboeuf, 258.

10. *OC*, vol. 9, p. 399.

11. *OC*, vol. 9, p. 286.

12. Carroy, *Hypnose*, 73.

13. See Jeanne des Anges, *Soeur Jeanne des Anges: Supérieure des Ursulines de Loudun (XVIIe siècle): Autobiographie d'une hystérique possédée (Bibliothèque diabolique–collection Bourneville)*, annotations Gabriel Legué and Georges Gilles de la Tourette, préface Jean-Martin Charcot (Paris: Progrès médical, 1886).

14. "*Pièce*" commonly means a room or play, but may also designate other artworks ("*pièce de sculpture*," "*pièce de théâtre*"). Delboeuf, 258.

15. *OC*, vol. 3, pp. 336–7; Marshall, "Kleist," 261–281, "Archaeology," 92–111.

16. In Ovid's *Metamorphoses*, the sculpture of Galatea made by the artist Pygmalion came to life as he kissed it. The myth was a popular topic of nineteenth century art, notably Jean-Léon Gérôme's erotic 1890 painting.

17. Paul Richer, *Études cliniques sur la grande hystérie ou l'hystéro-épilepsie* (Paris: Delahaye et Lecroisnier, 1885), 670; *OC*, vol. 9, pp. 441–3.

18. Jean-Michel Oughourlian, *The Puppet of Desire* (Stanford: Stanford University Press, 1991), 212–213.

19. Fulgence Raymond et al, "Inauguration du monument élevé à la mémoire du professeur J.-M. Charcot," *NIPS*, 11 (1898): 410–418.
20. Jean-Martin and Paul Richer, *Contribution de l'hypnotisme chez les hystériques* (Nendeln Liechtenstein: Kraus Reprint, 1978), 405.
21. *OC*, vol. 9, p. 446.
22. Robertson, 500.
23. Richet, "Démoniaques," 368.
24. Carroy, *Hypnose*, 93–96; Marshall, "Kleist," 261–281.
25. Richet, "Démoniaques," 369; Georges Gilles de la Tourette and Damain, "Un danseur monomane," *Annales d'hygiène publique et de médecine légale*, 3.29 (1893): 268–276.
26. *OC*, vol. 11, pp. 81–100.
27. *OC*, vol. 11, p. 125.
28. Delboeuf, 124–7; Richet, "Démoniaques," 368.
29. *OC*, vol. 9, p. 387; Richer, *Études* (1885), 684; Meige, "Genèse," 201–6.
30. Alfred Binet, "Reflexions sur le paradoxe de Diderot," *Année psychologique*, 3 (1897): 295.
31. Anon, "Revue clinique hebdomadaire: Leçons de M. Charcot à la Salpêtrière sur l'idée et sur le langage," *Gazette des hôpitaux* (28 June 1884): 593–4, collection of J.-M. Charcot, Bibliothèque Charcot; see also Alfred Binet, "Les maladies du langage après travaux récens," *Revue des deux mondes* (1 January 1892): 116–132; Jean-Martin Charcot, and Alfred Binet, "Un calculateur du type visuel," *Revue philosophique de la France et de l'étranger*, XXXV (1893): 590–4.
32. Janet, 586.
33. *OC*, vol. 3, p. 191; Freud, vol. 3, pp. 12–13; Janet, 590–1.
34. Joseph Séglas, *Leçons clinique sur les maladies mentales et nerveuses* (Paris, 1895), 581.
35. Séglas, 54.
36. F. Lhermitte and Jean-Louis Signoret, "L'aphasie de J.-M. Charcot à Th. Alajouanine," *Revue neurologique*, 138.12 (1982): 893–919.
37. Janet, 584.
38. *OC*, vol. 12, pp. 162–191.
39. See Marshall, "Beyond the Theatre of Desire," 42–60.
40. *OC*, vol. 12, p. 353.
41. Raymond et al, "Inauguration," 317–323.
42. Raymond, 75.
43. Edouard Brissaud and Henry Meige, "La discipline psycho-motrice," extrait des *Archives générales de médecine* (26 May 1903), 1–4.
44. Charcot and Gilles de la Tourette also developed a vibrating helmet and chair. Historian Rachel Maines correctly identifies these machines as precursors to genital vibrators. She fails, however, to distinguish between

genital massage and the bodily applications developed at the Salpêtrière. There is no evidence that Charcot and his peers applied these devices in a sexual manner, whilst there is much to suggest they did not. A.C., "La médecine vibratoire," *Chronique médical,* 6.2 (15 January 1899): 33–42; Rachel Maines, *The Technology of Orgasm* (Baltimore: Johns Hopkins University Press, 1999).

45. Butler, *Bodies,* 244.
46. Janet, 587.
47. Paul-Camille-Hippolyte Brouardel, Georges Gilles de la Tourette, et al, "Dangers des représentations de l'hypnotisme," *Tribune médicale* (1889): 46, collection of J.-M. Charcot, Bibliothèque Charcot.
48. *OC,* vol. 9, p. 480.
49. *OC,* vol. 13, pp. 234–255.
50. *OC,* vol. 9, p. 476.
51. *OC,* vol. 9, p. 477.
52. The best account of this extraordinary theatre of ritual possession and exorcism remains Michel de Certeau, *The Possession at Loudun* (Chicago: Chicago University Press, 2000).
53. Gustave Flaubert [1857], *Madame Bovary: A Story of a Provincial Life,* trans. Alan Russell (Harmondsworth: Penguin, 1981).
54. *OC,* vol. 1, p. 342.
55. Richer, *Études* (1881), 620.
56. *OC,* vol. 9, p. 480.
57. *OC,* vol. 9, p. 479.
58. *OC,* vol. 13, p. 254.
59. See Marshall, "Priestesses," 410–426.
60. Meige, *Possédées noires,* 86.
61. *OC,* vol. 1, p. 342.
62. Meige, *Possédées noires,* 28.
63. Ibid., 30.
64. Ibid., 47.
65. Michael Scott, *Delphi* (Princeton: Princeton University Press, 2014), 263–278.
66. Henry Meige, *La Pythie de Delphes* (Luxembourg: J. Beffort, 1921), 7–8. John Collier painted an especially famous image of the prophetess falling into trance in 1891, a copy of which is currently held at the Art Gallery of South Australia, Adelaide.
67. Meige, *Possédées noires,* 87.
68. Ibid., 28–40.
69. Ibid., 30.
70. Henry Meige, "Les possédées des dieux dans l'art antique," *NIPS,* 7 (1894): 35.

71. Léon Roblot, "Recherches originales et pratiques sur la gymnastique et les divers sports à la fin du XIXe siècle," in Jean-Martin Charcot, Étienne-Jules Marey, Mathias Duval et al, eds, *Les sciences biologiques à la fin du XIXe siècle* (Paris: Société d'éditions scientifiques, 1893), 655–673.

72. Lucien Arréat, untitled review of Max Nordau's *Degenerescence* (Berlin: 1892), in *Revue philosophique de la France et de l'étranger*, XXXV (1893): 434–9; Todd Presner, "'Clear heads, solid stomachs, and hard muscles': Max Nordau and the Aesthetics of Jewish Regeneration," *Modernism/ Modernity*, 10.2 (2003): 269–296.

73. Max Nordau [1892], *Degeneration* (NY: Howard Fertig, 1968), 15.

74. Ibid., 17–30.

75. Robertson, 494.

76. *OC*, vol. 3, p. 16, vol. 9, p. 224, vol. 13, pp. 489, 522.

77. Raymond, 71.

78. Richer, *Études* (1881), 187–8.

79. *OC*, vol. 1, pp. 282–304, vol. 12, p. 138.

80. Joseph Silverman, "Charcot's Comments on the Therapeutic Role of Isolation in the Treatment of Anorexia Nervosa," *International Journal of Eating Disorders*, 21 (1997): 297–8.

81. Raymond, 71.

82. Charles Richet, *L'homme et l'intelligence* (Paris: Alcan, 1884), 237.

83. Baudouin, "Quelques," 520.

84. Nordau, 538–559.

CHAPTER 8

Theatrical Appearances and Degenerative Synaesthesia: Munthe and Daudet

1 The Anti-theatrical Critique

Historians have suggested many reasons for the rapid decline of Charcot's teachings following his death. However, there has been little discussion of the role that Charcot's theatrical diagnosis and pedagogy played in this devaluation. Whilst Félix Platel's short, influential article comparing Charcot to Wagner is well known, for a more sustained anti-theatrical critique one must look to the biographical sketches offered by Charcot's former students Axel Munthe and Léon Daudet. Although Daudet's attack relates Charcot's practice to wider issues of nationalism and race in a manner absent in Munthe's critique, the opinions offered by these two critics are remarkably similar. Both are striking in how they decry the spectacular, theatrical aspects of Charcot's discourse as a particular weakness in their former teacher's practice. It is the work of these writers that is the subject of this chapter. The anti-theatrical character of their discourse demonstrates that the tension between performance and medical description was recognized by several of Charcot's peers, who did not

An earlier version of the material on Munthe here appeared as Jonathan W. Marshall, "Hypnotic Performance and the Falsity of Appearances: The Aesthetics of Medical Spectatorship and Axel Munthe's Critique of Jean-Martin Charcot," in Catriona MacLeod et al, eds, *Elective Affinities* (Amsterdam: Rodopi, 2009), 221–242, and is reproduced here by kind permission of Brill and Rodopi publishers.

© The Editor(s) (if applicable) and The Author(s) 2016   187
J.W. Marshall, *Performing Neurology*,
DOI 10.1057/978-1-137-51762-3_8

accept the neuropathologist's attempt to resolve such conflicts through his magisterial, defamiliarizing presentation style and rigorous practice. Performance emerges as a particularly vexatious contaminant of Charcot's discourse—a contaminant which his former students would have preferred expunged from the neurologist's otherwise insightful observations. They were themselves not free from such faults, however, their own accounts having a distinctly theatrical quality.

Munthe's primary objection to performative discourse revolved around questions of truth and falsehood. To trust externalized performance was to be deceived by appearances and so become complicit with dangerously infective, iatrogenic hysterical and hypnotic pathologies. Performance did not exist in dialogue with medicine, but was alien to diagnostic veracity. Daudet, however, was disturbed by the iatrogenic synaesthesia sustained by such theatrical environments. The totalizing sensorial assault of scientific spectacle and related practices threatened to consume the audience within a fundamentally Jewish miasma of physical, racial, and psychological indeterminacy. The object of Munthe's criticism was primarily Charcot, whereas Daudet denounced French medical discourse and its effects within society as a whole. Daudet and his peers were, in Butler's terms, haunted by the "specter of the subject's deconstitution" through performance.

2   A HYSTERICAL MELODRAMA

Munthe was a successful, peripatetic physician of Swedish origin whose semi-fictionalized biography, *The Story of San Michele* (1929), is still in print today, having been translated into more than fifty-five languages. Munthe attended Charcot's lectures and visited the wards between approximately 1879 and 1883, performing "experiments in post-hypnotic suggestion and telepathy" on the patients.[1] Although he parted with Charcot on extremely bad terms, he continued to represent himself as "a pupil of Charcot's." However, Munthe's practice was more closely based on that of Charcot's rival Hippolyte Bernheim, whom Munthe also visited; it seems likely that Munthe's shift in allegiance to the Nancy school of hypnosis is in fact what led to the split between himself and Charcot.

Munthe confessed in his introduction to altering events to make them more "sensational," and his account of the dispute between himself and Charcot appears to have been embellished in this way. However, Munthe was hardly unusual in this respect, and his style echoes that of other major literary diarists such as Charcot's friends Jules Claretie and the Goncourt brothers—or indeed Daudet's own reminiscences, which were published as *Memoirs of the Literary, Political, Artistic and Medical Milieu* (*Souvenirs des milieux littéraires, politiques, artistiques et médicaux*) in 1915. Indeed, the status of Munthe and Daudet as authors of both literary works and medical accounts makes their writings particularly insightful sources through which to examine Charcot's own aesthetics, which both authors found wanting.

Munthe's approach to medical visualization was opposed to that of Charcot. This was partly attributable to the Swede's own poor vision. Munthe's poor eyesight deteriorated over the years, and he was blind from 1922 until surgery restored partial vision in one eye in 1934. Whilst Charcot used photography extensively within his practice, Munthe related that:

I have never taken any interest even in the photographs of my friends, I can at will reproduce their un-retouched features on my retina with far more exactitude than can the best of photographers. For the student of psychology an ordinary photograph of a human face is besides of scant value.[2]

Whilst Salpêtrière photographer Albert Londe claimed that the photographic plate is the "savant's true retina," Munthe found photographs to constitute a degraded, "retouched" form of mimesis—a second-order representation in Platonic terms—at one remove from the world of superficial appearances.[3] This level of reality was itself but a pallid reflection, of "scant value" in observing the essential human nature lying behind visible features. It was such essential, non-apparent qualities with which his own practice was concerned.

However, Munthe did recognize that Charcot's own use of visual analysis aided the elder physician:

Charcot … was almost uncanny in the way he went straight to the root of the evil, often … only after a rapid glance at the patient from his cold eagle eyes. During the last years of his life maybe he relied too much upon his eye, the examination of his patients was often too rapid and superficial.[4]

Munthe was suitably impressed by Charcot's "almost uncanny" ability to paradoxically use his gaze to look beyond appearances and so identify "the root of the evil"—what Henry Meige had described as "the essential contours" of a disease and all of the "elements necessary for its expression" (see Chap. 3).[5] Munthe nevertheless concluded that Charcot came to rely "too much upon his eye," focusing only upon "superficial" details and thus being deceived regarding the essence of illness, of which appearances only offered an imperfect picture. Like the chained prisoners of Plato's cave, Charcot mistook the visible shadows he observed for the real, unseen performers.

Munthe also differed from Charcot in explicitly acknowledging the sexual danger which the largely male medical profession faced in administering psychic and physical treatment to impressionable, mentally unbalanced women. Munthe noted of Charcot that "Sharing the fate of all nerve specialists he was surrounded by a bodyguard of neurotic ladies, hero-worshippers at all costs."[6] Given the poor recovery rate for neurasthenics and hysterics, Charcot had around him a veritable entourage of such "helpless women" who were "too willing to be influenced by their doctor ... [and] to hero-worship him." Munthe reflected that "Sooner or later" these dependent patients begged that Charcot have them photographed, just as their peers had been, and "there is nothing to be done, 'il faut passer là,' as Charcot used to say with his grim smile." Photography thus appeared in Munthe's account not as an aid to objective analysis, but as a sign of the physician indulging the entreaties of his hysterical patients. Nevertheless, Charcot's patrician distance caused him to remain aloof from any more problematic entanglements: "Luckily for him he was absolutely indifferent to women." Unlike the scandalous eighteenth century Parisian hypnotist Anton Mesmer, Charcot was unsullied by accusations of sexual impropriety. It was rather in the realm of performance and exhibitionism that his famed indifference came undone.

Munthe only slightly overstated the case in claiming that during the early 1880s "Charcot's famous *Leçons du Mardi* in the Salpêtrière" were "just then devoted chiefly to his *grand hystérie* and to hypnotism."[7] The Swede observed that audiences to Charcot's presentations were offered such bizarre proofs as patients who:

smelt with delight a bottle of ammonia when told it was rose water, others would eat a piece of charcoal when presented to them as chocolate. Another would ... lift her skirts with a shriek of terror when a glove was thrown at her feet with the suggestion of being a snake. Another would walk with a top-hat in her arms rocking it to and fro and kissing it tenderly when she was told it was her baby.[8]

The *Iconographie photographique* indeed featured sketches by M. Loreau of such hypnotically provoked hallucinations (Fig. 7.1).[9] Munthe was uncomfortable regarding the melodramatic nature of these demonstrations, specifically identifying them as "stage performances" in order to distinguish them from proper scientific pedagogy. The fact that hysterics were enacting essentially fictional, delusional dramas rendered their performances, in Munthe's eyes, more suited to the world of the conventional stage than science. Munthe claimed that Charcot's lessons on hypnosis were "nothing but an absurd farce, a hopeless muddle of truth and cheating."[10] Where Charcot tried to establish a distinction between performance-as-pathology versus his own presentation of these deceptive diseases, Munthe found the entire process muddled and intermixed. The essentially fictive nature of hysterioepileptic hypnotic behaviour reformulated Charcot's own representation of these phenomena in hysteria's own "absurd" image.

Munthe focused much of his narrative upon a particularly telling example of the falsely exaggerated theatrical quality of hysterioepilepsy at the Salpêtrière—an example which drew Munthe himself into the very histrionic melodramas that he deplored in Charcot's practice. Munthe cited a patient called Geneviève, although this was not the famous hysteric who featured in the *Iconographie photographique*. Geneviève Legrand described by Désiré Bourneville was an orphan, aged thirty-seven when the Swede arrived at the Salpêtrière.[11] The twenty-year-old subject described by Munthe was still in intermittent contact with her peasant parents, who believed that their daughter worked in the kitchens. Whilst it is possible that Munthe was referring to a different patient, Munthe's references to Geneviève's fame and to depictions of her in newspapers suggest that the individual represented in *The Story of San Michele* was more likely a fictional composite based upon the historic Legrand and other, younger patients such as Augustine Gleize (see Chap. 6). Munthe characterized this figure in highly critical terms:

Geneviève was sitting dangling her silk-stockinged legs from the long table in the middle of the ward with a copy of *Le Rire* in her lap with her own portrait on the title-page. At her side sat Lisette, another of the leading stars of the company. Geneviève's coquettishly arranged hair was adorned with a blue silk ribbon, a row of false pearls hung around her neck, her pale face was made up with rouge, her lips painted. To all appearances she looked more like an enterprising *midinette* [working-class girl with poor taste and lax morals] off to take a stroll on the Boulevards than the inmate of a hospital. Geneviève was the *prima donna* of the Tuesday stage performances, spoiled and petted by everybody, very pleased with herself and her surroundings.[12]

Munthe's description of Geneviève was, however, not markedly different from those proffered in the *Iconographie photographique* and elsewhere. Paul Régnard's photographs of the patients' "normal state" prior to their fits presented his readers with a gallery of well-groomed, working-class women dressed in their Sunday best. The subjects differentiated their modest, undistinguished dark dresses (mostly supplied by the hospice) with the few adornments they possessed—a string of pearls, teardrop earrings, a ribbon, a hair comb. A tendency towards extravagance was nevertheless apparent in Geneviève Legrand and the would-be aristocrat Suzanne N... from the *Iconographie*, the former of whom adopted a veil and a melancholy demeanour after her hallucinatory visitations by nocturnal, phantom lovers. Indeed, Bourneville frequently noted the narcissistic tendencies of the patients, recording that when Augustine has a seizure, "if she has a remission, she takes advantage of it to attach a ribbon to her straight-jacket; it distracts her, gives her pleasure."[13] Other commentators offered similar vignettes, recording hysterioepileptics' attention to dress, hairstyling, and conflicts between them over the possession of various adornments.

Whilst Munthe agreed with his peers that the subjects' exhibitionistic costume was a diagnostic trait of hysterioepilepsy at the Salpêtrière, he implied that it was "the Tuesday stage performances" which were primarily responsible for this, and not any underlying disease. This was an iatrogenic symptom, not an objective sign. Rather than discouraging such behaviour, Charcot and his assistants "spoiled and petted" Geneviève, lavishing attention on her and her exhibitionistic tendencies within the amphitheatre. It was not only the outward symptoms of Geneviève which caused her to resemble a *"prima donna."* She had effectively become one under Charcot's care, a tawdry performer complete with pancake make-up and a costume, featured on the cover of a magazine which specialized in theatre and caricature (*Le Rire*). Nor was Munthe alone in finding the relationship between theatrical journalism and the patients' behaviour close—Maurice Guillemot of *Le Paris illustré* likened visiting the Salpêtrière to leafing through a book of melodramatic, theatrical posters or *cartelli*:

> For the curious, the mad are clearly extras *di primo cartello* [of the highest billing] of this immense theatre of misery and pain which is the Salpêtrière ... Like portraits which one leafs through in turning the pages of an album ...[14]

Whilst Guillemot found this fascinating and intriguing, Munthe implied that the theatrical quality of hysterioepileptic pathology rendered the diagnostic category of hysteria itself misleading, composed entirely of sketched surfaces and deceptive outward displays, and unconnected with the essential traits of true clinical illness.

Munthe argued that hysterics manipulated their illness, consciously or subconsciously, so as to guarantee their status at the Salpêtrière. He claimed that when he brought Geneviève's parents to see her in the ward:

> she did not ... recognize them at first. Suddenly her face began to twitch and with a piercing scream she fell headlong on the floor in violent convulsions, to be followed immediately by Lisette in the classic *arc-en-ciel* [sic]. Obeying the law of imitation a couple of the other *hystériques* started to "*piquer* [be overcome by]" their attacks from their beds, one in convulsive laughter, one in a flood of tears.[15]

Munthe accepted that "Some of the subjects were no doubt real somnambulists faithfully carrying out in a waking state the various suggestions made to them during sleep," or in Bernheim's terms, "post-hypnotic suggestions." But most were:

> mere frauds, knowing quite well what they were expected to do, delighted to perform their various tricks in public, cheating both doctors and audience with the amazing cunning of the *hystériques*. They were always ready to "*piquer une attaque*" of Charcot's classical grande hystérie, *arc-en-ciel* [sic] and all, or exhibit his famous three stages of hypnotism: lethargy, catalepsy, somnambulism, all invented by the Master and hardly ever observed outside of the Salpêtrière.[16]

The patients' behaviour was moreover encouraged by the very setting and audience of the lectures, which Munthe found as exaggerated and exhibitionistic as the patients:

> The huge amphitheatre was filled to the last place with a multicoloured audience drawn from *tout* Paris, authors, journalists, leading actors, actresses, fashionable *demi-mondaines*, all full of curiosity to witness the startling phenomena of hypnotism almost forgotten since the days of Mesmer and Braid.[17]

Within these confusing mixed environments, actresses attended the lectures to observe the fictional performances of disordered and diseased patients, which the *comédiennes* would themselves go on to depict in their own performances outside of the Salpêtrière—as was the case with Sarah Bernhardt, who toured the wards to learn how to portray madness and somnambulism.[18]

The reflective tendency which Charcot and others had identified in hysterioepilepsy was therefore highly active within the Salpêtrière itself. Paul Richer conceded that patients tended to imitate the outward elements of their neighbours' in the wards. Munthe's description of the "leading stars of the company" as stage-managed by Charcot was not consistent, however, with Richer's comparatively mild characterization of the effects of performative imitation and mirroring as nothing more than "surface modifications" or "ornamentation" to an otherwise stable set of behaviours.[19] The vain "*midinette*" portrayed in Munthe's text deceived her doctors and frightened away anyone like her parents who might have disturbed her pampered situation.

Munthe therefore rejected Charcot's contention that the tendency to perform constituted an identifiable, pathological hysterioepileptic symptom. On the contrary, performance was an *impediment* or problem for medicine—if not an actual moral *vice* which overlay hysterical pathology proper. Far from revealing the true nature of pathology, performance stood in the way of diagnosis and treatment. The false, exhibitionistic tendencies of performance had to be unmasked before the root illness itself could be diagnosed and treated. Medicine did not therefore exist in a dialectic relationship with performance, as Charcot had argued. Performance was rather a third term, contrary to medicine and its proper subjects. The task of the physician was not therefore to analyse or reproduce performative exhibitionism within the clinic or the lecture theatre, but to look beyond this so as to examine essential behaviour and causality.

This contamination of medical practice at the Salpêtrière by performative falsehood was, for Munthe, partly due to the spatial coincidence and intermixing of different medical departments and discourses which Charcot promoted (see Chap. 3). Charcot and his followers prided themselves on the creation of a mutually supportive "Institute of Neurology," composed of interpenetrating specialist departments at the hospice. Munthe, however, strove to drive a wedge between the sections of Charcot's institute: "While condemning these Tuesday gala performances in the amphitheatre as unscientific and unworthy of the Salpêtrière, it would be unfair not to admit that serious work was done in the wards."[20] Existing largely beyond the gaze of "the public of *tout* Paris," the wards were, in Munthe's opinion, the site where the "serious work" of the hospice occurred. Here at least one might be able to "investigate many of the still obscure phenomena of hypnotism" and other neurological topics. Charcot's injudicious treatment of hysterioepilepsy, however, and the attention which he had lavished upon its external, performative symptoms had violated this delicate separation between the space proper to medical pedagogy (the private lecture room), that proper to popular spectatorship (theatres devoted to fictional "stage performances"), and that of clinical study (the closed ward). The large, open-plan wards of the Salpêtrière had indeed become virtually indistinguishable from Paris' wide "Boulevards" upon which "enterprising" young girls flirted, or the equally degraded space of the amphitheatre, for which Geneviève and Lisette had learnt "their various tricks." Visitors to the wards were greeted with the same disorientating, exhibitionistic cacophony which characterized the lectures.

Munthe noted that "Charcot was surely right" in his contention: "Experiments on hypnotism are not without their danger, to the subjects as well as to the spectators."[21] "Personally," he added, "I think public demonstrations of hypnotic phenomena should be forbidden by law." Munthe implicitly included Charcot's *own* lectures within such ill-advised "public demonstrations," though. Proper medical display should not have attracted the "multicoloured audience" present at Charcot's lessons. The "authors, journalists" and "leading actors" who frequented the Salpêtrière cultivated the toilette of "fashionable *demi-mondaines*" and other dubious social types, causing them to become virtually indistinguishable from the exhibitionistic patients whom they observed. As Fulgence Raymond had noted, hysteria tended to re-create itself in its own mirror image. Munthe found that the ward and the medical auditorium reflected each other at the Salpêtrière, and not simply the hysterical patient and the diasthesic witness observing events outside of the hospital.

The spatial contamination between ward, clinic, and lecture theatre was echoed by the mixed populace of the auditorium. Munthe felt, though, that hypnosis was relatively unproblematic where such an inappropriate mingling of dubious social classes did not occur. Unlike their lay peers, Munthe and other sedate, medical specialists were apparently immune to the effects of hysteria and hypnosis. Such cautious, learned spectators did not need the protection of law. This was a distinction which the younger physician found Charcot to be woefully inadequate in policing amongst his own audience. Like Charcot, Munthe felt that disengaged, critical spectatorship was possible. For the Swede, however, this could only be achieved in an even more rigorous, non-performative environment than the defamiliarizing theatre which Charcot strove to create through his own pedagogy. Charcot exposed an ill-prepared audience to potentially dangerous displays. The inherent excitability and dilettantism of spectators such as "leading … actresses" was likely to be exacerbated by Charcot's performances.

Munthe concluded his account of his time at the Salpêtrière by sketching a dramatic conflict between himself and Charcot. Munthe had concluded that Geneviève's status as one of the most celebrated subjects of the Tuesday lessons meant not only that she was unlikely to leave the hospital and return to the country of her own free will, but also that Charcot would have been reluctant to allow her to do so even if she had been amenable to the idea. Munthe resolved therefore to overrule the will of both Charcot and Geneviève by placing in her mind a post-hypnotic suggestion that she should attempt to rejoin her parents.

Charcot soon discovered Munthe's betrayal when a violent change in Geneviève's post-hypnotic demeanour caused the senior neurologist to investigate. After spending a sleepless night wondering why Geneviève had not come to his house on the way to the station as agreed, Munthe was summoned to Charcot's office. "Speaking very slowly, his deep voice trembling with rage," Charcot asserted that Munthe's unauthorized intervention upon behalf of Geneviève's parents constituted "a criminal offence, he ought to hand me over to the police but for the honor of the profession … he would … turn me out of the hospital, he wished never to set his eyes on me again."[22] The irony here then is that Munthe's account of how he allegedly tried to prevent one of Charcot's star patients from performing within these dubious settings was hardly any less melodramatic than the demonstrations themselves, its tone consistent with the very events which Munthe was at pains to critique. The passage was a moment of high drama and suspense within Munthe's otherwise largely sedate and wistful narrative. Charcot was not alone, it seems, in acting in a way consonant with the hysterical melodramas he treated. Munthe's discourse too was infected by a tendency towards neuropathological histrionics.

Munthe's semi-fictionalized account therefore eloquently reflected how the Salpêtrière itself was transformed into a massive theatre, complete with "leading stars" of the "highest billing," cunning girls, medical intrigues and rivalries, dramatic confrontations between protagonists, and surprising denouements—a hyperbolical, performative environment contaminated by hysteria at every level. Munthe found Charcot's pedagogy to be hopelessly contaminated by these trends, concluding that even the fact that "Charcot's theories" were "accepted without opposition by his blindfolded pupils and the public ... can only be explained as a sort of suggestion *en masse.*"[23] It was not only Charcot's hypnotized patients who engaged in performative excess, falsehood, and confusion. It was also Charcot himself who, hypnotized by his own vision of performative illness, in turn hypnotized those who came to see his presentations ("suggestion *en masse*"). Although Munthe constructed the chief means of this pathological transmission as vision, by becoming entranced by such superficial disease phenomena, Charcot and his peers had ironically become "blindfolded" to true reality. Where Charcot advocated a form of surgical vision, cutting away secondary signifiers to reveal the essential features of disease visible in performance, Munthe was distrustful of all visual and performative phenomena. Like Plato, Munthe formulated true sight as a primarily metaphoric process, largely unrelated to the vagaries and deceptions of literal eyesight as it functioned within a theatrical environment.

3   MEDICINE THAT LOOKS AND PSYCHOPHYSICAL CONTAGION

Léon Daudet's criticism of Charcot was more ambivalent but harsher than that of Munthe. Daudet had been a formal student of Charcot. However, his grievances against Charcot were also personal, political, and racial. Léon and his father—author and playwright Alphonse Daudet—resided a few doors from Charcot's Hôtel Varangeville and both families moved in the same well-to-do circles, socializing with the Goncourt brothers, the Zolas, August Rodin, and other prominent intellectuals, artists, and politicians. Both families were habitués of each other's weekly salons and the young Daudet played with Charcot's children at their homes in the Hôtels Chimay and Varangeville.[24] Alphonse, however, contracted syphilis, causing him to suffer from locomotor ataxia (tabes dorsalis). He was treated by Charcot using the latter's latest experimental treatment of suspension.[25] This painful process was pioneered in 1883 by the Odessa physician A. Motchoukowsky and was subsequently introduced at the Salpêtrière by Raymond. Patients were hung for a protracted period from a harness bearing their weight primarily through the skull, in the hope of forcing the diseased spinal column into the normal, relaxed posture dictated by gravity. Though encouraging results were achieved with some subjects, it produced in Alphonse nothing but excruciating pain and debilitating symptoms. Léon considered it a "grave error" to employ such methods in the context of his father's "physiological delicacy," whilst Mme Daudet personally admonished Charcot for prescribing such an "uncertain and atrocious ... nightmare" upon her husband. Further health complications arose in the family when Léon's son Philippe was diagnosed by Charcot's student Joseph Babinski as suffering from ambulatory automatism.[26] Philippe was to be found dead under suspicious circumstances in 1923, presumably having committed suicide.

Léon's sexual and professional life was equally tangled. Jean-Martin Charcot's daughter, Jeanne, allegedly proposed a sexual concubinage to Léon, which left Charcot *père* enraged.[27] Rather than pursue the liaison, in 1891 Léon married the much sought after Jeanne Hugo, granddaughter of celebrated Republican author Victor Hugo. However, Léon was unfaithful to his first wife and she alleged that he abused her physically and sexually. In 1894 she divorced him in favour of his confrere at the medical school, Jean-Baptiste Charcot, who was Jean-Martin's son, and whom Jeanne Hugo later separated from in 1906. Léon came to interpret the impediments to both his medical career and his social mobility as the product of a conspiracy inaugurated by the Charcots. When in 1890 Léon failed to graduate from extern to intern, he blamed the Charcots and discontinued his medical studies in favour of a career in writing and politics.

In place of the thesis a medical student would normally be required to compose as part of progression, Daudet wrote a monstrously carnal critique of Third Republic medicine—*Les morticoles* (1894). It was published in the same year as the much debated conviction for alleged treason of the Jewish officer Alfred Dreyfus. *Les morticoles* was described by journalist René Doumic as a "*succès de scandal*," and it remained in print for more than forty years.[28] Daudet sketched a Swiftian portrait of the fictional Republic of the Morticoles: an island nation supposedly united under the banner of "Liberty, Fraternity, Equality," but in fact thoroughly eaten away from the inside by the iatrogenic cancer of nihilistic, anticlerical materialism and Jewish venality:

> The Morticoles are a race of maniacs and hypochondriacs who have raised doctors to an absolute pre-eminence ... their Medical Faculty is simultaneously a parliament, a deity and a court of justice. The only monuments are hospitals.[29]

The population paid obeisance to their god at the "festival of matter." François Rabelais' warning that "Science without conscience is the ruin of the soul" served as the preface to Daudet's novel. It was an injunction which Léon contended that French society and medicine had ignored at the nation's peril, rendering previously healthy French bodies susceptible to disease, licentiousness, moral corruption, neurasthenia, degeneracy, and Jewish contamination. As one of the most powerful and well-connected physicians in France, Charcot provided an exemplar of these deplorable trends.

Leaving aside the increasingly venomous intrigues between the two families, tensions already existed between the Daudets and the Charcots due to the former's longstanding Catholic, right-wing sympathies. The Daudets sided against the Republican-affiliated Charcots in the national controversy around the 1894 trial of Dreyfus, and Léon emerged as a leading anti-Dreyfusard and anti-Semitic author. Léon not only followed his father in composing plays and novels, but moved on to become co-editor of the paper published by the integral royalist political party of l'Action française in 1908 and a member of the Chamber of Deputies, 1919–1924. The once friendly association between the families made Léon ambivalent regarding his former teacher. In his later career as a medical satirist, Daudet lost no opportunity to chastise Charcot for the latter's harsh, anticlerical materialism.

Daudet endorsed the claim made by Charcot and others that Jews had an enhanced hereditary disposition to neuropathology, particularly "ambulatory automatism" or dissociated wandering during fugue states. In his 1893 dissertation, Henry Meige retrospectively diagnosed this condition as the source of historic engravings and paintings of "the Wandering Jew," Ahasuerus.[30] Ironically, even some right-wing Jews and Zionists such as Max Nordau accepted that Jews suffered from hereditary weakness, arguing for the rejuvenation of the race through the strenuous, hygienic cultivation of physical strength and athleticism—the so-called "muscle Jew."[31] Charcot's model of neuropathological susceptibility and performative behaviours provided many critics with a useful critical tool, which Daudet employed to attack the Judaic degeneracy of the Third Republic, spread by rival authors like the Dreyfusard Émile Zola. Daudet, however, resisted Charcot's belief in widespread diasthesia amongst the general French population. This proposition provided one of the primary dramatic motivations which underlay the work of Zola and his fellow Naturalists. Daudet noted with distaste that Charcot explicitly praised Zola's study of degeneracy *L'assommoir* (*The Grog Shop)* (1878)—the seventh of Zola's *Rougon-Macquart* series—during one of the lectures at the Salpêtrière.[32] Daudet, however, would not accept that the hereditary stock of the French race was contaminated by not only external forces, but was also itself severely depleted and diasthesic—although the ill health which plagued his own family gave him good reason to fear that there might be some truth in these claims. Although many of Léon's values echoed those of his former master, he rejected both the more exhibitionistic and the overly materialist tendencies of French scientific discourse. In Daudet's opinion, the French soul was, in itself, essentially free from contagion. It was society, medicine, and racial mobility which required reform.

Daudet's description of Charcot's demonstrations in the author's medical diary, *Devant la douleur*, was comparatively sympathetic. Daudet noted with some surprise that Ignotus had attacked Charcot for "being a charlatan who puts his hysterics on show!" an allegation that left Charcot extremely unsettled at the following salon which Daudet attended.[33] The author concluded that "He was accused of playing to the gallery [*cabotinage*]. The phrase is small and trivial for a mind and a spirit of such stature." Whilst Daudet felt there was some measure of truth in Platel's criticism, he considered it a more accurate description of the work of Charcot's former colleague on the 1876 Biology Society committee, Jules Luys. The patients of the latter seemed to Daudet to be drawn from "all the nervous simulators of Paris, wily women, debauched to their bones … well-versed in the comedies of the false attack."[34] These demonstrations were in Daudet's eyes nothing but "enormous farces" in which "students prompted magical experiences in their young subjects." By contrast, Charcot emerged as a relatively restrained, proper demonstrator, his cool medical demeanour marred predominantly by his lack of overt sympathy for his patients.

Despite Daudet's apparent generosity towards Charcot within *Devant la douleur*, the author presented a grotesquely exaggerated portrait of Charcot in *Les morticoles*. The neuropathologist became "Foutange." The title was a pun on the words "*foutre*"—meaning "fucked," "complete chaos," or "crazy"—in combination with "*ange*," meaning "angel." Fout-ange therefore represented a mad or fallen angel of sorts. Daudet's protagonist in *Les morticoles* stated that this Charcot substitute "excites a vast curiosity" by presenting his lectures within an "amphitheatre, rigged up like a performance venue" or "*salle de spectacle*." People therefore attended these lessons "for fun" and not to learn.[35] Upon the fictional stage rested illustrations of grotesque poses provided by "Tismet" (Paul Richer, a possible reference to the charlatan hypnotist portrayed in *Kismet*), alongside of which was propped a sensationalistic sign advertising the grand dame of hysterioepilepsy, "ROSALIE" (based on the famous Salpêtrière patient Rosalie Leroux; see Chap. 7):

"ROSALIE

"ROSALIE

"MARVELLOUS EFFECTS ...

"THERAPEUTIC PERSUASION.

"DISCUSSION AND REFUTATION

"OF THE BOUSTIBRASIEN [Bernheimian] SYSTEM."[36]

That Foutange's staging of demoniacal convulsions and somnambulism was a source of popular amusement meant that Charcot's double lived up to his offensive title. The professional debate between Bernheim and Charcot had become a tawdry spectacle in which each strove to publicly master famous female patients such as Rosalie through hypnosis. It was nevertheless predominantly these female, hypnotized stars whom the audience came to see, and not the hypnotizers themselves. Even within this, Daudet's most damning treatise, the author declined to attack Charcot directly.

Daudet's anti-theatrical criticisms echoed those of Munthe, but where the Swede identified vision and appearances as the source of theatre's contaminating influence, the problem was more profound and tangible for Daudet. Foutange's spectators collectively "emanated a heat, a harmful odor, and an unhealthy desire to excite the nerves."[37] Theatre thus facilitated a disgusting psychophysical empathy between spectator and performer, as well as amongst the audience members themselves, in which the entire collectivity was metaphorically transformed into a noisome, pathological mass, emanating a single "odor."

Julia Kristeva argues that right-wing authors such as Daudet and Louis Ferdinand Céline—who modelled himself in part on Daudet and who also had a medical background—express a horror for the abject.[38] The abject represents a "primitive terror of maternal engulfment" that threatens the psychological and physical boundaries of first the infant "almost before those boundaries come into being"—in other words, whilst the individual is beginning to conceptualize him or herself as distinct from both the mother and those fluid, excremental inputs and outputs of his own body (shit, milk, urine, the maternal embrace, etc.).[39]

> The abject can be experienced in the loathing one feels for rotting food, filth, or excrement, defilement, muck, pus, and decay. It is not unrelated to the fear of death or of the corpse. It is the psychological foundation, Kristeva suggests, for religious concepts of sin, impurity, and pollution. To speak of it is to begin to speak of the unspeakable.[40]

The hysteric, with her grotesque, inchoate, and pre-linguistic forms of physical expression, her epigastric complications, swellings in the stomach and throat, and so on, incarnates this form of the abject, as does the Jew. Troubling concepts such as weakness, fear, and guilt are displaced onto rejected types, including women, Jews, and communists. Sander Gilman provides a related analysis of how the Jew was figured by modern anti-Semites more as a source of contamination and corporeal uncertainty than an entirely distinctive figure.[41] The ultimate fear is the Jew who, despite his or her disgusting qualities, can visually pass and so mimetically portray the Gentile subject, thereby mingling with other races and enacting literal and cultural miscegenation.

Without fully endorsing the complicated psychological theorizing which underpins these critical frameworks, it is clear that Daudet's career and his discussion of abject theatrical and racial contaminations echo many of these principals. Daudet's criticism of Charcot's lectures stems from a revulsion at the highly embodied, kinesthetic sympathies set in train by theatrical environments and the iatrogenic effects this had upon the individual's physiology. The French race was degraded by such spectacular relationships, which drew it into the ethnic miasma of the impure Jewish race. The Judaic taint was indeed not so much a racial contaminant as a violation of physical and racial distinctiveness itself. To become like the Jew was to be lost in the "unhealthy desire" and nervous excitation of a degraded and grotesquely heterogeneous, psychophysical multitude.

Writing shortly after the commencement of World War I, Daudet declared in his memoirs that even the Great Exhibition of 1889—commemorating the centenary of the 1789 Revolution which overthrew the monarchy—served only to "represent the triumph of ... the wog [*métèque*] and the Jew." A special bibliography of publications by prominent physicians was produced for this celebration of French science, medicine, and industry, and the first six volumes of Charcot's *Oeuvres complètes* were proudly displayed for sale in the pavilion.[42] Daudet, however, insisted there had been an "invasion" of the Medical Faculty by Jewish practitioners and their sympathizers, including Dr Germain Sée and "Boustibras [Botched/Dung-like]," the latter standing in for Hippolyte Bernheim within *Les morticoles*, and of whom Daudet's fictional hero declared, "I recognized there one of the kikes [*juifaillons*] who infest the land of the Morticoles."[43] Spectacular scientific displays like the Great Exhibition were therefore nothing but a cover for corrupt, nefarious forces inimical to the health of the French nation.

4   MEDICINE, SENSORY HEALTH, AND WAGNEROMANIA

It was not Charcot's lectures per se which acted as the most telling example of deracinating nervous spectacle for Daudet, but rather the operas of Richard Wagner. Wagner's works were hugely popular in 1880s Paris. Though Wagner's German origins presented an obstacle to his reception following the Franco-Prussian War of 1870–1871, many French nationalist composers such as Vincent d'Indy sought to adopt elements of Wagner's approach for their own ends.[44] By 1915, the mature Daudet was quick to critique Wagner, but his objections were not focused upon Wagner's German character as such. Léon confessed that as a young student, his heart too had been stirred by Wagner's "racial consciousness ... for having glimpsed, beyond the individual case, the vast, eternal laws that govern the races of mankind."[45] It was rather the overall ambience of Wagner's work and its musical intensity that troubled him. Daudet described it representing a widespread "scientifico-musical fever." Daudet argued that "Wagneromania" was in fact a consequence of the medical environment fostered during Charcot's lifetime and that an unhealthy obsession with the German's operas was particularly prevalent amongst his former medical peers.

Daudet concluded that although Wagnerian excitation was the apparent logical opposite of Charcot's harsh, unadorned medical materialism, the two approaches were closely allied if not essentially complicit with each other. During their studies, physicians were presented with a series of authors, all of whom preached the doctrine of an impending hereditary apocalypse. This hateful "Teutonic '*Kultur*,'" so prevalent within the Medical Faculty, was "typified" by Wagner's supporters such as Friedrich Nietzsche and other Germans, such as "that sinister being" the embryologist and proponent of evolutionary recapitulation, Ernst Haeckel, as well as Charcot's former student "the hideous Max Nordau," and others:[46]

> As a matter of fact, German metaphysics, German music, German embryology, German neurology formed one single mass of influence which in successive waves assailed the minds of my generation. After Hegel, Kant, Hartmann and Schopenhauer came Beethoven, Bach and Wagner. Following Wagner and his universe, the latter peopled by sensual abstractions and erotic visions, came ... [Carl] Weissman with his *Essays on Heredity*, [neurologist Wilheim] Erb, [physician Hermann] Nothnagel and the rest.[47]

Daudet's description of these various viewpoints as "one single mass of influence" highlighted the parallel he drew between Germanic ideology and the ill-defined miasma which Jewishness represented—Wagner's anti-Semitism notwithstanding. Wagner was indeed known to stage his works with the aim of producing a single, unified sense of operatic flow, fusing the discrete dramaturgical elements of libretto, music, set, performance, chorus, solo, and lighting into a single piece of *Gesamtkunstwerk*, or total artwork.

Although Daudet and others resisted the invasion of France by these indistinct waves of corrupt German discourses, the unrelenting materialist reductionism of Charcot and his peers created the ideal environment within which such mystic "sensual abstractions and erotic visions" might prosper:

> medicine which looks, or medicine of the spectator, headed the field. This was largely due to the widespread materialist, antireligious ambience, of a resigned or Stoic fatalism. The conditions of the nervous centers are the most directly in contact with the state of the patients' soul ... the atmosphere of faith, of miracle, of prayer, is an atmosphere of healing, rather than the atmosphere of skepticism, of incredulity, of atheism which is an atmosphere of catastrophe.[48]

Daudet echoed in this sense Munthe's denunciation of Charcot's emphasis on visual analysis, but the dangers which Daudet saw in this approach were both more widespread and more physically tangible. Wagner's fervid, mythological fantasies might seem to offer the "promise of deliverance" from the "Stoic ... atmosphere of catastrophe" promoted by the spiritually bereft "medicine which looks" as practiced by Charcot. Daudet went on to ridicule Charcot's student Charles Féré in *Les morticoles* by depicting Féré as the inflexible materialist "Ligottin [Trussed/Bound]," who argued that

"Painting is as useless as music. To represent nature, we have the healthy, loyal medium of photography."[49] Both the fervid excesses of Wagnerian opera and its apparent opposite in the inflexible visual materialism of medicine could generate in the viewer a dangerous craving for nervous excitation, depression, or sensual delusions.[50] There was an inverse relationship between the spartan mode of scientific aesthetics and the effects it had on the viewer. Daudet claimed that even the arch-materialist Charcot was affected by this trend. The neurologist possessed a certain "mystic sympathy," drawing him to study demonism, hypnosis, hypnotic transference, and super-sense, in opposition to his otherwise Positivist outlook.

Indeed, the desire to render oneself sensitive to tangible and intangible stimuli via the eyes, skin, and other senses lay behind the work of many of the Daudets' peers, such as the Decadents and the Goncourt brothers. The Goncourts, for example, claimed that through the intentional, systematic excitation of the senses, "One becomes ... a kind of skinned and chafed moral and sensitive being ... wounded by the slightest impression, all bloody and raw."[51] This potentially dangerous openness to external and internal impressions gave these authors special insight into the world, which they translated into art. Although Daudet explicitly rejected this approach as pathological, those experiences which shaped his own work were remarkably similar. Léon conceded, for example, that it was his father's syphilis that provided much of the intensity behind Alphonse's work, and Léon wrote of his own escapades at various brothels—notably an incident in Hamburg where he had a fateful encounter with an objectionable patron and which caused him to loath Germans forevermore.[52]

Despite seeing such aesthetic and medical tendencies as signs of weakness and degeneration, Léon's own authorial status derived from his encounter with death and pain. For students such as himself, versed in the texts of such on degeneration theory and evolutionary atavism, "the daily spectacle of illness, pain and death weighs heavily upon young and ardent imaginations," engendering within many of them introspective "euphoric poisons."[53] Daudet nevertheless implied in the title of his memoir that it was "the daily spectacle of illness ... and death" which had helped him to become an artist. He had stood in hospitals, "before the pain," whose brutal, fleshy reality was the stuff of his writing—as exemplified in his grotesquely carnal satire *Les morticoles*. Léon had indeed witnessed the dying spasms of his own father and pronounced him dead after examining Alphonse with a stethoscope.[54] Even so, Léon retained a distance from a complete fusion with these emotionally and sensorially stimulating events and surroundings; Léon stood *before* the pain. He did not par-take of it. Daudet's stance in this sense echoed that of his former teacher Charcot, who also sought to stand upon the stage alongside illness and death, whilst retaining a distance from it as both a lecturer and a physician (see Chap. 4). Daudet seems in this sense to have been attracted by the desire for an ecstatic union with the object of his gaze and with the operas which he had attended in his youth, but refused to give himself over to such a transfiguration because it ran the risk of erasing his national, racial, physical, and psychological identity.

5   THE DISEASED HOME

One of the most revealing details from Charcot's life which Daudet raised was his description of Charcot's taste in decor. Commentators routinely reflected upon the extravagant confusion of furnishings which adorned both Charcot's house—where he saw his private patients and hosted members of his circle—as well as at his public rooms within the Salpêtrière. Faithful students such as Maurice Debove claimed that the Charcots' "sumptuous mansion" was in fact "at once rich and severe."[55] Achilles Souques clarified this with the insistence that "the patina of time gave" the ornamentation a sense of "austerity."[56] Decorators Jean-Martin and Augustine were thereby credited with producing a deliberately restrained effect through the evocation of a tastefully faded, patrician opulence. Henry Meige explained that neither:

> luxury, nor splendor, nor modern comforts touched Charcot. He had no desire for ostentation. He appreciated above all simplicity—the charm of a harmoniously prepared home.[57]

Such positive commentators emphasized the logical harmony amongst the historical references which the couple cultivated through their adornments.

Charcot's library and adjoining study—which served as the private consulting rooms—were designed after the style of the Medici Library from Florence's Convent of San Lorenzo. This unity of design, how-ever, was not immediately apparent within the furnishings or their overall distribution, with the neurologist's study also including details modelled upon the Louvre and King René's chateau at Tascaron. Moreover, the only link between what contemporary art critic Gustave Goetschy char-acterized as the "art objects of all types and styles" and the design of

Charcot's Medicean Library lay in Jean-Martin's broadly antiquarian tastes.[58] Decorative devices featured in the *maison* were as various as objects originating from throughout the Orient (Siam, Japan, China, Tibet, India, and elsewhere); Dutch, Italian, and Arabic faience and other polychromatic enamels; sixteenth, seventeenth, and eighteenth century furniture; sixteenth and seventeenth century tapestries; and the heraldry of the Charcot family.

Meige implicitly conceded that there was a contradiction between the neurologist's harsh, spartan, rationalist medical practice and the décor of his family home. Indeed, Alfred Binet saw the increasingly widespread love of shallow spectacle and sensory stimulation as a sign of the perverse sexual compulsion of fetishism becoming increasingly prevalent. Fetishism was identified in 1882 by Charcot and Salpêtrière alienist Valentin Magnan as a neuropsychological pathology associated with general nervous debilitation, seizure, spasms, and fugue states.[59] Although hereditary in origin, Binet saw it as fostered and brought on in the sufferer by:

> the Byzantine taste for luxury, the excess of fashions, and the abuse of make-up, are different forms of a single desire, the desire so frequent in our epoch to augment the causes of excitation and pleasure. History and physiology teach us that these are marks of enfeeblement and decadence. The individual only searches with such avidity such strong excitation because his power of reaction has waned.[60]

In contrast to such depraved popular taste as was denounced by both Daudet and his former peers from the Salpêtrière, Charcot was painted by Meige as an almost saintly figure who transcended his surroundings, luxurious though they may have been. "Amidst that magnificence," Meige contended, "Charcot retained his cool simplicity."[61]

Meige's exoneration of Charcot from any possible taint stemming from his theatrical framing and home décor was, however, not accepted by Daudet and others. The professional hypnotist Charles Fiessinger observed that "If it was theatrical at the Salpêtrière, it was even more so at his home."[62] Charcot's supporter Georges Guillain conceded as much, noting that the dim, tinted glow filtering through the stained glass in the library produced:

> a slightly mysterious appearance, with lighting effects resembling those of a church. At the end of this room, Charcot sat behind a large desk; visitors and patients alike were awed and intimidated as much by the ambience as by the impenetrable mask of the Professor.[63]

The neurologist's mise en scène assured his status as a learned professor, wise in the history and lore of medicine.

Daudet, for his part, recalled childhood visits to the house, where he observed how:

> Ataxics and melancholics writhed about upon baroque prayer stools from the thirteenth century. Those with muscular atrophy stretched out their emaciated limbs upon griffons, heraldic devices or gargoyles. Imagine Gehenna in an old antique shop, the courtyard of pathological miracles lodged in a setting [*un décor*] from Victor Hugo. This spectacle and that of our [the children's] merry-making must have created a nightmarish impression in those millionaires who came to see the great master.[64]

Daudet drew attention to the sympathy between the patients who sat awaiting their turn within these gloomy surrounds and the striking, Rabelaisian mixture of late Renaissance tapestries; Gothic knick-knacks; dark, shadowy corners; and strong colours which surrounded them. "Ataxics and melancholics" blended into this hellish, medical stage set, their clawed limbs nestled beside the equally misshapen talons of carved "griffons ... gargoyles," producing a "spectacle" of "nightmarish" proportions.

Daudet portrayed this mutually reinforcing relationship between disease and medical environment even more vividly in *Les morticoles*. The city itself took on the appearance of a corpse under whose cracked, cobbled skin flowed not blood, but excrement, born by a sewage system as famous as that found in the real Paris itself:

> It is here ... The great, salubrious mouth, the cloaca through which flows the sewer system which was the glory of the Morticoles, and which was the envy of the whole world, preventing certain epidemics, but creating others even more terrible. If I were to lift up the rough skin of paving-stones, you would see underneath a powerful organism, the ensemble of electrical ducts, of engine power, steam, [and] water pipes, that our hosts have constructed in the image of those vessels of the human body that they spend their lives studying; these make the city look like a vast, outstretched cadaver.[65]

As in the accounts of the Salpêtrière discussed in Chap. 2, Daudet concluded that, as in the land of the Morticoles, so in Paris such environments were themselves diseased, the bodies of the sick becoming indistinguishable from the settings within which they lay. The doctors' offices in the vast "Hôpital Typhus," for example—which stood in for the Salpêtrière in *Les morticoles*—were "covered with … photographs and bizarre paintings representing scenes of human butchery."[66] Similarly, in his memoirs, Daudet reflected that Charcot's personal library was "filled with works on magic and demonology … An unhealthy atmosphere hung about it."[67]

Daudet recorded in *Devant la douleur* an incident that occurred as he sat in Charcot's apartments. Daudet gazed at Charcot:

> through the balcony grating at the sad, careworn man … by his lamp … all hunched up and motionless … with a facial expression that I had not associated with him before, at once burning and desperate. He had the look of one who had made a pact with the devil and was now at the moment of truth. He stayed like this for a good hour, then rose and with his heavy footsteps went out the door … I felt chilled to the bone.[68]

Léon claimed to have glimpsed through the metaphoric bars presented by the balcony railings a man entirely in accord with his surrounds. Charcot appeared to Daudet as an individual imprisoned by his own psychophysical obsessions. Within five years the Faustian neurologist was dead from cardiac angina. It was an apt end for the dramaturg of the Salpêtrière: to become one with his patients and décor of his house—a denouement which left Daudet both moved and horrified.

Viewed together, Daudet's writings offered a portrait of a more terrifying social environment than Munthe's more restrained distrust of vision according to Platonic principals. For Daudet, the spectatorship of neurasthenics and degenerates was not only deceptive and unbecoming of the dignity of medicine. Such theatrical scenarios fostered a debilitating absorption of the viewer with illness itself—a fusion far more troubling and extreme than the echoing of the Salpêtrière's wards with the boulevards and theatres of Paris which Munthe perceived. In Daudet's analysis, the world appeared as a diseased theatre set in which the bleak teachings and public lectures of morally blind materialists facilitated widespread Jewish contamination and feverish "scientifico-medical" opera. Charcot emerged from these critiques as an intensely problematic figure, who, although possessed of certain virtues, was in the final analysis the epitome of this deplorable situation—an unsympathetic, reductionist medical demonstrator whose practice readily blended into Wagnerian excess and degenerate Jewish physicality. It was ironic that Charcot, most renowned as a classifier of diseases one from another, was presented by Daudet as representative of trends which would, if unchecked, have erased the boundaries between spectator and object, audience and performer, Frenchman and foreigner, healthy and sick. The pedagogic and clinical medical theatre as interpreted through the lens of right-wing Third Republic ideology was a dangerous place indeed.

NOTES

1. Axel Munthe [1929], *The Story of San Michele* (London: John Murray, 1948), 12, 79, 169–170, 210; Gustave Munthe and Gudrun Uexküll, *The Story of Axel Munthe* (London: John Murray, 1953), 17–29, 183; Bengt Jangfeldt, *Axel Munthe* (Hildasholm/Borås: Hildasholm Museum/Centraltryckeriet, 2001), 1–16; Véronique Leroux-Hugon, "L'évasion manquée de Geneviève," *Frénésie*, 2.4 (1987): 103–112.
2. Munthe, 340.
3. Bernard and Gunthert, 65–98.
4. Munthe, 229.
5. Meige, "Charcot," 491.
6. Munthe, 230, 340.
7. Ibid., 239.
8. Ibid., 244.
9. *IPS*, vol. 3, pp. 164–184.
10. Munthe, 244.
11. *IPS*, vol. 1, pp. 49–58; Munthe, 245–252.
12. Munthe, 247.
13. *IPS*, vol. 2, p. 168.
14. Guillemot, 354–5.
15. Munthe, 247–8.
16. Ibid., 244.
17. Ibid., 239. This may be a reference to an anonymous caricature of Brouillet's painting in which Charcot faces a gigantic folded book or pamphlet inscribed with the phrase "TOUT PARIS." Olivier Walusinski, "Public Medical Shows," *Frontiers of Neurology and Neuroscience*, 33 (2014), <http://www. baillement.com/lettres/public_medical_shows.pdf>.
18. Anon, "Une heure chez Sarah Bernhardt," 609–618; Elin Diamond, "Realism and Hysteria," *Discourse*, 13.1 (Fall-Winter 1990–91): 59–92.
19. Richer, *Études* (1881), 187–8.
20. Munthe, 244–5.
21. Ibid., 259.
22. Ibid., 252.
23. Ibid., 245.

24. On the relationship between the two families, see Michel Bonduelle, "Charcot et les Daudet," *Presse médicale*, 22.32 (23 October 1993): 1641–1648, "Léon Daudet, mémorialiste de Charcot," *Revue du practicien*, 49 (1999): 804–7; Toby Gelfand, "Medical Nemesis, Paris, 1894: Léon Daudet's *Les morticoles*," *Bulletin of History of Medicine*, 60 (1986): 155–176; Kate Cambor, *Gilded Youth: Three Lives in France's Belle Époque* (NY: Farrar, 2009). On Léon Daudet himself, see François Broche, *Léon Daudet: Le dernier imprécateur* (Paris: Robert Laffont, 1992); Jean-Paul Clébert, *Les Daudet* (Paris: Presses de la Renaissance, 1988); Éric Vatré, *Léon Daudet ou le libre réactionnaire* (Paris: France-Empire, 1987); Eugen Weber, *Action française: Royalism and Reaction* (Stanford: Stanford University Press, 1962); Alphonse Roche, *Alphonse Daudet* (Boston: Twayne Publishers, 1976).

25. P. Jules Rengade, "Le nouveau traitement de l'ataxie," *Illustration*, 2404 (23 March 1889): 231–2; *OC*, vol. 13, pp. 199–218.

26. Clébert, 385–403; Broche, 381–3; Vatre, 208–210.

27. Clébert, 214, 262–4.

28. René Doumic, *Les Jeunes, études et portraits* (Paris, Perrin, 1896), reproduced on <http://obvil.paris-sorbonne.fr/corpus/critique/doumic_jeunes/body-8>.

29. Léon Daudet [1894], *Les morticoles* (Paris: Fasquelle, 1956), 7.

30. Meige, *Le juif errant*; Goldstein, "Wandering," 521–552.

31. Presner, 269–296.

32. Daudet, *Devant*, 115; *OC*, vol. 13, p. 88. Zola was more directly influenced by the work of Claude Bernard than Charcot, though he nevertheless drew on much of Charcot's work as well; see Stanton Garner, "Physiologies of the Modern: Zola, Experimental Medicine, and the Naturalist Stage," *Modern Drama*, 43 (Winter 2000): 529–542; Isabelle Delamotte, "La place de Charcot dans la documentation medical d'Émile Zola," *Cahiers naturalistes*, 73 (1999): 287–99; Bertrand Marquer, *Les romans de la Salpêtrière* (Geneva: Droz, 2008); Christopher Innes, ed., *A Sourcebook on Naturalist Theatre* (London: Routledge, 2000), 3–27, 43–53; Émile Zola, "The Experimental Novel" (1893), in Stephen Regan, ed., *The Nineteenth Century Novel* (London: Routledge, 2001), 104–117.

33. Daudet, *Devant*, 16.

34. Ibid., 10, 87.

35. Daudet, *Morticoles*, 160.

36. Ibid., 164.

37. Ibid., 162.

38. Kristeva, *Powers of Horror*; Frederic Vitroux, *Céline* (NY: Paragon, 1992), 214–222; Klaus Theweleit, *Male Fantasies* (Cambridge: Polity, 1987).

39. Diane Jonte-Pace, *Speaking the Unspeakable* (Berkeley: California University Press, 2001), 110.

40. Ibid., 110.
41. Sander Gilman, *The Jew's Body* (NY: Routledge, 1992).
42. Anon, *Exposition universelle de 1889: Index bibliographique des ouvrages, mémoires et publications diverses de MM. les médecins, chirurgiens et accoucheurs des hôpitaux et hospices* (Paris: Assistance Publique, 1889).
43. Daudet, *Morticoles*, 164.
44. Scott Messing, *Neoclassicism in Music* (Rochester, NY: Rochester University Press, 1996); Jane Fulcher, *French Cultural Politics and Music* (Oxford: Oxford University Press, 1999); Marshall, "Priestess," 410–426.
45. Daudet, *Devant*, 208.
46. Ibid., 207–219.
47. Ibid., 219.
48. Ibid., 230.
49. Daudet, *Morticoles*, 339–341.
50. Daudet, *Devant*, 207–208.
51. Debora Silverman, 36–38.
52. Vatré, 42–44.
53. Daudet, *Devant*, 202.
54. Roche, 137.
55. Debove, 16.
56. Achilles Souques, *Charcot intime*, extrait de *Presse médicale*, 42 (27 May 1925): 693–8 (Paris: Masson, 1925), 10.
57. Meige, "Charcot," 500.
58. Gustave Goetschy, "Les femmes du monde artistes: Madame Charcot," *Revue des arts décoratifs*, 20.1 (1900): 41–51; anon, "Catalogue des objets d'art et d'ameublement," catalogue for sale of materials from the Hôtel Varangeville (4–5 July 1900), stamped "Union centrale des arts décoratifs," collection of Bibliothèque Charcot.
59. J.-M. Charcot and Valentin Magnan, "Inversion du sens génitale," *Archives de neurologie* (January 1882; November 1882): 53–60, 296–322.
60. Alfred Binet, "Le fétishisme dans l'amour," *Revue philosophique*, 24 (1887): 266.
61. Meige, "Charcot," 501.
62. Charles Fiessinger, "Charcot jugé par le Dr Fiessinger, d'Oyonnax," *Revue de l'hypnotisme* (December 1896): 186.
63. Guillain, 30–31.
64. Daudet, *Devant*, 11.
65. Daudet, *Morticoles*, 104–5.
66. Ibid., 27.
67. Daudet, *Devant*, 14.
68. Ibid., 14.

CHAPTER 9

Charcot and the Theatre of Horror and Terror

1 FRENCH MEDICINE AND THE THEATRE

In previous chapters I explored the theatricality of Charcot's practice, the role of performative discourses, and dramaturgy at the Salpêtrière in both pedagogy and disease manifestations. In this chapter I turn to the theatre itself, focusing on the relationship between members of the Salpêtrière school and the horror theatre of the Grand Guignol. The Guignol was founded by Oscar Méténier four years after Charcot's death, enjoying great popularity from 1897 through the late 1930s, before its ignominious closure in 1962.[1] Above all, it was the plays of André de Latour de Lorde which assured the success of the Grand Guignol. De Lorde embarked on an extended collaboration with Charcot's former student Alfred Binet, 1905–1911, and their five plays made up the core of what de Lorde described as his Théâtre d'Épouvante—Theatre of Horror and Terror. These violent, sensationalistic works dealt with neuropsychological conditions and medical scenarios which turned out horribly wrong. They were nevertheless endorsed by Charcot's senior students, including Georges Gilles de la Tourette. The manner in which Tourette offered his support could, however, have come from the stage of the Théâtre d'Épouvante itself. His 1901 lecture at the Théâtre de l'Odéon on de Lorde's hypnosis-drama *The Sleeper* was marred by what the Odéon director described as a "cerebral fit" which rendered Tourette's speech all but incomprehensible, offering clear signs for those who could read them of his incipient madness and decline due to syphilitic degeneration of the

© The Editor(s) (if applicable) and The Author(s) 2016
J.W. Marshall, *Performing Neurology*,
DOI 10.1057/978-1-137-51762-3_9

213

nervous system.[2] Charcot's *chef de clinique*, Gilbert Ballet, offered more coherent support in the form of his preface to a collection by de Lorde and Binet titled *Madness in the Theatre* (1913), whilst Joseph Babinski assumed the pseudonym Olaf to collaborate with Pierre Palau on a script for the Guignol entitled *The Disturbed* (1921). Babinski's piece described the murderous pathological desires of a pair of sadomasochistic lesbian school mistresses. These works reveal a covert acknowledgement on the part of former Salpêtrière physicians of the infective potentials of medical practice and its theatrical or performative qualities. A close reading of the Théâtre d'Épouvante in light of Charcot's oeuvre reveals that, far from representing an eccentric postscript to the neuropathologist's practice—as has generally been implied—the work of de Lorde and Binet constituted the *logical culmination* of Charcot's practice in terms of style and form.

The works of de Lorde and Binet act to invert the hierarchy of doctor to patient, engulfing the audience in a radical form of catharsis so overwhelming as to constitute a virtual annihilation of the self through neuroaffective processes. These theatrical effects verged on being actively pathological according to the models developed by Charcot and his students.

Members of the French medical profession under the Third Republic tended to see themselves as patrician cultural leaders. Most were schooled in the classics at the national lycées, and many dabbled in poetry, the arts, and playwriting. Jean-Martin and Augustine Charcot were skilled enamellists and interior designers, whilst Charcot's former intern Charles Richet wrote the script for *Circe* (1905), the premiere of which featured France's leading actress, Sarah Bernhardt.[3] Major venues such as the Odéon and the Comédie Française (where Charcot's friend Jules Claretie was administrator, 1885–1913) acted as key sites for well-to-do socialization. Although Charcot was a great lover of dramatic texts by Goethe, Molière, and Shakespeare, he was not especially enamoured of the theatre itself. He preferred the physical displays of the cabaret and the Folies Bergère, to which he occasionally took his interns. As Maurice Debove observed, Charcot "was in this as elsewhere simple in his tastes."[4] Parisian interns and physicians could also find themselves stationed at the theatre in the role of the officially appointed *médecins de service* or house doctors, who were on call with ether, bromide, and smelling salts should spectators faint or have a hysterical crisis, which was reportedly not uncommon.[5] The directors of the Grand Guignol were to make much of this institution, boasting that their own *médecin de service* had swooned during a performance of de Lorde's *The Last Torture* (1904), and so was unavailable to revive anyone else. The Guignol was reputed to have an especially high following of spectators drawn from nurses, *infirmières,* and doctors. Outside of this, Salpêtrière physicians typically looked to theatre and performance as likely sites to encounter pathological cases. Meige scoured the fairs and circuses of Paris seeking exceptional types for Richer to study (see Chap. 5). Nordau and others took a dim view of dance forms based on epileptic movements which were popular within fin de siècle cabarets and dance halls. The Salpêtrière physicians were more support-ive of fictional portrayals of diseases which echoed their clinical descrip-tions and which could be read as cautionary tales. Richet, for example, commended Gustave Flaubert's depiction of hysteria in *Madame Bovary* (1856), whilst Charcot endorsed Zola's depiction of alcoholic nervous debilitation in *L'assommoir (The Grog Shop)* (1878).[6] It is indeed difficult to underestimate the influence which neuropsychological models had on French theatre and performance of the Belle Époque, even feeding in to Paul Margueritte's re-versioning of the clown Pierrot as an obsessed, alcoholic, and seizure-prone murderer of his wife, a one-man show which premiered before Alphonse Daudet and the Goncourts in 1887.[7] This fertilization of French entertainment and comedy by medical discourse was indicative of a widespread public fascination with neurasthenic disor-der and degeneration. By and large, though, the medical profession did not reciprocate this curiosity, members of the Salpêtrière school remaining relatively aloof from main-stage theatre and popular entertainment.

Outside of avant-garde cabaret and Decadent arts, theatre practitioners themselves largely strove to maintain a distinction between their own practice and anything that could be considered actually diseased or pathological. In contrast to the "convulsively" shaking and hallucinating Pierrot performed by Margueritte,[8] the famous French actors Ernest and Constant Coquelin recommended that when playing the part of a drunkard, one might:

> come on stage with the physiognomy of one who is a bit overwhelmed, the body slightly automatic ... be concentrated, obsessed, very anxious and worried, but not hallucinated: you are a theatrical subject, not a medical subject. You belong to the stage, not to Dr Charcot.[9]

Such theatre professionals tended to object to the vogue for dances such as "Epileptic Sour Herrings" or the grotesque facial tics and mugging of cabaret star Paul Habans, and sought to distinguish their own craft from such behaviour.[10]

The support offered by Charcot's former students to de Lorde and company would at first seem consistent with these patterns. Ballet, for example, commended the clinical accuracy of the Théâtre d'Épouvante works, remarking on the importance of Binet's medical insight as part of this collaboration. In his preface to *Madness in the Theatre*, Ballet proclaimed:

> it is not enough to have a familiarity with the theatre, it is also necessary to possess precise clinical knowledge. It is rare that one is at once a dramaturg, an expert and a doctor. M. André de Lorde who has all of the qualities of a man of the theatre to the highest degree, but is not a medical professional, has overcome this difficulty by associating himself with those who are so competent, notably Alfred Binet who is a psychologist of great merit as well as being in some respects a clinician.[11]

A cursory examination of the plays themselves, supporting essays, and the manner in which they were produced when staged at the Guignol itself demonstrates that a more ambiguous relationship between enervating stimulation and the theatrical representation of medicine was at play here. It was perhaps less a case of madness correctly depicted in the theatre, as Ballet implied, and more theatre as a form of cathartic madness.

2   MEDICAL HORROR AT THE THÉÂTRE DU GRAND GUIGNOL

Alfred Binet was a doctor whose collaboration with playwright André de Lorde produced a fully rounded dramaturgical project sometimes described as "*le théâtre médical.*" Independently wealthy, Binet was somewhat eccentric in that he worked as a paid volunteer both at the Salpêtrière and the Sorbonne's psychological laboratory at the École Pratique des Hautes Études (EPHE).[12] Binet's career was nevertheless distinguished, covering general psychology, physiology, hypnosis, magnetism, aphasia, and fetishism. At the EPHE he developed an IQ test for the Ministry of Education, presenting children with such daunting diagnostic challenges as "What is the first thing that you would do, if you came home after school and found your mother strangled and mutilated?"[13] It was in this capacity as a neuropsychologist that Binet met de Lorde, interviewing him as part of a study which he was conducting into the similarity between acting and the hypnotic state.[14]

De Lorde was the chief author associated with the Théâtre du Grand Guignol, a small institution established in 1897 when, following the closure of Andre Antoine's Naturalist Théâtre Libre, its co-founder Oscar Méténier moved to a nearby Montmartre venue at the end of the cul de sac on 20 bis rue Chaptal. Méténier's darkly satirical Naturalistic scripts laid bare the moral hypocrisy of forcing bourgeois morality onto struggling workers, the destitute, and the criminal classes. Méténier's own *comédies rosses* (sardonic theatre dealing with the urban characters) or *moeurs populaires* (manners and mores of the lowest strata of society) were soon replaced by a programme of alternating short farces and horror plays at the Grand Guignol, typically consisting of five one-act performances per night.[15] For ten francs, audiences could attend a programme running from nine until midnight. Although the institution experienced many peaks and troughs prior to its final closure in 1962, by the 1930s the Grand Guignol ceased to be home to a distinctive dramaturgical style. Its aesthetic (though not financial) peak was during the period shortly after Charcot's death in the years leading up to the Great War. It was at this time that Charcot's peers from the Salpêtrière and elsewhere became regular patrons and supporters of the little theatre, composing criticism, writings, as well as giving public lectures on the work.

As popular mass cultural productions, the publications associated with de Lorde and the Grand Guignol were produced in a dizzying variety of iterations. Scripts were issued singly or in different editions, both with essays by Salpêtrière staff and without.[16] Many exist in at least two forms: a short, one-act version presented within the Grand Guignol's mixed programs; and a longer rendition presented at another venue such as the Théâtre Sarah Bernhardt (now the Théâtre de la Ville) or the Théâtre Ambigu. Moreover, de Lorde's status as the Grand Guignol's renowned "Prince of Terror" has tended to overshadow his collaborations, which were extensive, including not just Binet but also playwrights Henri Bauche, Charles Foley, and others. Several of the plays mounted under the banner of the Théâtre d'Épouvante were also known by multiple titles. *A Crime in a Madhouse* (1915), for example, is known to have been co-authored by Binet and de Lorde. It was later restaged as *The Infernal Ones, The Diabolical Ones,* and *The Old Women,* and at some period during these revivals, the two-act play script of de Lorde and Binet was transformed into a one-act piece with a different ending, sometimes attributed to de Lorde alone. Four other plays can be definitively attributed to both men— *The Obsession* (1905), *The Horrible Experiment* (1909), *The Mysterious*

Man (1910), and *The Invisible Beings* (1912). De Lorde's *A Lesson at the Salpêtrière* (1908) and *The System of Doctor Goudron and Professor Plume* (1903) were published in a compilation alongside the pair's collaborative works as *Le Théâtre d'Épouvante* (1909). All of these works therefore made up the Théâtre d'Épouvante, and all were staged at some time at the Théâtre du Grand Guignol. Although Binet was not directly credited as an author of *A Lesson,* de Lorde dedicated the play to Binet. The playwright drew upon Binet's specialist knowledge of Charcot's concepts, and the neuropsychologist often attended rehearsals to offer commentary and advice.[17] De Lorde gained access to the wards of the Salpêtrière, Bicêtre, and la Charité through Binet and other connections, and claimed himself to have acted as a lay participant "to numerous experiments conducted by Charcot, Pierre Janet, and many others."[18] The Salpêtrière school and the Grand Guignol were also linked through the work of illustrator Adrien Barrère, who produced a series of extremely popular, titillating caricatures of senior medical figures such as Edouard Brissaud, Paul Brouardel, Charles Richet, Maurice Debove, Jules Dejerine, Victor Cornil, and others, crowding over nude female patients, or clutching body parts and embryos in preservation jars.[19] Barrère also worked as a designer, producing posters for the Guignol classics of *The System of Dr Goudron* and *A Crime in the Madhouse,* as well as advertisements for cabaret performers and theatres. Given the long affiliation between de Lorde and Binet, it is likely that the playwright also consulted Binet on the typologies of madness depicted in his one-act version of *System of Dr Goudron,* prior to expanding it into the longer, two-act version published in *Le Théâtre d'Épouvante* collection.

The texts of the Théâtre d'Épouvante were therefore predominantly staged according to the dramaturgical principles first developed at the Grand Guignol. Max Maurey was the inaugural director of most of de Lorde's works and replaced Méténier as chief dramaturg of the Grand Guignol, 1898–1914. Camile Choisy took over as artistic director 1914–1930 and 1940–1944, sharing much the same dramaturgical values. Maurey and Choisy favoured a sparse, Naturalistic staging, close in many ways to that which André Antoine had pioneered at the Théâtre Libre. Real objects frequently served as stage properties at the Grand Guignol too, and several plays were devised specifically to take advantage of a surgical suite which the director had secured.[20] Noting de Lorde's professed aim to echo the Naturalists by applying scientific principles and findings to the stage, Henry François of *La revue théâtrale* (1904) claimed that de Lorde's works were "not so much in the category of 'slices of life' as 'slices of death.'"[21]

After a minimal, bald exposition, the action of the one-act plays of the Grand Guignol moved almost immediately to an inevitable, appalling conclusion, whilst the longer productions of the Théâtre d'Épouvante itself typically contained a middle section in which medical and moral dilemmas were explored in more detail. Both versions, however, channelled the dramaturgical action into a final, extreme, horrific *tableau vivant*. Maurey explicitly described the Grand Guignol's dramaturgical iconography in the terms of popular science, arguing in 1913 that the institution served "for all the world as a museum of horrors"—not unlike Charcot's own "museum of living pathology."[22]

These tightly focused shows exhibited a disconcerting dramaturgical duality which was essential to their success. As the historian František Deák observes:

Two tendencies were always present ... the naturalistic and the melodramatic ... The verisimilitude of the situation demanded concentration upon realistic detail ... but in the expressions of horror, in the situations of torture, madness and violent death, actors had to be able to produce a rather difficult scale of expressions and sounds.[23]

The convincing horrific effects for which the Grand Guignol was renowned were achieved not only by the actors' ability to combine melodramatic or hysterical performance with Naturalism. Ingenious prosthetic and technical means were employed, with acid-scarred visages, retractable blades, a patented secret blood recipe, and more, all featuring upon the small stage of rue Chaptal. Fresh sheep's eyes were used for scenes involving eye gouging—not least because of their propensity to bounce when they struck the stage.[24] The gestures and facial expressions of the actors were often strongly emphasized, as was the case in much contemporary cinema. Charcot's own medical presentations had been characterized by a contradictory dialectic between the neuropathologist's spartan, scientific dramaturgy and the potentially infective performative excesses of his patients. The Théâtre d'Épouvante, however, revelled in the fruitful interplay between these apparently opposed dramaturgical forces, employing Naturalistic devices to effect an overpowering *fusion* of realism and baroque horror.

The lighting at the Grand Guignol was extremely low, partly to facilitate the macabre illusions and surprising entrances which were a feature of the theatre. Contrary to the developing conventions of Naturalism, footlights such as were used at the Salpêtrière were also employed at the Grand Guignol in order to exaggerate physiognomic expression, throwing faces into shadowy relief with light from below, whilst diffuse, often coloured sidelights marked out the space itself.

The Grand Guignol was situated in a renovated Jansenist chapel. The décor was conducive to much the same Gothic atmosphere as that of Charcot's own home—but here, the unnerving psychophysiological effects produced by such an environment constituted a deliberate, dramaturgical strategy rather than an incidental side effect. Choisy's secretary, Camillo Antona-Traversi, gave a particularly rich account of these effects and their relation to neuropsychology in his 1933 history of the theatre:

> The spectator, who, for the first time, penetrates into the little room at the cul de sac of Chaptal is seized, upon his entry, by a vague feeling of disquiet. Because it is strange, this long, narrow room, with its walls hung with dark fabric, its severe wooden carvings, with its two mysterious doors, always closed, at each side of the stage, and its two unexpected angels who smile enigmatically at us from high up on the ceiling.
>
> It is then that, upon the striking of three blows, all of the lights in the house abruptly go out; and it is for those seconds, before the curtain rises, that we feel the great thrill.
>
> We are a bundle of nerves, the arcs of myelin are stretched to breaking point. One anxiously awaits the first shock which will launch the little arrow of emotion into the target of the brain. In the midst of this sudden darkness, where the pallor of the faces resembles ghostly white blotches, in the impressive silence, broken from time to time by bursts of nervous laughter from some lady wishing to disguise her inquietude, the air is impregnated with an anxiety which weighs heavily upon damp brows. All the cries of pain, the screams of terror, the groans of agony seem to come from out of the walls in which they hide ... The curtain rises, the spectator is "well prepared": all of the effects will bear fruit.[25]

Like Wagnerian opera, performance at the Grand Guignol constituted a totalizing, immersive theatrical experience, in which the elements of theatrical attendance, ritual, anticipation, décor, sound, lighting, text, and performance came together so as to produce a single, literally unnerving, sensorial experience. Nerve fibres were transformed into taut "arcs of myelin ... stretched to breaking point," one's sense of spatial awareness was ruptured by an all-pervading soundscape with no clear point of origin, and the patron was transformed into a highly suggestible subject (a "bundle of nerves"), similar in psychophysiology to the neurasthenic, the hysterioepileptic, or the hypnotized individual. In such a condition, normally *unpleasurable* or even *pathological* traumas offered the spectator potential *relief* from this highly charged synaesthetic state—"the first shock which will launch the ... arrow of emotion into the target of the brain."

The plays of de Lorde and Binet dealt with the intrigues of the asylum, psychopaths, heredity, radical electrotherapy, and—most striking of all—hysterioepileptic hypnosis as presented by Charcot himself. Many of the positions dramatized by de Lorde and Binet were commonplace in Third Republic debates regarding mental innervation. The pros and cons of incarceration in the face of libertarian principles were represented in *The Mysterious Man,* for example, with sequestration invidiously likened to imprisonment. *The Mysterious Man* was, however, unusual in its unresolved pessimism and ambiguity. Historians François Rivière and Gabrielle Wittkop observe that it was "less a play with a thesis than an exposition of a problem for which there is still no viable solution: what are the criteria which would permit one to free a patient who appears cured, without placing everyone around him in danger?"[26] The threat the mad posed to life and liberty was bloodily staged in this and other plays. As historian Mel Gordon observes, within de Lorde's "seemingly naturalistic world, madness was a human constant that had the power to overthrow any social contract at any time," be it that of family, class, medical institutions, and knowledge—or even the authority of the Guignol's supporters like the unfortunate Tourette.[27] It was the presentation of these issues as part of a coherent dramaturgical project that set de Lorde and Binet apart from their peers, rendering their work a perverse critique and celebration of the forces set in motion by Charcot's own practice. Binet and de Lorde repeatedly staged mental illness as a pathological, performative phenomenon which not only infected society and those predisposed to illness, but which tainted medicine itself. The distinction between medical discourse and its object was tenuous, if not unsustainable, in this context.

The scripts of de Lorde and Binet contained detailed notes on the dramaturgy developed by Maurey in consultation with the authors. The artists employed an unadorned, almost idiomatic theatrical language which melded Naturalism with melodrama. Photographs of the major productions show the stage was typically adorned with a smattering of clichéd properties and Naturalistic details, set in front of simple, generalized backdrops which collectively represented specific social spaces such as the family home or a medical ward. A physician's office at his home, for example, was signified by "Severe furniture … a marble bust of Hippocrates … surgical instruments," chemical flagons, and electrostimulation equipment.[28] Similar pieces of theatrical shorthand appeared throughout the Théâtre d'Épouvante, as in *The Mysterious Man* (a bust of Hippocrates), *The System* (electrical equipment, "severe" furnishings, embossed books), and *A Lesson* ("flagons," specimen jars). The Legion of Honor also was a frequent symbol of medical authority. Like many of his peers, Charcot was awarded the Legion in 1892. In the Théâtre d'Épouvante, however, the badge became a potentially deceptive or ironic signifier of medical hubris or impersonation, often worn by those pretending to assume the mantle of medical authority. Medical space and authority was reduced by Binet, de Lorde, and Maurey to a small number of interchangeable, treacherous performative signs, readily available for actors to pick up and invoke.

The Mysterious Man followed conventions widespread in popular literature regarding the depiction of the classic mad types of the asylum. As we have seen, the Salpêtrière was often depicted in the lay press and fiction as a theatre, populated by readily identifiable mad types and actors "of the highest billing"—as the journalist Maurice Guillemot of *Le Paris illustré* put it in 1887. Common characters in these accounts included those suffering from delusions of demoniacal possession, individuals believing themselves to be Napoleon or Christ, Ophelia-like women mumbling over flowers, raging maniacs, hunched introspective melancholics, religious ecstatics, anarchists, and dishevelled hysterical women.[29] *The Mysterious Man* featured a coprolaliac such as had been described by Gilles de la Tourette in his landmark description of Tourette's syndrome, another man yelling, "Long live the Republic!" (precisely the same symptom as was named by Guillemot), one loudly threatening to kill passers-by, an individual laughing uncontrollably, an agitated figure sporting a Russian beard known as the Cossack, and a patient of whom the chief surveillant noted, "We call him the General because of his mania for command."[30] Although the audience was alerted to the comic folly of these madmen, their conceits were shown to have real social effects. When the clamour of the mad became difficult to manage, the surveillants enlisted the General to help subdue the Cossack and his peers. Whilst the Legion of Honor worn by the General was fake, his ability to command was not. The General masterfully escorted the Cossack out of the room, whilst the surveillant in chief (played by the Guignol's stage manager and special effects expert

Paul Ratineau) only managed to escape the other inmates by slamming the door on them. The authority which the General performed through his dress and demeanour was therefore of comparable force and social reality to that of the surveillant within the context of the parodic asylum.

A more troubling inversion of medical authority was dramatized in *The System of Dr Goudron*. The piece opened with two journalists being introduced to Legion-holder Dr Goudron and his collaborator Professor Plume (Tarr and Fether in the original 1845 story by Edgar Allan Poe, from which de Lorde adapted the play). Goudron's ease with medical language, philosophy, and the surrounds of the alienist's office caused the journalists to readily accept his claim that he was director of the asylum. Like Charcot, Goudron performed his authority with conviction. He explained that his system rested upon "encouraging" the delusions of the mad until the patients eventually gave up their "ruse" and "hypocrisy."[31] The psychiatrist Philippe Pinel had suggested a comparable method during his term at the Salpêtrière, advocating such curative ruses as placing a snake in the motions of those who believed they had a serpent inside of them.[32] In the play, however, this method was so grotesquely exaggerated as to be of dubious therapeutic value. Goudron, for example, advocated simply feeding grain to an inmate who thought he was a chicken. Goudron informed the journalists that he had just restrained a patient who was obsessed with the thought that he was the head physician of the asylum. As Goudron began to exhibit the tic of stuttering, however, it became clear that it was *he* who was in fact the dangerous, raging patient referred to. The patient Goudron—much like the General—had made his delusion a reality.

The interchangeability of doctor and patient, the normal and its monstrous or psychopathic other, was a frequent motif in the work of de Lorde and Binet. Stage directions noted that each of Goudron's entourage "has a tic or a barely perceptible mania."[33] Mme Joyeuse, for example, was constantly sniffing a flower; Eugenie's eyes fluttered; Robert remained motionless except for periodically rifling through his pockets; whilst Professor Plume appeared mildly beatified and uncoordinated, repeating the last words of each of Goudron's sentences until his voice reached an unnerving crescendo. Similarly, the evil hysterics depicted in *A Crime in the Madhouse* each had "nervous tics of the face."[34] These figures disrupted the normal spectacular economy of the asylum. One of the journalists in *The System of Dr. Goudron* criticized how the asylum had become a place of tawdry entertainment and theatre: "one comes to see them [the insane] as though they are curious beasts! ... We don't have that right!"[35] Unlike the other figures within the production, or the inmates described by Guillement in *Le Paris illustré*, the insanity of these more successful performers in de Lorde's play was difficult to see. The mad characters themselves claimed to be horrified by the idea of gazing upon *les aliénés*. Joyeuse observed, "I could not look a madman in the face," whilst her companion exclaimed, "Madness! What an *épouvantable* illness!"[36]

The patient who had been impersonating the real Dr Goudron throughout the play initially offered his medical system as a humane alternative to the horrors of straightjackets and douches. Yet it was precisely these therapies which the guards finally prescribed for the lapsed psychopath.[37] This (false) Goudron had moreover complained that his own patient wished to assume *his* position as director, biting the alleged false director during their conflict. When the guards unmasked this Goudron as being one of the inmates, however, it became clear that the man which this false Goudron had claimed was his patient was in fact the *real* asylum director himself. Completing the inversion, it was the mad patient who had formerly been impersonating Goudron who now bit the psychiatric wardens as they dragged him away, echoing the violence which the real doctor had previously inflicted upon the psychopath during their struggle for dominance over the asylum.

As in *A Lesson at the Salpêtrière*, this inversion of roles was constructed so as to invite comparison with practices carried out at Charcot's hospice and elsewhere. The final irony of the play was provided by the revelation of the corpse of the real asylum director in the photographic darkroom attached to his office—a "horrible cadaver, mutilated, torn, the face slashed by a razor."[38] In a terrible mockery of physiognomic discourse as documented in the *Iconographie photographique de la Salpêtrière*, *Le Paris illustré*, and elsewhere, it was the psychiatrist's body that the guards and the audience now gazed upon, a picture violently engraved in flesh by theatrical madness. This disruption of the spectacular economy was sealed by the act of Plume and Goudron gouging out the eye of one of the journalists before he and his companion were saved by the guards. This is the image that features in Barrère's famous 1903 poster for the play. Recalling the famous blinding scenes of both *King Lear* and *Oedipus tyrannus,* the false physicians punished the journalist for attempting to share the psychiatrist's gaze. The play ended with the actors echoing the reaction of the spectators in the auditorium to the alienist's corpse: "They recoil completely horrified." The act of on stage characters bearing witness to horror concluded virtually all of the plays from the Théâtre d'Épouvante. Dread in the face of the effects of mental innervation all but erased the boundary between the medical spectator and horrible object of his gaze. The psychopathic Goudron's last words as he was dragged off stage were, "I am the master, do you hear me? I am the master!" which echoed through the venue with piercing irony. The Théâtre d'Épouvante constituted nothing less than a monstrous hall of mirrors, or echo chamber, in which spectator and object, doctor and patient, reflected each other.

The most remarkable play from the Théâtre d'Épouvante, however, was *A Lesson at the Salpêtrière*. The title recalled that of the most famous illustration of Charcot's lesson, but the work of de Lorde and Binet stood in stark contrast to the objective, unemotional qualities of André Brouillet's painting. Marbois—the savant of the play—was modelled on Charcot and was explicitly named as Charcot's successor in the script. Like his predecessor, Marbois was adorned with a Legion of Honor. He too was a distant, authoritative figure, unseen for a great deal of the production, yet constantly referred to by those on stage.

Both *A Crime in the Madhouse* and *A Lesson at the Salpêtrière* explored the paradox of double negation: the hysteric who cried wolf, if you will. Both dealt with the problematic status of hysterical speech. The pathological and performative status of the condition rendered hysterical testimony inherently suspect. When characters accused others of brutalizing them, they were not believed. The sympathetic doctor of the *Lesson* was named Bernard, presumably after Charcot's eminent peer Claude Bernard. He too boasted a Legion of Honor. The patient Claire Camu informed him that her hysterical contracture has been rendered somatic—and therefore real—by electrical shocks applied to the parietal region of her brain by Marbois' assistant Nicolo. Bernard probed the veracity of the hysteric's case, using the needle test seen in the demonstrations mounted by Charcot and others to determine the anaesthesia of Claire's arm. This scene paradoxically dramatized the destruction of sensibility effected by Nicolo's heartless experiments. Claire's face contracted with pain, her eyes filled with tears—yet this was not caused by physical pain. Rather it was Claire's awareness of the *absence* of organic pain that engendered an even more intense expression of emotional pain. Sobbing, she proclaimed to Bernard, "No, I assure you that I cannot" feel it.[39] Pain, truth, and sadism became pathetically intertwined within this theatrical exchange.

The play ended with a variant on the melodramatic formula where the hysterical victim confronted Nicolo with evidence of his crime. In this case, however, the proof was her paralysed limb, which was both a classic sign of hysterioepilepsy itself, as well as of permanent organic damage.[40] Nicolo was nevertheless thrown by the presentation of this ambiguous sign of his guilt, recognizing its *true* cause. Claire broke free of the *infirmières* to throw acid upon his face. Although Claire was to have been the subject of the lesson, it was Nicolo and his patron Marbois who ended up taking on her role. After Nicolo was disfigured, Marbois did not hypnotize Claire as he had planned to do, but instead began acting like a somnambule himself. "Unnerved by the scene," Marbois nevertheless retained "his professorial authority." In a slightly tremulous voice he explained that in "cases such as this" one must first neutralize the acid with a base. The violation of vivisectionist protocol carried out by Nicolo under the cover of hysterical delusion transformed Marbois and Nicolo into patients mounted within their own display.

The performativity of neuropathology here provided several occasions for black humour within *A Lesson at the Salpêtrière*. During an earlier farcical sequence, two of the interns mused over the links between hysteria and sexuality. Literary works such as Goethe's *Faustus* or Clarétie's *Loves of an Intern* frequently noted the desire of university students to enliven their studies through sexual conquests. *A Lesson at the Salpêtrière* was no exception, with the young men reflecting that:

> *BERNIER*: ... to have a hysteric for a mistress, that would disgust me!
> *GASQUET*: You are right there, my friend, contrary to what bourgeois think, when one wants a hot-blooded woman, it is not among hysterics that one must search.[41]

Hysteria was shown to disrupt not only the spectacular economy of disease and its medical analysis, but also normative gender constructions and sexuality. Despite the allure of their charismatic young patients, the interns remained certain of the unsuitability of the residents for their amours.

Bernier was later tricked by his comrades into making advances towards Tatiana, an Eastern medical student who represented the new modern woman as she appeared within the medical hierarchy. Tatiana smoked and was openly derisive of Bernier's attentions.[42] She was the epitome of cool detachment in comparison to the melodramatic inmates she studied. If hysterioepilepsy represented a hyper-feminization of the female sufferer, Tatiana's modern self-restraint represented its antithesis. She exhibited a femininity stripped of its normal exterior signs and outward behaviour.

The contemporary journal *Les annales politiques et littéraires* recorded a similarly disorientating encounter with a medical woman at the Salpêtrière. The journalist noticed amongst the audience for one of Charcot's hysterical presentations a woman who:

> wears the white apron of the interns; her blond hair full of curls, her accentuated features, not without grace, her bearing decidedly gives her the look of a young man; this medical student chats familiarly with her brother students.[43]

The intern's presence was doubly problematic in this journalistic account because the lecture in question began with the presentation of a *male* hysteric (a young man), before a female patient was then introduced and "the dream began." Men working in the medical profession found Tatiana and her real-life sisters difficult to read—especially sexually inexperienced students like Bernier. The brotherhood of medicine was rendered confusing by the presence of such women, a number of whom worked with Charcot and his assistants on hysteria and other topics. Such women violated the transparency of normative femininity. The performative restraint of these figures rendered them as opaque as their pathologically excessive others, whom Charcot regularly proffered to his viewers.

Tatiana's appearance in the play was not merely a creative flourish added by the authors. Charcot publicly advocated the right of "exceptional women" to be physicians, and at least five of the first women to enter medicine were associated with neuropathology at the Salpêtrière. Neuroanatomist Augusta Marie née Klumpke, for example, was the first female intern and served as effective co-professor of neuropathology at the Salpêtrière with her husband Jules Dejerine, 1913–1917.[44] *Les hommes d'aujourd'hui* listed her as a member of Charcot's entourage or "charcoterie" in 1890.[45] Tatiana was most likely based upon Russian extern Glafira Abricossoff, whose thesis of accreditation explored the historiography of hysterioepileptic pathology.[46] It was moreover common for recovered patients to work in the institutions where they had been residents.[47] When nurses became sick, they were commonly interned at their former place of employment. The most famous instance of this was the demonstration subject Blanche Wittman, who worked in the Salpêtrière photographic laboratory and later succumbed to cancer caused by unshielded radiography devices. The sympathetic nurse depicted by Binet and de Lorde in *A Crime in a Madhouse* provided another such case, being a recovered patient now charged with protecting her former peers from the poor treat-ment they received from the religious sisters employed at the unreformed asylum where she worked. These and other cases dramatized the instabil-ity of the separation between patient and medic, appearance and essence.

Hysteria's status as an illness at once closely allied to, yet nominally unrelated to, sexuality arose several times within *A Lesson at the Salpêtrière*. Marbois, for example, rejected Claire's assertion of mistreatment by citing the example of a hysterioepileptic who falsely accused a doctor of deflow-ering her—a particularly potent example in that it set somatic evidence against the patient's immaterial imaginings.[48] His student Gasquet also reiterated Charcot's adage that, far from being nymphomaniacs, hysterics had a horror of intercourse.

The most remarkable depiction of hysterioepilepsy, though, was offered in a scene where Bernard introduced both the audience and his assistant Roland (played again by Ratineau) to the obliging young patient Suzanne (possibly based on Suzanne N...).[49] The episode was striking in how—like hysterioepilepsy itself—it possessed an exaggerated length and power not altogether concomitant with its role within the narrative. Historian Jaqueline Carroy-Thirard tellingly notes that Suzanne's main function was to highlight Claire's innocence: "the coquettish woman, a liar and provocative, is contrasted with the poor victim."[50] This does not fully do justice to the highly ambiguous presentation of Suzanne by de Lorde and Binet, however.

Like the hysteric later presented by Marbois in his lecture, Suzanne was dressed "coquettishly."[51] Marbois was annoyed by this—but Bernard accepted it with cool equanimity. Missing the opportunity to perform for the public as often as she would like, Suzanne asked Bernard:

> *SUZANNE:* Tell me then, m'sieu, why does M. Marbois no longer have me come to the lesson... Why doesn't he put me to sleep any more?
> *BERNARD:* Because you upstage him...
> *SUZANNE (unable to stop herself from laughing):* Oh! m'sieu!
> *BERNARD (to Roland):* This little bitch is a marvelous simulator ... She plays for us the great play of hypnotism with its periods (*She laughs*).[52]

Suzanne remained unfazed by Bernard's insulting epithet, teasingly admonishing him in return: "That's not nice." Moreover, she answered him in this fashion immediately before acceding to his request for a dem-onstration of hysterical hypnosis for the benefit of Roland. Bernard in turn tolerated Suzanne's disrespectful, insinuating behaviour so that he might present Suzanne's symptoms to Roland—despite the fact that Bernard explicitly identified these actions as the product of her skills as a "simulatrice." Indeed, the relationship between doctor and patient appeared highly ambiguous, and Bernard seemed to flirt with her.

Bernard offered the patient sweets in exchange for her performance. Suzanne began by teasingly proffering her tongue. Bernard triumphantly proclaimed to Roland that this represented "Anesthesia of the sense of taste!"—a classic hysterioepileptic symptom.[53] This pattern continued throughout, with Bernard naming each state, whilst Suzanne related the symptoms "with the voice of a fairground spruiker [*du barnum*] delivering a pitch." Although Bernard did not actually hypnotize her, she commenced by explaining, "When you tell me to sleep, I fall like a stone, like this" and then promptly collapsed into a chair. Bernard instructed Roland that she had entered stage "Number one, lethargy!" Suzanne added that she could not hear anything and was unresponsive to external stimuli, though this was patently false. Bernard then identified catalepsy—again without intervening to produce Suzanne's transition out of lethargy—whilst Suzanne herself named the final state of ecstasy. In her pseudo-delirium, Suzanne adopted "a soft and song-like voice," murmuring about flowers and birds before crying out for her mother.

Suzanne's performance accorded precisely with the procession of classic poses and symptoms of hysterical hypnosis identified by Charcot and his peers (Table 7.1). The patient's ability to simulate these phenomena without being hypnotized, though, cast serious doubt upon the reality of Charcot's classification. The dubious quality of clinical hypnosis was further emphasized by its representation here within the explicitly *fictive* frame of the play. It was not only the hysteric who could reproduce the symptoms of hypnosis, but also the Grand Guignol actress who played her, throwing into question the reality of Charcot's own presentations.

If Suzanne was indeed nothing but a carnivalesque charlatan, then Bernard was shown to have no qualms in adopting the role of Barnum to her freak show. The critique offered by de Lorde and Binet was therefore not simply to unmask the falsehood of hysteria. Rather, the condition was shown to be an illness which drew the doctor in, making him party to an amusing but troubling disease of simulation. The playwrights can therefore be interpreted as not so much attacking hysterioepilepsy as highlighting the complex, destabilizing theatrical reciprocity it engendered—

perhaps unsurprising given that Binet himself had hypnotized patients on Charcot's behalf at the Salpêtrière.

3 RADICAL CATHARSIS

The critical deformation of medical discourse which was effected by the texts performed at the Grand Guignol was only surpassed by the disturbing nature of the philosophy which drove them. De Lorde's theatrical principles brought together science, horror, neurology, modernity, Aristotelian aesthetics, and popular representation in an unnerving critique of normative social existence. De Lorde's foreword to *Le Théâtre d'Épouvante* explained how he derived his theatrical methodology from his upbringing. His father was a doctor who had tried to cure his son's fear of death by placing the young author in the mortuary attached to the former's practice.[54] Binet recorded that he had the same boyhood experience, having been forced to touch a cadaver in a morgue by his father, who was also a physician. De Lorde went on to watch women in mourning and helped in the preparation of his grandmother for display in a coffin. Previously de Lorde's fears had been only "germs," but in a classic hysterogenic encounter they came to fruition when he first looked upon the face of a corpse.

Charcot was highly skeptical of the idea that a visual shock alone could produce any form of illness. Emotional traumas were in his terminology "provocative agents; the true cause does not lie there, it is in the predisposition, in nervous heredity."[55] A disturbing sight could engender the expression of an otherwise unrelated latent hereditary disposition to illness (diasthesia). Charcot was ambivalent regarding whether such degeneracy would inevitably be expressed or not, but the pattern was the same. Hereditary illnesses were not in themselves incurable, but neuropathological degeneracy was associated with a vast array of tenacious conditions whose manifestation was almost invariably brought on by a physical or moral-psychic shock. In the *Iconographie photographique* in particular, precipitating circumstances frequently revolved around a spectacular scenario. The first fit experienced by the hysterioepileptic Rosalie Leroux, for example, was precipitated by her confrontation with an enraged dog. Her condition was later confirmed when she saw the corpse of a woman who had been murdered by her husband.[56]

The fearsome encounters with death experienced by de Lorde and Binet therefore made them prime candidates for neuropathological degeneration. De Lorde came to base his technique on both Aristotelian catharsis and the still extant medical practice of prescribing purgatives to effect a physical catharsis:

> Pharmacists have come to condense strong doses of very violent or powerful drugs into certain '*comprimés*' [concentrated doses or pills] of a very small volume, easy to absorb: likewise, I try … to fabricate '*comprimés*' of terror.[57]

The programme of the Grand Guignol itself was described in these terms. Farces were interleaved with violent melodramas, acting according to the principle of "Scottish showers," or alternating hot-and-cold douching.[58] This ancient hygienic technique of shocking subjects out of their psychophysiological disequilibrium remained a therapeutic standard at asylums like the Salpêtrière and the many hydrotherapy facilities scattered throughout Europe and America. Charcot routinely referred his well-to-do patients to the spas of Lamalou Les Bains, in which he had a commercial interest. Although the humeral theory behind gastrointestinal purgatives, phlebotomy (bloodletting), and douching had been overturned, the lack of truly effective alternative therapies meant that all of these venerable techniques continued to be used. Only the development of electroshock, insulin shock, psychoactive drugs, and lobotomy during the twentieth century led to the abandonment of these methods.

De Lorde's modification of Aristotelian dramaturgy proceeded directly from ideas proposed by the physicians closest to him. In Binet's 1896 study "Fear Amongst Children," the physician noted the dangers of representations of fear for those ill-prepared to withstand them.[59] An attack of fear closely resembled a miniature hysterical seizure, and was spread through "contagion by example," communicating itself by the viewing in another individual of such theatrical signs as "gestures, by physiognomic expressions … producing epidemics of fear comparable to epidemics of nervous illness, chorea, convulsions." However, this could be abated by the sight of one who resisted the urge to succumb to such psychophysical reactions. In showing "an absolute calm," a resolute teacher or school mistress could avoid "a general panic" in her class, engendering a sympathetic physical and psychological response in her students. In more mature subjects, the aim was to acclimatize individuals through measured exposure to the representation of fears. Binet published the results of tests he had conducted upon his own daughter, a disturbing combination of paternity and medical experimentation which echoed his own upbringing as well as that of de Lorde. Binet argued that such experiences could "toughen the character ... and progressively stimulate the habit of courage." Charles Richet similarly claimed that individuals could harness the "vital force" which was provided by normal, low levels of fear: "habituating themselves to danger, envisaging as often as possible, without bravado, but without sadness, the image of death that awaits us all."[60] Excess fear, however, remained pathological for both authors.

De Lorde concurred, claiming that staging works "with no other reason than to torture the nerves" was reprehensible.[61] Nevertheless, fear could serve as a "method" for the generation and layering of other, more complicated emotional effects. De Lorde's *comprimés* were designed to have an effect beyond that of the *phamakos* of tragic theatre which Aristotle had prescribed to purge the angst and the built-up tension from the social body. De Lorde's works, on the contrary, effected a radical process akin to that which gave rise to neuropathologies. The author argued that his plays were designed to cause a "shaking of the whole nervous system" or "paroxysm" such as one experienced in seizure.[62] Such a play "suspends us on the edge of a bottomless abyss; vertigo seizes us, anguish makes our throat contract." The spectator's spatial awareness was destabilized as he or she lost the faculty for speech and language, the throat becoming constricted with psychophysical "anguish."[63] De Lorde observed that he had to keep his works short not only to maximize their effectiveness, but also to prevent long-term damage to the audience.

If the doctrines of de Lorde and Binet were vaguely disquieting from a medical perspective, they paled in comparison to what was proposed in Albert Sorel's preface to the *Théâtre d'Épouvante* collection. In addition to being a playwright and theatre critic, Sorel was a respected historian of post-Revolutionary France and a member of such prestigious institutions as the French Academy, the Institute, and the Academy of Moral and Political Sciences. Despite his reputable credentials, his febrile manifesto on the Théâtre d'Épouvante verged on the avant-garde in extolling a radical, violent aesthetic.

Sorel followed Aristotle in characterizing theatre as a form of ritual exorcism. It was not Aristotle's social agon that Sorel argued was managed by the theatre, though. Rather, it was fear itself: "Throughout time men have been haunted by fear, and the only way that they have found to divert themselves is by producing representations, in the theatre, of the objects of their terror."[64] Modern theatre, however, offered something which approached the pure "Idea" of fear itself. In de Lorde's words, Poe had discovered a new, modern sensibility: "the fear of being afraid" itself.[65] Sorel claimed that "The fears that we thought banished, come back at us from everywhere, intrusive, multiplied, like figures in a hall of mirrors, like sounds in an echo chamber."[66] In the progression from antiquity to modernity, fear had been transformed. Playwrights had evolved from invoking fear through representations of antique gods, to the devils of the Middle Ages, to Renaissance poisoners, to the popular melodramas staged along Montmartre's Boulevard du Crime in the early nineteenth century, to a veritable *mise en abyme* of images—concluding with something even more intangible than a hall of mirrors: a collection of sounds which receded into the darkness before coming back at the listener. As Antona-Traversi observed, an important element of the dramaturgy of the Grand Guignol was indeed the skilful orchestration of sound effects, often produced from distant chambers far from the stage itself in order to maximize their indistinct, non-localized, immersive quality. Spectators at the Théâtre du Grand Guignol were menaced by an all-encompassing presence which rendered everything strange and dangerous as its vibrations moved throughout the space.

Sorel claimed that "bourgeois order and conjugal serenity" did threaten society with the loss of fear altogether. The bourgeoisie had become obsessed with such banalities as "a grand bed" and "elections."[67] For Sorel it was the loss of fear itself—and not the decadence which bourgeois doctors such as Charcot had decried—which menaced Western society. "Humanity protests however and reclaims fear" as part of "a natural law. The masses have a nostalgia for panic; the world, a nostalgia for *frisson*." Sketching a vision of anguished audiences emerging from their homes en masse, in search of fearful stimulation, Sorel described a scene in which:

> From all directions, at the hour when night falls, at the hour when the worms and specters rise up, coming for our fathers, along the boulevard du Crime, one hears rising towards the heights of Montmartre this desolate clamor: "Oh! who will unchain the monsters? who will reopen the box of phantoms? who will give us back fear, overwhelming fear, stupefying fear, the good old fear of our forebears?"[68]

Greeting the crowds, de Lorde stepped forward to answer: "It was I" who was to adopt this role as a modern-day Pandora.

Sorel's account inverted the symbolism traditionally associated with the act of unchaining in post-Enlightenment society. Pinel had emancipated the madwomen of the Salpêtrière by striking the chains from them, whilst Charcot was attributed a similar role in lifting the chains of prejudice from hysterioepilepsy and demonism. De Lorde, however, critiqued such medical hubris, unchaining the theatrical terror which continued to haunt the projects of his medical predecessors. In de Lorde's words, it was through the work of modern investigators into hypnosis and altered states such as "Mesmer ... Braid and Charcot" that "the ancient forms of fear, the marvel of mystery, have returned" and which de Lorde and Binet now explored in plays like *A Lesson at the Salpêtrière*, and which caused Tourette to be banished to an asylum in Lausanne.[69]

De Lorde emerged from Sorel's description as a new charismatic prophet, imbued with an aura of sadomasochistic power, who drew upon primal human urges lying at the fringes of modern civilization: "here are wellsprings of night and terror more inexhaustible than the sources of light of all the oil fields of the Caucasus or the land of the Mormons."[70] Even such talismans of modern progress as oil or the New World were rendered dark and mysterious through their association with distant lands such as the Caucasus, or curious religious groups such as the Mormons. Science and fear were not, therefore, simply antagonistic. They were part of a complex dialectic in which each generated, sustained, and undermined the other. The "good fear of our forebears" was a necessary correlative to science and vice-versa. Fear without science would lead to the collapse of civilization, to men dying of that most primal of terrors: the fear of death. Scientific mastery was, however, an illusion, engendering bourgeois complacency and the dilution of human strength through comforts both material and sexual ("conjugal serenity" and "a grand bed").

In response, Sorel proposed a model of society as a deeply riven, agonistic alliance in which people were menaced at every turn by an infinity of dangers, both subtle and gross. The encroachment of events like natural disasters into the sensorium of the individual was already intense through the new media of telegraphy, photography, and phonography. De Lorde directly commented upon this trend with the earthquake disaster play *The Terrible Earth* (1907), or the earlier *On the Telephone* (1901), in which a husband listens helplessly to the sound of his family on the other end of the line as they are brutalized and murdered by tramps. Sorel reflected that this intrusion of fear into daily life was occurring again: "Today, by telegraph without wires, tomorrow telephone without ... fibers, then by the motor-powered cinematograph [*cinématographe automobile*], one will perceive everything."⁷¹ Sorel's speculation of what was to come was so fervid as to recall Jules Verne's science fictions, moving from the pseudo-neural fibres of early radio telegraphy to Sorel's "*cinématographe automobile*"—a film theatre unleashed from its geographic moorings as it roared across the countryside, dispensing visions painful and pleasurable wherever it travelled. Even more than its predecessors, this bewildering device would reproduce, multiply, and cyberneticize the human sensorium, moving across time and space to transmit images and text caught within the gaze of its cinematic eye. Sorel likened such sensory prostheses to sirens which radiated fiercely affective "cries of agony," enabling the individual to "feel the burns from the fire, the chill of the water ... one experiences asphyxiation oneself." The expansion of the senses led to an interpenetration of reality and pathological delusion: "Life ... becomes a true hallucination."

Sorel likened the state engendered in the individual by the phantasmagoria of modern existence to that of hypnosis or suggestion. One became engrossed in an "insurmountable obsession, the obsession of going mad without knowing, without having the time to call for the doctor."⁷² This topic was indeed given a theatrical representation by de Lorde and Binet in *The Obsession*. An otherwise normal man was so terrified by the possibility that his son might inherit his tendency to fantasize about murdering his offspring that he went mad and killed his child. In the equally fervid Grand Guignol classic of *The Last Torture*, de Lorde portrayed a French consul to China who was so terrified at the outrages likely to be inflicted upon his loved ones during the Boxer Rebellion that he shot his wife and daughter, only to discover that the approaching army was that of the European allies, and not the savage hordes. The man therefore went mad.

Sorel pointed out that in a world where one could not distinguish between good and bad microbes, even the most materially secure bourgeois was under threat. One could be an influential politician like the French consul, living in an otherwise stable country, bathed in contentment and power, amusing oneself by playing tennis with young ladies. But then:

> A shot from a cannon comes from you know not where, the war begins and you do not know why, you ask the girl on the telephone, she does not respond, and already appearing at the top of your wall the hideous heads of savages have suddenly arrived—and you only just have time to take out your revolver if you want to spare your children the last torture.

> What a nightmare! and how amusing it is for them [the bourgeoisie] to experience the agony![73]

Such topics made up "the *divertissements* of the Théâtre d'Épouvante."

Sorel echoed de Lorde's comments regarding the attractive power of fearful spectacle in his description of an average night at the Théâtre d'Épouvante. On a rainy evening one left the wet, darkened street for the "small, illuminated theatre" of Montmartre's Grand Guignol. One's friends waited inside and there one discovered that:

> you are afraid of everything, afraid to stay, afraid to leave, afraid to appear to be afraid, afraid of not having the air of one who is afraid, which would be to "disqualify" your nerves; afraid of not being able to return home, afraid of being there [at home] alone.[74]

Sorel characterized theatrical terror as causing an almost complete rupture of the self or one's belief in one's ability to exert power over oneself in any way. The Théâtre d'Épouvante defied both representation and normal cathartic identification. As the *Revue théâtrale* critic observed, "One not only witnesses the drama, one lives it."[75] Fear effected a truly radical form of violent catharsis. Writers on degeneration varying from Charcot to Léon Daudet and even Binet had warned of the dangers of psychonervous overstimulation, but Sorel advocated precisely such a condition, whereby the theatrical stimulation of the senses would lead to a veritable explosion of uncontrollable nervous energy. Sorel's theatrical catharsis did not therefore act by purging dangerous thoughts or emotions. Rather, it set in train a radical process of neuropsychological self-annihilation. Theatrical trauma forced the psyche to rebuild itself. This renewed psychophysical being would emerge stronger from this theatrical *auto da fè*, better prepared to face the hysteria of modern existence.

Although Charcot influenced early twentieth century cabaret performers, cinematographers, and avant-garde theatre workers such as Habans, the Naturalists, and others, the Théâtre d'Épouvante was by far the most specifically medical of these forms, directly contributed to by Charcot's own senior assistants and students. The collaboration of de Lorde and Binet upon the Théâtre d'Épouvante demonstrated that following Charcot's death, such senior *anciens* from the Salpêtrière as Ballet, Babinski, and even Gilles de la Tourette welcomed the melodramatic abandonment of that patrician separation from the theatre which Charcot had once promoted.

The Théâtre d'Épouvante represented a carnivalesque eruption of the forces which Charcot had put in motion through his use of a theatrical method for diagnosis and pedagogy. This was a popular form which could nevertheless readily spill over into avant-garde aesthetics, constituting a radical, almost pathological assault on normative values and medical ideas of healthy physiology. Audiences to the plays of de Lorde and Binet were sensorially stimulated by their surrounds and horrified by the spectacle, becoming deeply implicated in the covalent exchanges between physician and patient, spectator and object, which were dramatized through the medically informed, totalizing mise en scène. Whilst Charcot had resisted the interpenetration of pathological performance and medical theatre, his separation between the two did not survive him.

NOTES

1. Scholarship on the Grand Guignol has been marred by lack of acknowledgement and eccentric publishing and referencing. The following are the best sources: François Rivière and Gabrielle Wittkop, *Grand Guignol* (Paris: Henri Veyrier, 1979); Mel Gordon, *The Grand Guignol: Theatre of Fear and Terror* (NY: Da Capo, 1997); Richard Hand and Michael Wilson, *Grand-Guignol: The French Theatre of Horror* (Exeter, UK: Exeter University Press, 2002); Christian Bourgois, ed., *Le théâtre: Cahiers dirigés par Arrabal*, 2 (Paris: 1969).

2. Rivière and Wittkop, 79; Chenivesse, 436–7; Pierre Palau and Olaf (pseudonym of Joseph Babinski), *Les Détraquées* (Paris: 1958).

3. Charles Richet, *Circé* (Paris: Carqueiranne, 1920).

4. Debove, 16.

5. Various, *Service médical des théâtres, cafés-concérts, cirques, etc., de Paris: Agenda 1904* (Paris: Trouette, 1905), 223. Abel Faivre's famous caricature of this event—"Au théâtre des supplices," *Journal* (13 December 1904)—was extensively republished in Grand Guignol programs and fliers.

6. Richet, "Démoniaques," 349; *OC*, vol. 13, p. 88.

7. Paul Margueritte, *Pierrot, assassin de sa femme* (Paris: Paul Schmidt, 1882); Daniel Gerould, "Paul Margueritte and *Pierrot Assassin of His Wife*," *TDR: The Drama Review*, 23.1 (March 1979): 103–112; Marshall, "'World'" 60–85.

8. L. Marc, "Pierrot, assassin de sa femme," *Illustration*, 2300 (26 March 1887): 209–216.

9. Ernest Coquelin and Constant Coquelin, *L'art de dire le monologue* (Paris: Ollendorff, 1884), 92.

10. See Gordon, *Why the French*, 85–90.

11. André de Lorde with Alfred Binet et al., *La folie au théâtre*, préface Gilbert Ballet (Paris: Fontemoing, 1913), VI.
12. Carroy, *Hypnose*, 112–117; Finger, *Origins*, 312–3.
13. Mel Gordon, vii.
14. Theta Wolf, "A New Perspective on Alfred Binet," *Psychological Record*, 32 (1982): 399–400; Alfred Binet, "Reflexions," 279–95.
15. See Daniel Gerould, "Oscar Méténier and *comédie rosse*," *TDR: The Drama Review*, 28.1 (Spring 1984): 15–19.
16. See, for example, Andre de Lorde with Alfred Binet et al, *Théâtre d'Épouvante: Une leçon à la Salpêtrière. L'obsession. La dormeuse. Au rat mort. Le système du docteur Goudron et du professeur Plume. La dernière torture. Sur la dalle*, préface Albert Sorel (Paris: Charpentier et Fasquelle, 1909), *La folie au théâtre: L'homme mystérieux. La petite roque. Les invisibles*, préface Gilbert Ballet (Paris: Fontemoing, 1913), *Théâtre de la peur: L'horrible expérience. Baraterie. L'acquittée*, préface Alfred Binet (Paris: Figuière, 1924), *Théâtre de la mort: L'illustre Professeur Truchard. L'homme mystérieux*, préface André Antoine (Paris: Figuière, 1928).
17. Agnès Pierron, *Les nuits blanche du Grand Guignol* (Paris: Seuil, 2002), 89.
18. Agnès Pierron, *Le théâtre medical du prince de la terreur* (Paris: Les empêcheurs de penser en rond, 1996), 4. David Le Vay, "Adrien Barrère: A French Medical Caricaturist," *The Practitioner*, 207 (July 1971): 106–138; Pierron, *Nuits*, 8–9, 74–87, 122–3, 138–9; Carol Gouspy, "La représentation du chanteur de charme et du scieur," *Image and Narrative*, 20 (December 2007), <http://www.imageandnarrative.be/inarchive/affiche_findesiecle/gouspy.htm>.
19. Mel Gordon, 9.
20. Bourgois, ed., 114.
21. Camillo Antona-Traversi, *L'histoire du Grand-Guignol* (Paris/Reims: Libraire théâtrale, 1933), 78.
22. František Deák, "Théâtre du Grand Guignol," *TDR: The Drama Review*, 18.1 (March 1974): 42.
23. Mel Gordon, 47.
24. Antona-Traversi, 76–77.
25. Rivière and Wittkop, 24–25.
26. Mel Gordon, 113.
27. De Lorde and Binet, *Théâtre*, 2, 221, passim.
28. Guillemot, 335–355.
29. De Lorde et al., *Folie*, 61.
30. De Lorde and Binet, *Théâtre*, 240–1.
31. Goldstein, *Console and Classify*, 81–93.
32. De Lorde and Binet, *Théâtre*, 237–243.
33. André de Lorde and Alfred Binet, *Un crime dans une maison de fous* (Paris: Libraire théâtrale, 1927), 14.

34. De Lorde and Binet, *Théâtre*, 225.
35. Ibid., 238.
36. Ibid., 234–6, 252.
37. Ibid., 253–8.
38. Ibid., 45.
39. Ibid., 74–81.
40. Ibid., 12–13.
41. Ibid., 54–55. On the relationship between feminism, the New Woman, and hysteria, see Gilman et al, 286–344.
42. X [Pont-Calé], 12. Goetz, "Charcot and the Myth," 1678–1685; Nathalie Pigeard-Micault, "L'entrée des femmes à l'école de médecine" (2007), reproduced on <http://www.biusante.parisdescartes.fr/histmed/medica/femmesmed.htm>.
43. Pont-Calé, up.
44. Glafira Abricossoff, *L'hystérie au XVIIe et XVIIIe siècles* (Paris: Steinheil, 1897). Another candidate would be Sophie Woltke, who worked extensively on hypnosis with Charcot's secretary, Georges Guinon.
45. Micale, "Salpêtrière," 718; Freud, Vol. 3, p. 14.
46. De Lorde and Binet, *Théâtre*, 76.
47. Ibid., 33–35.
48. Carroy-Thirard, "Hystérie," 306.
49. De Lorde and Binet, *Théâtre*, 64–65.
50. Ibid., 34.
51. Ibid., 33–35.
52. De Lorde and Binet, *Théâtre*, XIX–XX; Wolf, 400.
53. Charcot and Richer, *Contribution*, 7, 22–23.
54. *IPS*, vol. 1, pp. 14–15, *IPS*, vol. 3, p. 118; Richer, *Études* (1881), 117–122.
55. "*Comprimé*" translates as "pill," though its precise definition includes any form of concentrated medicine or tonic (from "*comprimer*": to compress), and it was this sense of a strong dose which de Lorde was emphasizing. De Lorde and Binet, *Théâtre*, XXV.
56. Mel Gordon, 16–18.
57. Alfred Binet, "La peur chez les enfants," *Année psychologique*, 2 (1896): 223–254.
58. Charles Richet, "La peur: Étude psychologique," *Revue des deux mondes*, 76 (July 1886): 87–117.
59. Antona-Traversi, 82.
60. De Lorde and Binet, *Théâtre*, XXIV.
61. André de Lorde, "La peur dans la littérature," *Revue mondiale* (15 March 1927): 124.
62. De Lorde and Binet, *Théâtre*, IX.
63. De Lorde, "Peur," 124.

64. De Lorde and Binet, *Théâtre*, XII.
65. Ibid., *Théâtre*, X.
66. Ibid., XI–XII.
67. De Lorde, "Peur," 120; Walusinski, "Georges Gilles de la Tourette," unpaginated.
68. De Lorde and Binet, *Théâtre*, XII.
69. Ibid., XIII.
70. Ibid., XIII–XIV.
71. Ibid., XIV–XV.
72. Ibid., XV.
73. Bourgois, ed., 114.

CHAPTER 10

Conclusion
Medical Visibility and the Infectious Appeal of Art

Charcot developed a dramaturgical diagnostic model for several reasons, chief amongst which was the formalistic consistency between using theatrical methods for the presentation and description of the shaking, "dancing" body in movement. The paradox involved in rationally recording what is today described as the "staging" of neuropathological symptoms, whose primary trait is their disorderly, irrational, stochastic distribution in time, space, and the body, has yet to be entirely solved. It seems inevitable that a degree of "fiction" will intrude, at least at a rhetorical level. The variations contained within generalized nosological archetypes as performed by individual patients still erode the stability of modern disease classifications. Charcot was and remains an exemplar of the skilful observation and diagnosis of neurophysiological symptoms, just as he remains an exemplar of the problems which this aspect of clinical practice involves. His theatrical skills, however, have meant that his influence extends far beyond neurology. These formal processes of his practice have had at least as much influence upon the arts as medicine.

The rapid decline of Charcot's status following his death in 1893 was in large part attributable to his role as the head of a school, and his construction of hysterioepilepsy. It had become clear by 1890 that Charcot's association of hysterical pathology with hypnosis was in error, and that the rival Nancy school led by Hippolyte Bernheim was correct in seeing hypnosis as an essentially non-pathological state. By the twentieth century, the remarkable symptoms that Charcot had observed

© The Editor(s) (if applicable) and The Author(s) 2016   241
J.W. Marshall, *Performing Neurology*,
DOI 10.1057/978-1-137-51762-3_10

in hysterioepileptics were difficult to identify beyond a small number of elderly patients at the Salpêtrière. Those discussing post-traumatic stress disorders increasingly tended to work within a Janetian, Freudian, or other psychological paradigm, as opposed to Charcot's neurophysiological approach.[1] Neurology and physiology were further transformed by the discovery of the role of neurochemistry and hormones—also pioneered at the Salpêtrière by Meige, Marie, and Brissaud, who examined the function of the thymus and thyroid.

Charcot was, moreover, a victim of his own success. The iron rule he had striven to exert throughout the Salpêtrière and the Parisian medical fraternity was beginning to crack even before his death. Charles Bouchard, a former Salpêtrière intern, successfully opposed his teacher in 1892 when Bouchard blocked the theses of aggregation proffered by both Babinski and Gilles de la Tourette in favour of his own students.[2] Charcot's death left a power vacuum which many rushed to fill. Former colleagues like Babinski and Joseph Jules Dejerine—the latter more closely associated with Charcot's early collaborator Alfred Vulpian—discovered that the best way to rise within this environment was to disavow close sympathy with the deceased master of the Salpêtrière. Gilles de la Tourette's spectacular decline removed Charcot's main defender, although both Binet and Meige continued to profess Charcot's model into the 1920s. The subtle distinctions between the work of Charcot, Bernheim, and others tended to be lost in much of this debate, Charcot's neuropathological model remaining an undercurrent within the discussion of hysteria, hypnosis, trauma, and altered states throughout the early twentieth century.[3]

More recent developments in the neurosciences suggest that the dichotomy between the dynamic psychological approach developed by Freud, versus Charcot's more materialist somatic perspective, may yet be reconciled.[4] The contribution of Charcot and his colleagues continues to be re-evaluated, and today the work of Pierre Janet—who developed an alternative model of psycho-cognition out of Charcot's somatic models—again occupies a significant place within theories of neuroaffectivity and identity. Charcot's more physical model of trauma has also since been reconsidered in light of the later diagnostic category of post-traumatic stress disorder. Much of the evidence for these new developments comes not from anatomoclinical investigation itself, nor Charcot's innovations in choreo-analysis, but rather twentieth century developments in brain imaging. Physicians today can literally visualize mental processes within the living subject in ways Charcot could only dream of. Through such innovations in visualizing the body, the first tremulous steps in neurology made by Charcot and his associates have given rise to a highly sophisticated collection of neurocognitive models and treatments.

Within fifty years of Charcot's death, for example, film had all but eclipsed the theatre as the socially pre-eminent form of dramatic and visual representation of the body. Where film-makers had striven to produce movies which resembled performances from the stage or music hall, now the reverse was true. The filmic technologies developed at the Salpêtrière were no longer an addition to, but rather a replacement for, the literally present performative body. Printed works—accompanied by reproductions of not just photographs, but X-rays and other materials—no longer tended to supplement the live lecture, but served instead as the authoritative version for public circulation. The years 1894–1900 also saw the production of the first radiographs, electrocardiographs, and even so-called "phonocardiographs" at the Salpêtrière. X-ray photography—pioneered at the hospice by Londe and others—enabled physicians to look directly into the tissues and internal mechanisms of the living body prior to autopsy or surgical intervention. Where Charcot, Richer, and Marey developed subtle ways of reading internal physiological activity from external signs, radiography increasingly pushed aside the importance of these approaches.

Discoveries driven by these developments in neuroimaging have led cognitive scientists of our own era to posit that important parts of human aesthetic response are "hard-wired" into neural function. Vilayanur Ramachandran's concept of "mirror neurons" is the most famous of these theories, a model which parallels to some degree Charcot's concept that the neurosensory body is a system which takes up patterns perceived in other individuals and stimuli. Ramachandran argues that by observing either a real event or its aesthetic representation, a sympathetic reaction may be generated within the nervous system. Witnessing as in a theatre or other scenario encourages neurophysical replication or mimicry—although for Ramachandran, this is more of an aesthetic filter than an open reflex mechanism, and only "great" works of art fully activate these systems. Bruce McConachie and others have more recently attempted to deploy some of these models as the beginnings of something like a global heuristic of theatrical aesthetics.[5] Few authors within the arts, however, share Ramachandran's confidence that neurocognitive principles might offer a universally applicable master key to the description of how audiences approach art or theatre. The close correlation between Charcot's neuroreflexive model of aesthetics, and the values of Charcot's own patrician milieu, provide a cautionary tale against any overconfidence that neuro-biology might offer unambiguous data upon which a universal aesthetic theory could be founded. For Charcot, Richer, and others, though, good health largely coincided with balanced, athletic neoclassicism.

The transition from the theatre of Charcot's own medical prac-tice, performed at the decaying, melancholy venue of the Salpêtrière, into the horrific spectacles and Gothic mise en scène of the Théâtre d'Épouvante, was not great, constituting a shift in intent and degree rather than nature. The same dramaturgical dichotomies informed and energized performance at both sites. Charcot's disciplinary vision sought to bring within medical science a series of previously resistant terms and objects: neurology, athleticism, the living moving body, the grotesque body, theatrical pedagogy, theatrical diagnosis, and sci-entifically based aesthetics. Like many other fin de siècle visionaries, Charcot's reach exceeded his grasp. The contradictions which he strove to overcome proved so insoluble that the historiography of his career has been characterized by attempts to either extol or purge these aspects of his practice ever since.

Nor was the continued blurring of the separation between Charcot's work and the grotesque theatre of horror after his death a purely ret-rospective insight based upon later theories of the performative or the carnivalesque. The work of Munthe, Daudet, Platel, Binet, and Ballet demonstrates that those close to Charcot recognized the contradic-tions between dramaturgical diagnosis and the pursuit of medical truth, between pedagogy and the hygienic protection of the kinesthetic specta-tor. By striving to both medicalize theatre and to theatricalize medicine, Charcot made it possible for theatre to pathologize and disrupt his own practice. The works of Wagner, Binet, and de Lorde—and later Artaud, the Surrealists, the Futurists, and others—offered a glimpse of just what such a pathologization could lead to, kinesthetically engulfing the specta-tor so that the distinction between audience and actor was systematically violated and inverted.

Ironically then, the true heirs to Charcot in terms of his *dramaturgical* and *iconographic* principals would come not from the sciences, but from amongst those artists such as Charcot would have previously diagnosed as diseased. The infectious dramaturgical forces which Charcot released flourished across the twentieth century avant-garde. Whilst neurologists were reluctant to invoke such concepts in the wake of his death, artists would not be so coy—then, or now.

NOTES

1. Mark Micale, "Charcot and *les névroses traumatiques*," *Revue neurologique*, 150.8–9 (1994): 498–505; Charcot, *Charcot*, 116–7.

2. Vicente Iragui, "The Charcot-Bouchard Controversy," *Archives of Neurology*, 43 (March 1986): 290–5; Goetz et al, 307–332; Bernard Brais, "Jean-Martin Charcot et le césarisme de Faculté," 3–27, unpublished article communicated to the French Neurology Society, Paris (9–11 June 1993), collection of the Bibliothèque Charcot; Christopher Goetz, "The Salpêtrière in the Wake of Charcot's Death," *Neurology*, 37 (March 1987): 444–7; Daniela Barberis, "Changing Practices of Commemoration in Neurology," *Osiris*, 14 (1999): 102–117.

3. See, for example, Chadwick Hansen, *Witchcraft at Salem* (NY: Braziller, 1969). I have explored this topic in more detail in "Kleist's *Übermarionetten*," 261–281, "Archaeology of the Abstract Body," 92–111, and "Priestesses," 410–426.

4. For a survey of this literature, see Alistair Fox, *Speaking Pictures: Neuropsychoanalysis and Authorship in Film and Literature* (Indianapolis: Indiana University Press, 2016).

5. Vilayanur Ramachandran and W. Hirstein, "The Science of Art: A Neurological Theory of Aesthetic Experience," *Journal of Consciousness Studies*, 6.6–7 (1999): 15–51; Bruce McConachie, *Theatre and Mind* (London: Palgrave Macmillan, 2012). Significantly, Ramachandran and his supporters ignore the existence of communities who enjoy otherwise atypical aesthetic forms, such as noise music, feedback, drone music, or the contemporary avant-garde in general—although there is considerable psychoanalytic work on this topic, such as Scott Wilson, *Stop Making Sense* (London: Karnac, 2015) and Jonathan W. Marshall, "Sonic Pleasure, Absence and the History of the Self: An Alternative Approach to the Criticism of Sound Art," *Sound Scripts*, 3 (2011): 6–25.

BIBLIOGRAPHY

IRREGULAR PUBLICATIONS: "*MÉLANGES*"

French medical publishing was often by individualized subscription, so there is some inconsistency regarding references. The Bibliothèque Inter-Universitaire de Médecine, Paris (BIUM), has a rich collection of "*mélanges,*" or individually bound collections of pamphlets, mostly from the major medical publishing houses of Baillière, Masson, Félix Alcan, Adrien Delahaye and Émile Lecroisnier. These are limited editions of essays, articles, and speeches, sometimes simultaneously published within a journal, or submitted to a congress. Where these are used, any journal edition which is listed on the title page of the pamphlet has also been indicated in the bibliography, as in: Henry Meige, *Sur le gigantisme*, extrait de *Archives générales de médecine* (October 1902) Paris: Albouy, 1903, mélange, collection of BIUM.

CONTRACTIONS

IPS, vols 1–3	Désiré-Magloire Bourneville and Paul Régnard, *Iconographie photographique de la Salpêtrière* (Paris: Progrès médical, 1875–1880), 3 vols
NIPS (1888–1918) vols 1–19	*Nouvelle iconographie photographique de la Salpêtrière* (Paris: Progrès médical, 1888–1918), 19 vols
RPHP (1869–1876) vols 1–8	A. de Montméja, P. Jules Rengade, Désiré-Magloire Bourneville et al, eds, *Revue Photographique des Hôpitaux de Paris* (Paris: Delahaye, 1869–1876), 8 vols

© The Editor(s) (if applicable) and The Author(s) 2016
J.W. Marshall, *Performing Neurology*,
DOI 10.1057/978-1-137-51762-3

Primary Sources

Abricossoff, Glafira. *L'hystérie au XVIIe et XVIIIe siècles*. Paris: Steinheil, 1897.

A.C. "La médecine vibratoire," *Chronique médical* 6.2 (January 15, 1899): 33–42.

Anon, "Catalogue des objets d'art et d'ameublement," catalogue for sale of materials from the Hôtel Varangeville (July 4–5, 1900), stamped: "Union centrale des arts décoratifs"; collection of Bibliothèque Charcot.

Anon, "Un drame de l'hypnotisme," *Pays illustré*, December 8, 1893, 1ff.

Anon. *Exposition universelle de 1889: Index bibliographique des ouvrages, mémoires et publications diverses de MM. les médecins, chirurgiens et accoucheurs des hôpitaux et hospices*. Paris: AP, 1889.

Anon, "La femme 'à la crinière de cheval,'" *Monde illustré*, August 5, 1893, back-page (unpaginated).

Anon, "Revue clinique hebdomadaire: Leçons de M. Charcot à la Salpêtrière sur l'idée et sur le langage," *Gazette des hôpitaux*, June 28, 1884, 593–4, collection of Jean-Martin Charcot, Bibliothèque Charcot.

Anon. *La revue d'amour*, souvenir program. Paris: Éditions artistiques de Paris, 1933, unpaginated, possession of the author.

Anon. "RICHER (Paul-Marie-Louis-Pierre)," In *Les biographies médicales*, edited by Maurice Genty and Paul Busquet, vol. 5, 65–76. Paris: Baillière, 1930–36.

Anon. "Une heure chez Sarah Bernhardt," *Chronique médicale* 4.19 (October 1, 1897), 609–616.

Antona-Traversi, Camillo. *L'Histoire du Grand-Guignol*. Paris Reims: Librairie théâtrale, 1933.

Arréat, Lucien. "Untitled review of Max Nordau's *Degenerescence* (Berlin: 1892)," *Revue philosophique de la France et de l'étranger* XXXV (1893): 434–9.

Avril, Jane [1933]. *Mes mémoires*. Paris: Association Les Bourlapapey, 2014. www.ebooks-bnr.com.

Ballu, Roger. "Le salon de 1887: Supplément," *L'illustration* 2305 (April 30, 1887): unpaginated.

Baudouin, Alphonse. "Quelques souvenirs de la Salpêtrière," *Paris médical* 56.21 (May 23, 1925): 517–520.

Bellugue, P. "Henry Meige," *Presse médicale* 29–30 (April 2–5, 1941): 372–4.

Binet, Alfred. "Le fétishisme dans l'amour: Étude de psychologie morbide," *Revue philosophique* 24 (1887): 143–167, 252–274.

———. "Les maladies du langage après travaux récens," *Revue des deux mondes* (January 1, 1892): 116–132.

———. "La peur chez les enfants," *Année psychologique* 2 (1896): 223–254.

———. "Reflexions sur le paradoxe de Diderot," *Année psychologique* 3 (1897): 279–95.

Bois, Jules. *Le monde invisible*. Paris: Flammarion, 1902.

Boucher, Louis. *La Salpêtrière: Son histoire*. Paris: Progrès médical, 1883.

Bourneville, Désiré-Magloire. "Étude sur les arthropathies," *RPHP* 3 (1871): 9–18, 67–77, 120–4, 243–49.

———. "J.-M. Charcot," *Archives de neurologie* 26.79 (September 1893): 177–210.

———. *Science et Miracle: Louise Lateau ou la stigmatisée belge.* Paris: Progrès médical, 1875.

Brissaud, Edouard, and Henry Meige, "La discipline psycho-motrice," extrait des *Archives générales de médecine* (26 May 1903), mélange, collection of BIUM.

———. *Gigantisme et acromégalie,* extrait de *Journal de médecine et de chirurgie pratique* (January 25, 1895) (Paris: A. Coccoz, 1895), mélange, collection of BIUM.

Brissaud, Edouard, and Pierre Marie. "Nécrologie: J.-M. Charcot," *Revue neurologique* 1.16 (August 31, 1893): 30–31.

Brouardel, Paul-Camille-Hippolyte et al., "Dangers des représentations de l'hypnotisme," *Tribune médicale* (1889): 46, collection of Jean-Martin Charcot, Bibliothèque Charcot.

Cartaz, A. "Du somnambulisme et du magnétisme: À propos du cours du Dr Charcot à la Salpêtrière," *La Nature* 7.1 (1879): 104–106.

Charcot, Jean-Martin. *Charcot the Clinician: The Tuesday Lessons: Excerpts from Nine Case Presentations on General Neurology Delivered at the Salpêtrière Hospital in 1887–1888.* Translated, edited, and commentary by Christopher Goetz. NY: Raven, 1987.

———. "Clinique médicale: De la contracture hystérique," *RPHP* 3 (1871): 193–203

———. *Oeuvres complètes.* Edited by Désiré-Magloire Bourneville et al. 13 vols. Paris: Progrès médical, 1888–1894.

———. *OC. Tome I. Leçons sur le maladies du système nerveux.* Edited by Désiré-Magloire Bourneville. Paris: Progrès médical, 1892.

———. *OC. Tome II. Leçons sur le maladies du système nerveux.* Edited by Désiré-Magloire Bourneville. Paris: Progrès médical, 1894.

———. *OC. Tome III. Leçons sur le maladies du système nerveux.* Edited by Joseph Babinski, Désiré Antoine François Bernard, Charles Féré, Georges Guinon, Pierre Marie, and Georges Gilles de la Tourette. Paris: Progrès médical, 1890.

———. *OC. Tome IV. Leçons sur le maladies du système nerveux.* Edited by Désiré-Magloire Bourneville and Edouard Brissaud. Paris: Progrès médical, 1893.

———. *OC. Tome V. Maladies des poumons et du système vasculaire.* Edited by Désiré-Magloire Bourneville. Paris: Progrès médical, 1888.

———. *OC. Tome VI. Maladies du foie et des reins.* Edited by Désiré-Magloire Bourneville, A. Sevestre, and Edouard Brissaud. Paris: Progrès médical, 1891.

———. *OC. Tome VII. Maladies des vieillards. Goutte et rhumatisme.* Edited by Désiré-Magloire Bourneville. Paris: Progrès médical, 1890.

————. *OC. Tome VIII. Maladies infectieuses, affections de la peu, kyste hydatiques, estomac et rate, théraputique.* Edited by Désiré-Magloire Bourneville. Paris: Progrès médical, 1889.

————. *OC. Tome IX. Hémorragie et ramollissement du cerveau, métallothérapie et hypnotisme, électrothérapie.* Edited by Désiré-Magloire Bourneville. Paris: Progrès médical, 1890.

————. *OC. Tome X. Hospice de la Salpêtrière: Clinique des maladies du système nerveux. Leçons du professeur, mémoires, notes et observations. Tome I.* Edited by Georges Guinon et al. Paris: Progrès médical, 1892.

————. *OC. Tome XI. Hospice de la Salpêtrière: Clinique des maladies du système nerveux. Leçons du professeur, mémoires, notes et observations. Tome II.* Edited by Georges Guinon and Achilles Souques. Paris: Progrès médical, 1893.

————. *OC. Tome XII. Leçons du mardi à la Salpêtrière policlinique 1887–1888.* Edited by Blin, Jean-Baptiste Charcot and Henri Colin, préface Joseph Babinski, 2nd ed. Paris: Progrès médical, 1892.

————. *OC. Tome XII. Leçons du mardi à la Salpêtrière. Professeur Charcot. Policlinique 1887–1888. Notes de cours de MM. Blin, [Jean-Baptiste] Charcot et [Henri] Colin. Tome I.* lithographic proof, collection of Bibliothèque Charcot, Paris: Progrès médical, 1887.

————. *OC. Tome XIII. Leçons du mardi à la Salpêtrière policlinique 1888–1889.* Paris: Progrès médical, 1889.

Charcot, Jean-Martin, and Alfred Binet. "Un calculateur du type visuel," *Revue philosophique de la France et de l'étranger* XXXV (1893): 590–4.

Charcot, Jean-Martin, and Paul Richer. *Contribution de l'hypnotisme chez les hystériques.* Nendeln Liechtenstein: Kraus Reprint, 1978.

————. *"Les démoniaques dans l'art" suivi de "La foi qui guérit,"* facsimile reproduction; edited and commentary by Georges Didi-Huberman and Pierre Fédida. Paris: Macula, 1984.

————. *Les difformes et les malades dans l'art.* Facsimile ed. Amsterdam: N.V. Boekhandel et antiquariaat, 1972.

————. "Le mascaron grotesque de l'église Santa Maria Formosa," *NIPS* 1 (1888): 87–92.

Charcot, Jean-Martin, and Jules Luys, Amédée Victor Dumontpallier, et al, "Rapport fait à la Société de Biologie sur la métalloscopie du docteur Burq," *Comptes-rendus des séances et mémoires de la Société de Biologie* 6.4 (1877): 1–24 and 6.5 (1878): 1–22.

Charcot, Jean-Martin, and Valentin Magnan. "Inversion du sens génitale," *Archives de neurologie* 3.7 (January 1882): 53–60 and 4.12 (November 1882): 296–322.

Claretie, Jules. *Les amours d'un interne.* Paris: Ollendorf, 1902.

————. "Charcot, le consolateur," *Annales politiques et littéraires* 21 (1903): 179–180.

————. *La vie à Paris.* Paris: Victor Harvard, 1881.

Christiansen, Viggo. *Centenaire de J.-M. Charcot*. Paris: Masson, 1925.

Coquelin, Ernest, and Constant Coquelin. *L'art de dire le monologue*. Paris: Ollendorff, 1884.

Courmelles, Foveau de. *Hypnotism*. London: Routledge, 1895.

Courrière, Berthe de. "Néron: Prince de la science," *Mercure de France* (October 9, 1893): 144–6.

Dana, C. L., "Charcot," *Medical Record* (September 9, 1893): 351–2.

Daudet, Léon. *Devant la douleur: Souvenirs des milieux littéraires, politiques, artistiques et médicaux de 1880 à 1905*. Paris: Nouvelle librairie nationale, 1915.

———. [1894]. *Les morticoles*. Paris: Fasquelle, 1956.

Debove, Maurice. "Éloge de J.-M. Charcot," *Mémoires de l'Académie de médecine* 39 (1901): 1–19.

Delboeuf, Joseph. "Une visite à la Salpêtrière," *Revue de Belgique* 54 (October 15, 1886): 122–147, 259–275.

Dequillebecq, Léon. "Une matinée à la Salpêtrière," *Annales politiques et littéraires* 21.531 (August 27, 1893): 135–6.

Diderot, Denis, ed. *Encyclopédie; ou Dictionnaire raisonné des sciences, des arts, et des métiers, par une société de gens de lettres*. Paris: Briasson et al 1751–65.

Doumic, René. *Les Jeunes, études et portraits* (Paris, Perrin et Cie, 1896). reproduced on http://obvil.paris-sorbonne.frcorpuscritiquedoumic_jeunesbody-8.

Duchenne de Boulogne, and Guillaume-Benjamin. *The Mechanism of Human Facial Expression*. Translated, edited, and commentary by R. Andrew Cuthbertson. Cambridge: Cambridge University Press, 1990.

Duval, Mathias [1891]. *Précis d'anatomie à l'usage des artistes*. Paris: L.-H. May, 1900.

Fiessinger, Charles. "Charcot jugé par le Dr Fiessinger, d'Oyonnax," *Revue de l'hypnotisme* 11.6 (December 1896): 186–7.

Féré, Charles. "J.-M. Charcot et son oeuvre," *Revue des deux mondes* 122 (March 15, 1893): 410–424.

———. "Review of *Iconographie photographique de la Salpêtrière* (service de M. Charcot) par Bourneville et Régnard," *Archives de neurologie* 1 (1881): 625–633.

Fleury, Maurice de. *Introduction à la médecine de l'esprit*. Paris: Baillière, 1898.

Flaubert, Gustave [1857]. *Madame Bovary: A Story of a Provincial Life*. Translated by Alan Russell. Harmondsworth: Penguin, 1981.

Freud, Sigmund. *The Standard Edition of the Complete Psychological Works of Sigmund Freud*. Edited and translated by James Strachey. London: Hogarth Press, 1973.

Gamgee, Arthur. "An Account of a Demonstration on the Phenomena of Hysterio-Epilepsy," *British Medical Journal* 2 (October 12, 1878): 545–8.

Gilles de la Tourette, Georges. *L'épilogue d'un procès célèbre (affaire Eyraud-Bompard)*. Paris: Progrès médical, 1891.

———. "Jean-Martin Charcot," *NIPS* 6 (1893): 241–250.

Gilles de la Tourette, Georges, and Damain. "Un danseur monomane," *Annales d'hygiène publique et de médecine légale* 3.29 (1893): 268–276.

Goetschy, Gustave. "Les femmes du monde artistes: Madame Charcot," *Revue des arts decoratifs* 20.1 (1900): 41–51.

Grimm, Thomas. "Le magnétisme," *Petit Journal* 699 (February 15, 1882): 1ff.

Guérin, Alexandre. "Une visite à la Salpêtrière," *Revue illustrée* 4.40, 4.42 (August 1, 1887; September 1, 1887): 97–103, 171–7.

Guinon, Georges. "Charcot intime," *Paris médical* 56.21 (May 23, 1925): 511–516.

Guillain, Georges. *J.-M. Charcot 1825–1893: His Life—His Work*. Translated by Pearce Bailey. NY: Paul Hoeber, 1959.

Guillain, Georges, and Pierre Mathieu. *La Salpêtrière*. Paris: Masson, 1925.

Guillemot, Maurice. "À la Salpêtrière," *Paris illustré* 5.22 (September 24, 1887): 354–5.

Hamel, Maurice. "Le salon de 1887," *Gazette des beaux-arts* 35–36 (June 1887): 473–510, and (July 1887): 35–56.

Helme, François. *Les jardins de la médecine*. Paris: Vigot, 1907.

Henderson, Jane. "Personal Reminiscences of M. Charcot," *Glasgow Medical Journal* 40 (1893): 292–8.

Hugo, Victor [1862]. *Les misérables*. Translated by Isabel Hapgood. Adelaide: Adelaide University Press, 2014. Reproduced on https://ebooks.adelaide.edu. au/h/hugo/victor/lesmis/.

Ignotus [real name: Félix Platel], "Le cabotinage," *Figaro* (April 18, 1883): 1.

———. "M. Charcot," *Les hommes de mon temps*. Paris: Bureau du Figaro, from 1878; dating incomplete, 377–388.

Janet, Pierre. "Charcot: Son oeuvre philosophique," *Revue philosophique de la France et de l'étranger* XXXIX (June 1895): 569–604.

Jeanne des Anges, Soeur. *Soeur Jeanne des Anges: Supérieure des Ursulines de Loudun (XVIIe siècle): Autobiographie d'une hystérique possédée (Bibliothèque diabolique—collection Bourneville)*. Annotations Gabriel Legué and Georges Gilles de la Tourette, Préface Jean-Martin Charcot. Paris: Progrès médical, 1886.

Laurent, Léon. "Lanterne de projection et mégascope," *La Nature* 6.2 (1878): 69–70.

Levillain, Fernand. "Charcot et l'école de la Salpêtrière," *Revue encyclopédique* 4 (1894): 108–115.

Leyden, Ernst von. "Éloge de J.-M. Charcot," *Archives de médecine experimentale* 6 (1894): 151–4.

Londe, Albert. *La photographie médical*. Préface Jean-Martin Charcot. Paris: Gauthier-Villars, 1893.

———. "Le nouveau laboratoire de la Salpêtrière," *Nature* 21.7 (1893): 370–4.

Lorde, André de, "La peur dans la littérature," *Revue mondiale* (March 15, 1927): 118–128.

Lorde, André de, and Alfred Binet. *Un crime dans une maison de fous*. Paris: Libraire théâtrale, 1927.

Lorde, André de et al., *Théâtre d'Épouvante: Une leçon à la Salpêtrière. L'obsession. La dormeuse. Au rat mort. Le système du docteur Goudron et du professeur Plume. La dernière torture. Sur la dalle*. Préface Albert Sorel. Paris: Charpentier et Fasquelle, 1909.

Lorde, André de et al., *La folie au théâtre: L'homme mystérieux. La petite roque. Les invisibles*. Préface Gilbert Ballet. Paris: Fontemoing, 1913.

Lorde, André et al., *Théâtre de la mort: L'illustre Professeur Truchard. L'homme mystérieux*. Préface André Antoine. Paris: Figuière, 1928.

Lorde, André et al., *Théâtre de la peur: L'horrible expérience. Baraterie. L'acquittée*. Préface Alfred Binet. Paris: Figuière, 1924.

Lorde, André de, and Eugène Morel. *Terre d'épouvante*, in *L'illustration théâtrale: Journal d'actualités dramatiques. Suppléments* 70 (1907).

Lubimoff, A. *Le professeur Charcot: Étude scientifique et biologique*. Translated by Lydie Rostopchine. Paris: 1894.

Marc, L. "Pierrot, Assassin de sa femme," *L'illustration* 2300 (March 26, 1887): 209, 216.

Margueritte, Paul. *Pierrot, assassin de sa femme*. Paris: Paul Schmidt, 1882.

Marie, Pierre. "Éloge de J.-M. Charcot," *Bulletin de l'Académie de médecine* 93 (1925): 576–593.

M.D., "La suggestion criminelle: À propos d'un drame," *Petite république* (December 9, 1893): 1.

Meige, Henry. "Charcot artiste," *NIPS* 11 (1898): 489–516.

———. *École nationale supérieure des beaux-arts. Cours d'anatomie. Leçon d'ouverture (18 décembre 1922)*. Paris: Masson, 1923.

———. "Les 'écorchés,'" *Aesculape* 16 (1926): 1–7.

———. "La genèse des tics," *Journal de neurologie* (June 5, 1902): 201–6.

———. *L'infantilisme, le féminisme et les hermaphrodites antiques*, extrait de *L'anthropologie*, vol. VI. Paris: Masson, 1895. mélange, collection of BIUM.

———. *Le juif errant à la Salpêtrière*. Paris: Bataille, 1893.

———. "Les possédées des dieux dans l'art antique," *NIPS* 7 (1894): 35–64.

———. *Les possédées noires*. Paris: Schiller, 1894.

———. *La Pythie de Delphes*. Luxembourg: J. Beffort, 1921.

———. "Une révolution anatomique," *NIPS* 20 (1907): 97–115, 174–183.

———. *Sur le gigantisme*, extrait de *Archives générales de médecine* (October 1902). Paris: Albouy, 1903. mélange, collection of BIUM.

Meurville, Louis de, "Le docteur Charcot," *Gazette de France* (August 18, 1893): 1–2.

Munthe, Axel [1929]. *The Story of San Michele*. London: John Murray, 1948.

Norech. "Le Dr Charcot à la Salpêtrière," *Paris illustré* 5.1 (April 30, 1887): 14.

Nordau, Max [1892]. *Degeneration*. NY: Howard Fertig, 1968.

Palau, Pierre, and Olaf [pseudonym of Joseph Babinski]. *Les Détraquées*. Paris: 1958.

Peugniez, Paul-Aimé-Desiré. *J.-M. Charcot (1825–1893)*. Amiens: Picarde, 1893.

Platel, Félix, published under pseudonym of "Ignotus" (see above).

Pont-Calé. "Le professeur Charcot," *Hommes d'aujourd'hui* 7.343 (1890): 1–3.

Ranse, F. de. "*Iconographie photographique de la Salpêtrière* [revue]," *Progrès médical* 7 (1879): 331–332.

Raymond, Fulgence. *Leçons sur les maladies de système nerveux, Hospice de la Salpêtrière (année 1894–1895) par F. Raymond, première série*. Paris: Octave Don, 1896.

Raymond, Fulgence, et al., "Inauguration du monument élevé à la mémoire du professeur J.-M. Charcot," *NIPS* 11 (1898): 410–418.

Reenooz, C., "Charcot devoilé," *Revue scientifique des femmes* 1.6 (December 1888): 241–7.

Rengade, P. Jules. "Le nouveau traitement de l'ataxie," *Illustration* 2404 (March 23, 1889): 231–2.

Richard, H. "Richer (Paul-Marie-Louis-Pierre)," *Les Biographes médicales* 4.1 (January 1930): 65–76.

Richer, Paul, "L'anatomie et les arts plastiques," *Séance publique annuelle des Cinq Académies* (October 25, 1907).

———. *L'art et la médecine*. Paris: Gaultier, 1901.

———. *Artistic Anatomy*. Translated by Robert Hale. NY: Watson-Guptill, 1986.

———. *Canon des proportions du corps humain*. Paris: Delgrave, 1919.

———. *Dialogues sur l'art et la science*. Paris: Auxerre, 1897.

———. *École nationale et spéciale des beaux-arts: Cours d'anatomie. Leçon d'ouverture (25 novembre 1903)*. Paris: Masson, 1903.

———. *Études cliniques sur la grande hystérie ou l'hystéro-épilepsie*. Paris: Delahaye et Lecroisnier, 1881.

———. *Études cliniques sur la grande hystérie ou l'hystéro-épilepsie*. Paris: Delahaye et Lecroisnier, 1885.

———. "Locomotion humaine," In *Traité de physique biologique*, edited by Arsène d'Arsonval, Étienne-Jules Marey, et al., vol. 1. Paris: Masson, 1901–03.

———. *Nouvelle anatomie artistique*. 7 vols. Paris: Plon, 1889–1929.

———. *Paralysies et contractures hystériques* (Paris: 1882), manuscript copy submitted for the Medical Academy prize, collection of Bakken Museum and Library of Electricity in Life, Minneapolis.

———. *Physiologie artistique de l'homme en mouvement*. Paris: Octave Doin, 1895.

Richer, Paul, Georges Gilles de la Tourette, and Albert Londe. "Avertissement," *NIPS* 1 (1888): I–II.

Richet, Charles [1905]. *Circé*. Paris: Carqueiranne, 1920.

——. "Les démoniaques d'aujourd'hui," *Revue des deux mondes* 1.37 (January 15, 1880): 340–372.

——. *L'homme et l'intelligence.* Paris: Alcan, 1884.

——. "La peur: Étude psychologique," *Revue des deux mondes* 76 (July 1886): 87–117.

Roc, Étienne, "Professeur Mathias Duval," *Hommes d'aujourd'hui* 273 (1886): 1–4.

Robertson, George M., "Hypnotism at Paris and Nancy: Notes of a visit," *British Medical Journal* 38.163 (October 1892): 494–531.

Roblot, Léon, "Recherches originales et pratiques sur la gymnastique et les divers sports à la fin du XIXe siècle," In *Les sciences biologiques à la fin du XIXe siècle,* edited by Jean-Martin Charcot, Étienne-Jules Marey, Mathias Duval et al., 655–673. Paris: Société d'éditions scientifiques, 1893.

Séglas, Joseph. *Leçons clinique sur les maladies mentales et nerveuses (Salpêtrière 1887–1894).* Paris: Asselin et Houzeau, 1895.

Souques, Achilles. *Charcot intime,* extrait de *Presse médicale* 42 (May 27, 1925): 693–8. Paris: Masson, 1925. mélange, collection of BIUM.

Souques, Achilles, and Henry Meige. "Jean-Martin Charcot," *Biographies médicales* (May–July 1939): 321–352.

Starr, Moses Allen. "The Neurological Clinic at the Salpêtrière: Jean-Martin Charcot," In *The Physician Throughout the Ages,* edited by Arthur Selwyn-Brown, vol. 1, 651–654. New York: Capehart-Brown, 1928.

Starr, Moses Allen, et al. [23 November 1925]. "Minutes of Boston Medical History Club centenary meeting," *Boston Medical and Surgical Association* 194 (1926): 10–20.

Various. *Service médical des théâtres, cafés-concérts, cirques, etc., de Paris: Agenda 1904.* Paris: Trouette, 1905.

Véron, Pierre, Untitled eulogy of J.-M. Charcot, *Monde illustré* (August 26, 1893): 130–3.

Wagner, Richard. *Wagner on Music and Drama.* London: Victor Gollancz, 1970.

Watteville, A. de, "Critical Digests and Notices of Books: *Études cliniques sur la grande hystérie ou l'hystéro-épilepsie,* par le Dr Paul Richer," *Brain* IV (1882): 507–517.

Withington, C.F. "A Last Glimpse of Charcot at the Salpêtrière," *Boston Medical and Surgical Journal* CXXIX.8 (1893): 207.

X [possible pseudonym of Pont-Calé], "M. Charcot à la Salpêtrière," *Annales politiques et littéraires,* July 5, 1885, 12–13.

Zola, Émile. "The Experimental Novel" (1893), In *The Nineteenth Century Novel,* edited by Stephen Regan, 104–117. London: Routledge, 2001.

SECONDARY SOURCES

Apollonio, Umbro, ed. and trans. *Futurist Manifestoes*. London: Thames and Hudson, 1973.

Aragon, Louis, and André Breton. "Le cinquantenaire de l'hystérie (1878–1928)," *Révolution surréaliste* 4 (March 15, 1928): 20–22.

Artaud, Antonin. *The Theatre and its Double*. Translated by Mary Caroline Richards. NY: George Weidenfeld, 1958.

Aubenas, Sylvie, ed. *L'art du nu au XIXe siècle: Le photographe et son modèle*. Paris: Hazan/BNF, 1997.

Auerbach, Nina. *Private Theatricals*. Cambridge, MA: Harvard University Press, 1990.

Ballestriero, R. "Anatomical Models and Wax Venuses," *Journal of Anatomy* 216.2 (February 2010): 223–234.

Barberis, Daniela. "Changing Practices of Commemoration in Neurology," *Osiris* 14 (1999): 102–117.

Barish, Jonas. *The Antitheatrical Prejudice*. Berkley: California University Press, 1981.

Beizer, Janet. *Ventriloquized Bodies*. Ithaca: Cornell University Press, 1994.

Benjamin, Walter. *The Arcades Project*. Translated by Howard Eiland and Kevin McLaughlin. Cambridge, MA: Belknap, 1999.

Bernard, Denis, and André Gunthert. *L'instant rêvé Albert Londe*. Nîmes: Chambon, 1993.

Blau, Herbert. "The Audition of Dream and Events," *TDR: The Drama Review* 31.3 (1987): 59–72.

Bogousslavsky, Julien, ed. *Following Charcot*. Basel: Karger, 2011.

Bogousslavsky, Julien, et al., "Crime, Hysteria and *Belle Époque* Hypnotism," *European Neurology* 62 (2009): 193–199.

Bonduelle, Michel. "Charcot et les Daudet," *Presse médicale* 22.32 (October 23, 1993): 1641–1648.

———. "Léon Daudet, mémorialiste de Charcot," *Revue du practicien* 49 (1999): 804–7.

Bonduelle, Michel, and Toby Gelfand. "Hysteria Behind the Scenes: Jane Avril at the Salpêtrière," *Journal of the History of Neurosciences* 7.1 (1998): 35–42.

Bourgois, Christian, ed. *Le théâtre: Cahiers dirigés par [Fernando] Arrabal*. vol. 2. Paris: Théâtre Christian Bourgois, 1969.

Brais, Bernard. "Jean-Martin Charcot et le césarisme de Faculté." Unpublished article communicated to the French Neurology Society, Paris (June 9–11, 1993), collection of the Bibliothèque Charcot.

Braun, Marta. *Picturing Time*. Chicago: Chicago University Press, 1994.

Brecht, Bertolt. *Brecht on Theatre*. Edited and translated by John Willett. London: Methuen, 2001.

Broche, François. *Léon Daudet: Le dernier imprécateur.* Paris: Robert Laffont, 1992.

Bronfen, Elisabeth. *The Knotted Subject: Hysteria and its Discontents.* Princeton: Princeton University Press, 1998.

Bulfinch, Thomas. *Bulfinch's Mythology.* New York: Crowell, 1970.

Butler, Judith. *Bodies That Matter.* NY: Routledge, 1993.

———. *Excitable Speech.* NY: Routledge, 1997.

Callen, Anthea. "The Body and Difference," *Art History* 20.1 (March 1997): 23–60.

———. "Masculinity and Muscularity," *Paragraph* 26.1–2 (March–July 2003): 17–41.

Cambor, Kate. *Gilded Youth: Three Lives in France's Belle Époque.* NY: Farrar, 2009.

Carroy[-Thirard], Jacqueline. *Hypnose, suggestion et psychologie.* Paris: Presses universitaires de France, 1991.

———. "Hystérie, théâtre, littérature au dix-neuvième siècle," *Psychanalyse à l'université* 7.26 (March 1982): 299–317.

Cartwright, Lisa. *Screening the Body.* Minneapolis: Minnesota University Press, 1995.

Certeau, Michel de. *The Possession at Loudun.* Chicago: Chicago University Press, 2000.

Chemers, Michael. *Staging Stigma.* New York: Palgrave Macmillan, 2008.

Chenivesse, Pierre. "Grand Guignol et aliénisme," In *Psychiatries dans l'histoire*, edited by Jacques Arveiller, 431–438. Caen: Presses Universitaires de Caen, 2008.

Cixous, Hélène, and Catherine Clément. *The Newly Born Woman,* Translated by Betsy Wing. Minneapolis: Minnesota University Press, 1975.

Clébert, Jean-Paul. *Les Daudet.* Paris: Presses de la Renaissance, 1988.

Comar, Philippe, et al., *Figures du corps.* Paris: ENSBA, 2009.

Cooke, Lynne, and Peter Woolen, eds. *Visual Culture.* Seattle: Bay Press, 1995.

Crabtree, Adam. *From Mesmer to Freud.* New Haven: Yale University Press, 1993.

Creed, Barbara. *The Monstrous Feminine.* NY: Routledge, 1993.

Dagen, Philippe. "Le 'Premier artiste,'" *Romantisme* 84 (1994): 69–78.

Darnton, Robert. *The Great Cat Massacre.* NY: Basic Books, 1984.

———. *Mesmerism and the End of the Enlightenment.* Cambridge, MA: Harvard University Press, 1968.

Darwin, Charles [1872]. *The Expression of the Emotions in Man and Animals.* Edited and commentary by Paul Ekman and Phillip Prodger. London: HarperCollins, 1998.

Deák, František. "Théâtre du Grand Guignol," *TDR: The Drama Review* 18.1 (March 1974): 34–43.

Delamotte, Isabelle. "La place de Charcot dans la documentation medical d'Émile Zola," *Cahiers naturalistes* 73 (1999): 287–99.

Derrida, Jacques. *Writing and Difference*. Translated by Alan Bass. London: Routledge, 1978.

Diamond, Elin. "Realism and Hysteria," *Discourse* 13.1 (Fall-Winter 1990–1991): 59–92.

Didi-Huberman, Georges. *The Invention of Hysteria*. Translated by Alisa Hartz. Cambridge, MA: MIT, 2003.

Dingwell, Eric, ed. *Abnormal Hypnotic Phenomena*. 3 vols. London: Churchill, 1967.

Eade, Jane. "The Theatre of Death," *Oxford Art Journal* 36.1 (2013): 109–125.

Eco, Umberto. *On Ugliness*. London: Harvil Seeker, 2007.

Ellenberger, Henri. *The Discovery of the Unconscious*. London: Penguin, 1970.

Ellis, Jack. *The Physician-Legislators of France*. Cambridge: Cambridge University Press, 1990.

Elsaesser, Thomas, and Adam Barker, eds. *Early Cinema*. London: BFI, 1990.

Enquist, Per Olov. *The Book About Blanche and Marie*. NY: Overlook, 2007.

Finger, Stanley. *Origins of Neurosciences*. NY: Oxford University Press, 1994.

Foucault, Michel. *Archaeology of Knowledge*. Translated by A.M. Sheridan Smith. NY: Pantheon, 1972.

———. *The Birth of the Clinic*. Translated by A.M. Sheridan Smith. NY: Vintage, 1994.

———. *The History of Sexuality. Volume I. An Introduction*. Translated by Robert Hurley. London: Penguin, 1990.

———. *Madness and Civilization*. Translated by Richard Howard. NY: Vintage, 1988.

Fox, Alistair. *Speaking Pictures: Neuropsychoanalysis and Authorship in Film and Literature*. Indianapolis: Indiana University Press, 2016.

Freund, Philip. *The Birth of Theatre*. London: Peter Owen, 2003.

Frizot, Michel. *Étienne-Jules Marey*. Paris: Nathan, 2004.

Fulcher, Jane. *French Cultural Politics and Music*. Oxford: Oxford University Press, 1999.

Furse, Anna. *Augustine (Big Hysteria)*. Oxford: Routledge, 2013.

Garner, Stanton. "Physiologies of the Modern: Zola, Experimental Medicine, and the Naturalist Stage," *Modern Drama* 43 (Winter 2000): 529–542.

Gauld, Alan. *A History of Hypnosis*. Cambridge: Cambridge University Press, 1992.

Gates, John. "Non-Epileptic Seizures," *Epilepsy and Behavior* 3 (2002): 28–33.

Geertz, Clifford. *The Interpretation of Cultures*. London: Hutchinson, 1975.

Gelfand, Toby. "Medical Nemesis, Paris, 1894: Léon Daudet's *Les morticoles*," *Bulletin of History of Medicine* 60 (1986): 155–176.

———. "Mon cher docteur Freud," *Bulletin of the History of Medicine* 62.4 (Winter 1988): 563–588.

Germiniani, Francisco, et al., "Where is Gilles? Or, the Little Mistake in a Copy of Brouillet's painting *A Clinical Lesson at the Salpêtrière*," *Arquivos de Neuro-Psiquiatria* 71.5 (2013): 327–329.

Gerould, Daniel. "Oscar Méténier and *comédie rosse*," *TDR: The Drama Review* 28.1 (Spring 1984): 15–19.

———. "Paul Margueritte and *Pierrot Assassin of His Wife*," *TDR: The Drama Review* 23.1 (March 1979), 103–112.

Gilman, Sander. *The Jew's Body*. NY: Routledge, 1992.

———. *Seeing the Insane*. NY: John Wiley and Sons, 1982.

Gilman, Sander, et al., *Hysteria Beyond Freud*. LA: California, 1993.

Goetz, Christopher G. "Charcot and the Myth of Misogyny," *Neurology* 52 (May 1999): 1678–1685.

———. "Charcot: Scientifique bifrons," *Revue neurologique* 150.10 (1994): 485–9.

———. "The Salpêtrière in the Wake of Charcot's Death," *Neurology* 37 (March 1987): 444–7.

——— trans., ed. and commentary to Jean-Martin Charcot. *Charcot the Clinician: The Tuesday Lessons: Excerpts From Nine Case Presentations on General Neurology Delivered at the Salpêtrière Hospital in 1887–1888*. NY: Raven, 1987.

Goetz, Christopher G., Michel Bonduelle, and Toby Gelfand. *Charcot: Constructing Neurology*. NY: Oxford University Press, 1995.

Goldstein, Jan. *Console and Classify*. Cambridge: Cambridge University Press, 1987.

———. "Foucault Among the Sociologists," *History and Theory* 23 (1984):170–192.

———. "The Wandering Jew and the Problem of Psychiatric Anti-Semitism in Fin-de-Siècle France," *Journal of Contemporary History* 20 (1985): 521–552.

Gordon, Rae Beth. *Why the French Love Jerry Lewis*. Stanford: Stanford University Press, 2002.

Gordon, Mel. *The Grand Guignol: Theatre of Fear and Terror*. NY: Da Capo, 1997.

Gouspy, Carol. "La représentation du chanteur de charme et du scieur," *Image and Narrative* 20 (December 2007). http://www.imageandnarrative.beinar-chiveaffiche_findesieclegouspy.htm.

Grey, Thomas, ed. *Richard Wagner and his World*. Princeton: Princeton University Press, 2009.

Gunthert, André. *Albert Londe*. Paris: Nathan, 1999.

Hand, Richard, and Michael Wilson. *Grand-Guignol: The French Theatre of Horror*. Exeter, UK: Exeter University Press, 2002.

Hannaway, Caroline, and Ann La Berge, eds. *Constructing Paris Medicine*. Amsterdam: Rodopi, 1998.

Hansen, Chadwick, *Witchcraft at Salem*. NY: Braziller, 1969.

Harrington, Anne. *Medicine, Mind, and the Double Brain*. Princeton: Princeton University Press, 1987.

———. "Metals and Magnets in Medicine: Hysteria, Hypnosis and Medical Culture in *fin de siècle* Paris," *Psychological Medicine* 18 (1988): 21–38.

Harris, Ruth. *Murders and Madness: Medicine, Law, and Society in the fin de siècle.* Oxford: Clarendon, 1989.

———. "The 'Unconscious' and Catholicism in France," *Historical Journal* 47.2 (2004): 331–54.

Hayden, Michael. *Huntington's Chorea.* Berlin: Springer-Verlag, 1981.

Herbert, Stephen, ed. *A History of Pre-Cinema.* 3 vols. London: Routledge, 2001.

Herder, Wouter de. "History of Acromegaly," *Neuroendocrinology* (January 5, 2015): 1–11.

Hillman, Robert. "A Scientific Study of Mystery: The Role of the Medical and Popular Press in the Nancy-Salpêtrière Controversy on Hypnotism," *Bulletin of the History of Medicine* 39.2 (1965): 163–182.

Hunter, Dianne. *The Makings of "Dr. Charcot's Hysteria Shows".* NY: Mellen, 1998.

Hustvedt, Asti. *Medical Muses.* NY: Norton, 2011.

Innes, Christopher, ed. *A Sourcebook on Naturalist Theatre.* London: Routledge, 2000.

Iles, Chrissie, and Russell Roberts, eds. *In Visible Light: Photography and Classification.* Oxford: Museum of Modern Art Oxford, 1997.

Iragui, Vicente J. "The Charcot-Bouchard Controversy," *Archives of Neurology* 43 (March 1986): 290–5.

Irigaray, Luce. *That Sex Which is Not One.* Translated by Catherine Porter and Carolyn Burke. Ithaca: Cornell University Press, 1977.

Jangfeldt, Bengt. *Axel Munthe.* Hildasholm Borås: Hildasholm Museum Centraltryckeriet, 2001.

Johnson, Belinda. "Renaissance Body Matters," *International Journal of Sexuality and Gender Studies* 6.1 (2001): 77–94.

Johnson, Felicity, et al., *Anne Ferran.* Perth: Lawrence Wilson Art Gallery, 2014.

Jonte-Pace, Diane. *Speaking the Unspeakable.* Berkeley: California University Press, 2001.

Kelly, Mary, et al., *Interim.* NY: New Museum of Contemporary Art, 1997.

Klestinec, Cynthia. "Civility, Comportment, and the Anatomy Theater," *Renaissance Quarterly* 60 (2007): 434–463.

Kristeva, Julia. *Powers of Horror.* Translated by Leon Roudiez. NY: Columbia University Press, 1980.

Kushner, Howard. *A Cursing Brain?* Cambridge, MA: Harvard University Press, 2000.

Laissus, Yves. *Le musée national d'histoire naturelle.* Paris: Gallimard, 1995.

Lamers-Schütze, Petra, ed. *Encyclopaedia anatomica: Museo La Specola, Florence.* Köln: Taschen, 2001.

Lanska, Douglas. "Early Controversies Over Athetosis," *Tremor and Other Hyperkinetic Movement* 2 (2012) and 3 (2013).http://www.tremorjournal.org.

Lees, A. J. "Georges Gilles de la Tourette," *Revue Neurologique* 142.11 (1986): 808–16.

Lellouch, A. "Charcot, découvreur de maladies," *Revue neurologique* 150.8–9 (1994): 506–510.

Leroux-Hugon, Véronique. "L'évasion manquée de Geneviève, ou des aléas de la traduction," *Frénésie. Histoire de psychiatrie et psychanalyse* 2.4 (1987): 103–112.

Lhermitte, F., and Jean-Louis Signoret. "L'aphasie de J.-M. Charcot à Th. Alajouanine," *Revue neurologique* 138.12 (1982): 893–919.

Maines, Rachel. *The Technology of Orgasm.* Baltimore: Johns Hopkins University Press, 1999.

Mannoni, Laurent. *The Great Art of Light and Shadow.* Translated by Richard Crangle. Exeter: Exeter University Press, 2000.

Marneffe, Daphne de. "Looking and Listening: The Construction of Clinical Knowledge in Charcot and Freud," *Signs* 17.1 (Autumn 1991): 71–111.

Marquer, Bertrand. *Les romans de la Salpêtrière.* Geneva: Droz, 2008.

Marsh, Anne. *Pat Brassington.* Hobart: Quintus, 2006.

Marshall, Jonathan W. "The Archaeology of the Abstract Body: Parascientific Discourse and the Legacy of Dr J.-M. Charcot, 1876–1969," *French History and Civilization: Papers from the George Rudé Seminar* 3 (2009): 92–111. Reproduced on http://www.h-france.netruderudevolumeiiiMarshallVol3.pdf.

———. "Beyond the Theatre of Desire: Hysterical Performativity and Perverse Choreography in the Writings of the Salpêtrière School, 1862–1893," In *Fin de siècle Sexuality: The Making of a Central Problem,* edited by Peter Cryle and Christopher E. Forth, 42–60. Newark: Delaware University Press, 2008.

———. "Dynamic Medicine and Theatrical Form at the *fin de siècle*: A Formal Analysis of Dr Jean-Martin Charcot's Pedagogy, 1862–1893," *Modernism/Modernity* 15.1 (January 2008): 131–153.

———. "Hypnotic Performance and the Falsity of Appearances: The Aesthetics of Medical Spectatorship and Axel Munthe's Critique of Jean-Martin Charcot," In *Elective Affinities,* edited by Catriona MacLeod et al., 221–242. Amsterdam: Rodopi, 2009.

———. "Kleist's *Übermarionetten* and Schrenck-Notzing's *Traumtänzerin*: Nervous Mechanics and Hypnotic Performance Under Modernism," In *Heinrich von Kleist and Modernity,* edited by Bernd Fischer and Tim Mehigan, 261–281. Rochester: Camden House, 2011.

———. "Performing Hysteria," *Proceedings of the Western Society of French History* 28 (2002): 19–26.

———. "The Priestesses of Apollo and the Heirs of Aesculapius: Medical Art-Historical Approaches to Ancient Choreography After Charcot," *Forum for Modern Language Studies* 43.4 (October 2007): 410–426.

———. "Sonic Pleasure, Absence and the History of the Self: An Alternative Approach to the Criticism of Sound Art," *Sound Scripts* 3 (2011): 6–25.

———. "The Theatre of the Athletic Nude: The Teaching and Study of Anatomy at the École des Beaux-Arts, Paris, 1873–1940," *Being There: ADSA (Australasian Association for theatre and Drama Studies) Conference Proceedings* (June 2008). http://ses.library.usyd.edu.aubitstream212325111ADSA2006_Marshall.pdf.

————. "'The World of the Neurological Pavilion': Hauntology and European Modernism *'mal tourné,"* *TDR: The Drama Review* 57.4 (Winter 2013), 60–85.

Matlock, Jann. *Scenes of Seduction.* NY: Columbia University Press, 1994.

McCarren, Felicia. "The 'Symptomatic Act' circa 1900: Hysteria, Hypnosis, Electricity and Dance," *Critical Inquiry* (Summer 1995): 748–774.

McConachie, Bruce. *Theatre and Mind.* London: Palgrave Macmillan, 2012.

Messing, Scott. *Neoclassicism in Music.* Rochester, NY: Rochester University Press, 1996.

Micale, Mark. *Approaching Hysteria.* Princeton: Princeton University Press, 1995.

————. "Charcot and *les névroses traumatiques,"* *Revue neurologique* 150.8–9 (1994): 498–505.

————. "Charcot and the Idea of Hysteria in the Male," *Medical History* 34 (1990): 363–411.

————. "Hysteria Male/Hysteria Female," In *Science and Sensibility,* edited by Marina Benjamin, 200–242. Oxford: Blackwell, 1991.

————. "The Salpêtrière in the Age of Charcot," *Journal of Contemporary History* 20 (1985): 703–731.

Miller, Julian, et al., "Some Aspects of Charcot's Influence on Freud," *Journal of the American Psychoanalytic Association* 17.2 (1969): 608–23.

Munthe, Gustave, and Gudrun Uexküll. *The Story of Axel Munthe.* London: John Murray, 1953.

Murray, Timothy, ed. *Mimesis, Masochism, and Mime.* Ann Arbor: Michigan University Press, 1997.

Nye, Robert. *Crime, Madness, and Politics in Modern France.* Princeton: Princeton University Press 1984.

Oughourlian, Jean-Michel. *The Puppet of Desire.* Translated by Eugene Webb. Stanford: Stanford University Press, 1991.

Parker, James. "The Hotel de Varengeville Room and the Room from the Palais Paar," *Metropolitan Museum of Art Bulletin* (November 1969): 129–146.

Pick, Daniel. *Faces of Degeneration.* Cambridge: Cambridge University Press, 1989.

Pigeard-Micault, Nathalie, "L'entrée des femmes à l'école de médecine" (2007), reproduced on http://www.biusante.parisdescartes.frhistmedmedicafemmesmed.htm.

Pierron, Agnès. *Les nuits blanche du Grand Guignol.* Paris: Seuil, 2002.

————. *Le théâtre medical du prince de la terreur.* Paris: Les empêcheurs de penser en rond, 1996.

Plato, "The Allegory of the Cave," from *Republic,* VII.514.a.2 to VII.517.a.7, translated by Thomas Sheehan. Reproduced on https://web.stanford.edu/class/ihum40/cave.pdf.

Presner, Todd. "'Clear heads, solid stomachs, and hard muscles': Max Nordau and the Aesthetics of Jewish Regeneration," *Modernism/Modernity* 10.2 (2003): 269–296.

Ramachandran, Vilayanur, and W. Hirstein. "The Science of Art: A Neurological Theory of Aesthetic Experience," *Journal of Consciousness Studies* 6.6–7 (1999): 15–51.

Rivière, François, and Gabrielle Wittkop. *Grand Guignol*. Paris: Henri Veyrier, 1979.

Roach, Joseph. *The Player's Passion*. Delaware: Delaware University Press, 1985.

Roche, Alphonse. *Alphonse Daudet*. Boston: Twayne Publishers, 1976.

Rose, F. Clifford, ed. *A Short History of Neurology*. Butterworth Heinemann: Oxford, 1999.

Rose, F. Clifford, and W. F. Bynum, eds. *Historical Abstracts of the Neurosciences*. NY: Raven, 1980.

Roth, Michael. "Hysterical Remembering," *Modernism/Modernity* 3.2 (May 1996): 1–30.

Schechner, Richard. *Performance Studies*. London: Routledge, 2013.

Schade, Sigrid. "Charcot and the Spectacle of the Hysterical Body," *Art History* 18.4 (December 1995): 499–517.

Schwartz, Vanessa. *Spectacular Realities*. LA: California University Press, 1998.

Scott, Michael. *Delphi*. Princeton: Princeton University Press, 2014.

Shapiro, Ann-Louise. *Breaking the Codes*. Stanford: Stanford University Press, 1996.

Showalter, Elaine. *The Female Malady*. London: Virago, 1988.

———. *Hystories*. NY: Columbia University Press, 1997.

Silverman, Debora. *Art nouveau in fin-de-siècle France*. Berkeley: California University Press, 1989.

Silverman, Joseph. "Charcot's Comments on the Therapeutic Role of Isolation in the Treatment of Anorexia Nervosa," *International Journal of Eating Disorders* 21 (1997): 295–8.

Simon-Dhouailly, Nadine, ed. *Le leçon de Charcot: Voyage dans une toile*, catalogue d'exposition. Paris: Musée de l'Assistance publique des hôpitaux de Paris, 1986.

Smith-Rosenberg, Caroll. "The Hysterical Woman," *Social Research* 39 (Winter 1975): 652–678.

Sowerwine, Charles. *France Since 1870*. Houndmills: Palgrave, 2001.

Stallybrass, Peter, and Allon White, *The Politics and Poetics of Transgression*. London: Methuen, 1986.

Taylor, Katherine. *In the Theater of Criminal Justice*. Princeton: Princeton University Press, 1993.

Temkin, Owsei. *The Falling Sickness: A History of Epilepsy*. Baltimore: Johns Hopkins, 1971.

Theweleit, Klaus. *Male Fantasies*. Cambridge: Polity, 1987.

Trillat, Étienne. *Histoire de l'hystérie*. Paris: Seghers, 1986.

Various. *Musée de l'Assistance publique de Paris*, catalogue d'exposition. Paris: Musée de l'Assistance publique des hôpitaux de Paris, 1998.

Vatré, Éric. *Léon Daudet ou le libre réactionnaire*. Paris: France-Empire, 1987.

Vay, David Le. "Adrien Barrère: A French Medical Caricaturist," *The Practitioner* 207 (July 1971): 106–138.

Veith, Ilza. *Hysteria: The History of a Disease*. Chicago: Chicago University Press, 1965.

Vessier, Maximilien. *La Pitié-Salpêtrière: Quatre siècles d'histoire et d'histoires*. Préface Daniel Widlöcher. Paris: Groupe hospitalier Pitié-Salpêtrière, 1999.

Vitroux, Frédéric. *Céline*. NY: Paragon, 1992.

Wald, Christina. *Hysteria, Trauma and Melancholia*. Houndmills: Palgrave Macmillan, 2007.

Waller, John. *A Time to Dance, a Time to Die*. London: Icon, 2009.

Walusinski, Olivier, "Georges Gilles de la Tourette," *Histoire des sciences médicales* (2015). Reproduced on www.baillement.comrecherchegdt_sfhm.pdf.

———. "Public Medical Shows," *Frontiers of Neurology and Neuroscience* 33 (2014). http://www.baillement.comlettrespublic_medical_shows.pdf.

Weber, Eugen. *Action française: Royalism and Reaction*. Stanford: Stanford University Press, 1962.

Wilson, Scott. *Stop Making Sense*. London: Karnac, 2015.

Winocour, Alice, dir., *Augustine,* film (France: 2012).

Winter, Alison. *Mesmerized: Powers of the Mind in Victorian Britain*. Chicago: Chicago University Press, 1998.

Wolf, Theta. "A New Perspective on Alfred Binet," *Psychological Record* 32 (1982), 397–407.

Yates, Frances A. *The Art of Memory*. London: Routledge, 1966.

INDEX

Printed by Printforce, the Netherlands